THE ECONOMIC THEORY OF EMINENT DOMAIN

This book surveys the contributions that economic theory has made to the often contentious debate over the government's use of its power of eminent domain, as prescribed by the Fifth Amendment. It addresses such questions as: When should the government be allowed to take private property without the owner's consent? Does it depend on how the land will be used? And what amount of compensation, if any, is the landowner entitled to receive? The recent case of *Kelo v. New London* (2005) revitalized the debate, but it was only the latest skirmish in the ongoing struggle between advocates of strong governmental powers to acquire private property in the public interest and private property rights advocates. Written for a general audience, the book advances a coherent theory that views eminent domain within the context of the government's proper role in an economic system whose primary objective is to achieve efficient land use.

Thomas J. Miceli is Professor of Economics at the University of Connecticut in Storrs, where he has taught since 1987. He is a recognized scholar in the fields of law and economics and urban economics, and he has published widely in such journals as *The Journal of Legal Studies*, *The Journal of Law and Economics*, and *The Rand Journal of Economics*. *The Economic Theory of Eminent Domain* is his fifth book. Professor Miceli received his PhD from Brown University in 1988.

The Economic Theory of Eminent Domain

Private Property, Public Use

THOMAS J. MICELI

University of Connecticut

CAMBRIDGE UNIVERSITY PRESS
Cambridge, New York, Melbourne, Madrid, Cape Town,
Singapore, São Paulo, Delhi, Tokyo, Mexico City

Cambridge University Press
32 Avenue of the Americas, New York, NY 10013-2473, USA

www.cambridge.org
Information on this title: www.cambridge.org/9780521182973

First published 2011

Printed in the United States of America

A catalog record for this publication is available from the British Library.

Library of Congress Cataloging in Publication Data
Miceli, Thomas J.
The economic theory of eminent domain: private property,
public use / Thomas J. Miceli.
p.   cm.
Includes bibliographical references and index.
ISBN 978-0-521-18297-3 (pbk.)
1. Eminent domain – United States.   2. Eminent
domain – Economic aspects.   I. Title.
KF5599.M45   2011
343.73'0252–dc22   2010054309

ISBN 978-1-107-00525-9 Hardback
ISBN 978-0-521-18297-3 Paperback

To Ana Maria,
whom I can never fully compensate

Contents

Tables and Figures

Preface

The Fifth Amendment of the U.S. Constitution gives the government the power to take private property for public use as long as it pays the owner just compensation. Though never popular, the government's exercise of this power for the purpose of constructing highways, hospitals, or other truly public projects is generally unquestioned. The recent case of *Kelo v. New London* (2005), however, pushed the limits of what constitutes an acceptable public use. In that case, the city sought to use eminent domain to acquire several private residences and small businesses in order to clear the way for a redevelopment project whose primary beneficiary was a large pharmaceutical company. In a 5–4 decision, the U.S. Supreme Court nevertheless upheld the city's right to take the property based on the enhanced tax revenues and new jobs that the project promised. The public outcry against this decision, and its apparent expansion of the government's power over private property, was loud and immediate, and was soon followed by political efforts in many states to curb the perceived abuse of eminent domain.

The *Kelo* case and its aftermath, however, was only the latest skirmish in the ongoing debate about the limits of eminent domain, pitting proponents of strong governmental powers to acquire or regulate property in the public interest on one side against private property rights advocates on the other. The legal terrain is well trod, yet there continues to be a lack of consensus on certain key issues, owing in part to their unavoidable political dimension. The goal of this book is to ask whether economic theory can help provide workable answers that transcend political affiliations. That eminent domain has an economic dimension is undeniable, considering that at its basis it is concerned with the transfer of land or other property interests from one user to another. An economic approach to takings focuses on whether, or under what conditions, a forced transfer (for that is what eminent domain allows) is preferred to voluntary (or market) exchange as a means of achieving the maximum value of the property in question.

In adopting this perspective, I do not wish to suggest that economic efficiency is the only criterion by which eminent domain should be evaluated, nor do I wish to minimize the political or philosophical dimensions of the debate over this contentious subject. Rather, I hope to illustrate the power of economic theory to provide both a positive (descriptive) and normative (prescriptive) approach to this issue, thereby clarifying the nature of the legal and political debate, if not entirely resolving it.

Economic analysis of eminent domain has a long history, but research in this area has accelerated in the past quarter century as economists have brought increasingly sophisticated tools to bear on the subject. This book attempts to synthesize that research, but it is more than just a literature review. Rather, it seeks to advance a coherent perspective that embeds eminent domain within a larger economic theory of exchange that draws on insights gained from the wider field of law and economics, which in recent decades has had an increasing influence on the study of nearly all areas of law.

The book is aimed at a broad audience that includes legal scholars, economists, and general readers with an interest in how economics can inform legal debates. To accommodate readers with such diverse backgrounds, I have written the main text in an entirely non-technical way, with limited use of numerical examples to illustrate some of the more formal aspects of the various economic models. For economists interested in technical details, an appendix contains formal proofs of the key results that reflect the state-of-the-art of research in this area. (The appendix reproduces some material that previously appeared in a substantially shorter and more technical survey of the economics of eminent domain; see Miceli and Segerson 2007a.)

From a personal perspective, this book is the culmination of nearly twenty years of my own research on the economics of eminent domain. I was first exposed to the topic as an undergraduate in a law and economics course taught by Richard Adelstein, and my interest was revived by the publication of the seminal article by Blume, Rubinfeld, and Shapiro in 1984 while I was a graduate student. I therefore naturally turned to the subject as a new assistant professor in search of a research agenda, and I have worked on it more or less steadily ever since. Much of my work in this area has been done in collaboration with Kathy Segerson, whose insights are reflected throughout this book, as are the comments of Perry Shapiro and several anonymous reviewers who read and provided valuable feedback on the entire manuscript. I also want to thank Scott Parris, who expressed enthusiasm for the project at its early stages and shepherded it through the review and publication process. As usual, my greatest thanks are to Ana, Tommy, and Nick, whose continual support is of incalculable value.

West Hartford, CT
Summer 2010

ONE

Introduction

A Framework for Analysis

When a social decision to redirect economic resources entails painfully obvious opportunity costs, how shall those costs ultimately be distributed among all members of society?

Frank Michelman (1967, p. 1169)

The problem to which the eminent domain clause is directed is that of political obligation and organization. What are the reasons for the formation of the state? What can the state demand of the individual citizens whom it governs and represents?

Richard Epstein (1985, p. 3)

Property rights are fundamental to both law and economics. From the perspective of law, property rights define and protect those things that people can and cannot do with the assets under their control, including, but not limited to, land. From the perspective of economics, property rights provide incentives for people to use their assets in an efficient way. Some reflection, however, should reveal that these are two ways of saying the same thing. The incentive function of property rights ultimately resides in the legal protections that they afford to owners, particularly in terms of their right to exclude others (including the government) from infringing on their chosen use. In this way, property rights ensure that their holders will be able to enjoy the fruits of their efforts. Private property rights therefore represent an important pre-requisite for both efficient exchange and development of land, which are the fundamental sources of economic value. As Robert Ellickson (1993, p. 1327) has observed, private property provides incentives for "people to 'do the right thing' with the earth's surface."

There are cases, however, where one person's unrestricted use of his or her property imposes costs on others. For example, certain uses of property involve the production of smoke, noise, or other forms of pollution that may cause harm to nearby residents or to the environment. These cost

1

spillovers, or externalities (as economists call them), create potential inefficiencies in land use and therefore provide a possible justification for the government to impose limits on what owners can do with their property. And even though such restrictions may reduce the value of the specific properties on which they are imposed, their goal, if properly structured, is to increase overall efficiency.

Inefficiencies in land use can also arise when land that is currently privately owned becomes more valuable for public use. For example, as an economy develops, it becomes desirable for some amount of land to be devoted to the construction of highways, railroads, and airports, which are freely available to all. Or people may desire to set aside some amount of undeveloped land for recreational use or as an undisturbed sanctuary for wildlife. In these cases as well, unrestricted private property may impede the production of such "public goods" on a voluntary basis, so economists have long recognized that there may be a role for the government to step in and ensure that these goods are provided in the efficient quantity.

The government's response to both of the previously mentioned problems – namely, regulating externalities and providing public goods – generally involves its asking private property owners to give up some or all of their property rights in the collective interest. That is, owners are either required to limit those things that they can do with their property, or they are compelled to surrender some or all of it to the government for public use. Such acquisitions of rights by the government are justified on efficiency grounds for the reasons just described, but the specific terms under which the acquisition occurs are open to debate. For example, under what circumstances are landowners whose rights are acquired entitled to compensation for the resulting loss in value? And if they are so entitled, how should the amount or form of compensation be determined? Providing answers to these questions is where the issue of eminent domain arises, for this power describes the constitutional limits of the government's ability to take private property without the owner's consent. The problem is that the language of the Fifth Amendment's takings clause is sufficiently vague that courts are left with considerable discretion in applying those limits. Consequently, the government's exercise of its taking power has generated extensive case law and scholarship, both legal and economic, seeking to define its appropriate scope. The purpose of this book is to see what light economic theory can shed on this issue based on the goal of achieving an efficient use of land. (For readers unfamiliar with the idea of economic efficiency, the appendix to this chapter provides a brief overview of the key concepts.)

1.1. The Takings Clause

The concluding clause of the Fifth Amendment to the U.S. Constitution states "nor shall private property be taken for public use, without just compensation." This is referred to as the Eminent Domain, or Takings Clause. Notice that the clause is phrased as a limitation on a power that is inherent to the government, rather than the granting of a new power (Meltz et al., 1999, p. 14). The idea that the sovereign could seize private property for the state's use originated in English common law and was imported by the American colonies. Even after independence, though, uncompensated takings by legislatures were accepted based on the republican notion that individual property rights were secondary to the common good. Only later did the liberal belief in the primacy of private property, and the concomitant need to protect it from legislative infringement, begin to emerge as the predominant viewpoint among the founding fathers, led by James Madison. The Fifth Amendment's Takings Clause was the culmination of this ideological trend (Treanor, 1985).

The specific protections of private property that the clause announced were, first, that the taken property must be put to *public use*, and second, that the owner must be paid *just compensation*. However, no further guidance was provided as to the specific meanings of the phrases "public use" or "just compensation." Thus, it has been left to the courts and legal scholars to define these terms, and much ink has been spilled in that effort. The question of interest here is what economic theory has to say about these limits.

Although the Takings Clause is phrased as a limitation on the government's use of its power to acquire land, a proper inquiry into the nature of those limits necessarily begins by asking why the government should have the power in the first place. This question is especially appropriate in the context of a democratic system where the power of the state emanates from the citizens themselves. Thus, we are prompted to ask why, in such a system, a group of citizens, acting through the government, should have a power that none of them individually has – namely, to force another citizen or group of citizens to surrender or limit the use of their property. This way of framing the question forces us to examine the underlying economic rationale for eminent domain, which, as previously suggested, is based on the goal of achieving an efficient allocation and use of land.

The proper starting point for such an inquiry is the fundamental result from welfare economics, known as the Invisible Hand Theorem, which states that in a competitive market setting, voluntary (or market) exchange will result in an efficient allocation of resources.[1] In other words, when the conditions for perfect competition are in place, property rights will end up in the hands of those parties who value them most, or in those uses where they are most valuable, without the need for government intervention. This is a profound result because it establishes that when individual property owners pursue their own self-interests, the outcome will be socially optimal as regards the efficient use of economic resources. In such an environment, there is no apparent need for the government to intervene in the market for purposes of improving efficiency (though there may be a need or desire for it to intervene to achieve a more equitable distribution of wealth).

The requirement that exchange must take place within a competitive setting is critical, however, because it means that no parties can have market power (that is, neither buyers nor sellers can have an inordinate ability to affect the market price), and other sources of market failure, like externalities and public goods, must be absent. These qualifications are especially important for our purposes because, as suggested earlier, an economic theory of eminent domain (or, for that matter, any departure from voluntary exchange) must be based on its ability to overcome one or more of these market failures. The next section begins to lay the foundation for such a theory of eminent domain by examining the problem of externalities, and the various possible responses to them, in more detail. (I consider the problem of public good provision in Chapter 2.)

1.2. Theoretical Preliminaries: Externalities and the Coase Theorem

The economic theory of eminent domain to be advanced in this book is a component of the broader economic theory of *property rights* and *property law*. The distinction between these two is that property rights represent those things that one is entitled do with one's property (thus, they are sometimes referred to as "entitlements"), whereas property law represents the set of legal rules that enforce those rights or entitlements. As previously suggested, the economic theory of property law views these rules as being designed to maximize the value of property.[2] In most ordinary instances, this involves protecting an owner's right to *use* his property as he sees fit,

---

[1] The result is also called the First Fundamental Theorem of Welfare Economics (Feldman, 1980, chapter 3).

[2] For surveys of the economic theory of property law, see Lueck and Miceli (2007) and Miceli (2009a, chapter 6).

allowing him to *exclude* others from using it, and facilitating his ability to *transfer* the right to another user on mutually acceptable terms. As argued earlier, though, when externalities are present, an owner's intended use of his property imposes unintended costs (or benefits) on others. For example, a farmer's use of a certain chemical fertilizer to increase his crop yield may pollute his neighbor's water supply, or a rancher's allowing his cattle to graze freely may result in their straying onto a neighboring farmer's land, destroying his crops. The role of the law in the presence of these incompatible uses is to limit an owner's property rights so as to eliminate or minimize the resulting external cost.

Traditionally, economists viewed externalities as a problem that only the government could solve by coercive means, for example by imposing a tax or other form of regulation on the "cause" of the harm. This so-called Pigovian view of externalities is based on the idea, previously noted, that externalities necessarily lead to market failure and thus require the government to intervene to achieve an efficient outcome. For example, a polluting factory must be taxed; otherwise it will ignore the harm that its pollution causes to nearby residents and will therefore emit too much of it. Another way to say this is that, absent the tax, the factory will view pollution (and the resulting harm) as a free "input" into its production process and will therefore overuse that input. By imposing the tax, the government is in effect saying that pollution victims "own" the right to be free from the harm, and thus the factory has to "purchase" that right (via the tax) if it wants to continue polluting (even though the tax revenue is not necessarily paid to the victims). In this way, a "forced" transaction at a price set by the government replaces the hypothetical market transaction that ideally would have taken place between the factory and residents regarding the exchange of the right to pollute.

Ronald Coase made a fundamental contribution to the economic analysis of externalities when he re-examined this traditional Pigovian response to the problem of incompatible property rights (Coase, 1960). Coase's key insight was not that the Pigovian perspective as just described is wrong; rather, he suggested that it was incomplete. In particular, he argued that it is based on two implicit assumptions, neither of which is necessarily valid. The first assumption is that there is a well-defined "cause" of the external harm; that is, there is a clear injurer, the factory, and a clear victim, the residents. The second assumption is that government intervention is necessary to internalize the harm because the market will fail to do so. The role of these assumptions in the traditional Pigovian view of externalities, and Coase's re-interpretation of the problem, is best illustrated in terms of

Table 1.1. *Coase's farmer-rancher example*

Herd size	Total crop damage ($)	Marginal crop damage ($)
1	1	1
2	3	2
3	6	3
4	10	4

Coase's example of the conflict between a farmer and a rancher occupying adjacent parcels of land.

Consider a rancher whose cattle sometimes stray onto a neighboring farmer's land and damage his crops. Table 1.1 shows the resulting crop damage, both in total and at the margin, as a function of the rancher's herd size. (The marginal damage is simply the amount that the total damage increases with each additional steer.) Suppose that the marginal benefit to the rancher of adding additional cattle to his herd is a constant $3.50. That is, each new steer increases the rancher's profit by $3.50. Thus, the rancher's profit-maximizing herd size is four (its maximal size), which yields a total profit of $14.00 (4 × $3.50). Once the crop damage is accounted for, however, the socially optimal herd size – that is, the herd size that maximizes the joint value of ranching and farming – is three. This is true because, for each steer added to the herd up to three, the marginal benefit of $3.50 exceeds the marginal crop damage, but for the fourth steer, the marginal crop damage exceeds the marginal benefit. A joint owner of the ranch and farm would therefore choose a herd size of three because he would internalize both the benefit and cost of changes in the herd.[3]

When the activities are separately owned, however, we would expect the rancher to increase his herd to four because he would ignore the crop damage suffered by the farmer. This provides the rationale, according to the logic of the Pigovian view, for the government to intervene and impose a tax on ranching (or crop damage) so as to achieve the efficient herd size.

But let us consider more carefully the situation where the rancher is neither taxed nor otherwise held legally responsible for the crop damage. Is

---

[3] Another way to see that the optimal herd size is three is to compute the net benefit from ranching and farming as follows:

herd size	net benefit
1	$3.50 – $1 = $2.50
2	$7.00 – $3 = $4
3	$10.50 – $6 = $4.50 (the maximum)
4	$14 – $10 = $4

it necessarily true, as is implicit in the Pigovian view, that the rancher will increase the herd size to four in this case? Suppose that the rancher and farmer can bargain freely with one another. Specifically, suppose that when the herd size is four, the farmer offers to pay the rancher, say $3.75, to reduce his herd to three. Clearly, the rancher will accept this offer because it yields him more income than the $3.50 he could earn by retaining the fourth steer, and the farmer is also better off because he avoids the $4 in additional crop damage at a cost of $3.75. Thus, because both parties benefit from the transaction, it will occur. Additional bargains to reduce the herd size further are not possible, however, because the marginal benefit of steers exceeds the marginal crop damage for herd sizes of three or fewer. Thus, the herd size remains at three, which is efficient. What this example shows is that when bargaining is possible, the efficient outcome can always be achieved in an externality setting by a voluntary transaction, even when the literal source or cause of the harm (the rancher) is not held legally responsible for it. This conclusion, known as the Coase Theorem, is a fundamental element of the economic approach to property law, and indeed, of the economic approach to law in general.

Now recall the two implicit assumptions underlying the Pigovian view of externalities – first, that there is an identifiable cause of the harm (in this case, the rancher), and second, that government intervention is necessary to internalize it – and note that, in light of the Coase Theorem, neither is necessarily correct. This is true, first, because both the farmer and rancher are "causes" of the crop damage in the sense that both must be present for the damage to occur. In this sense, the harm is said to be "reciprocal."[4] The importance of this insight is that the assignment of responsibility for an external harm is not absolute, but in fact involves a value judgment regarding who is more deserving of legal protection. In other words, it involves a decision about who should pay for the damages. It follows that, although the legal rule for assigning liability will not affect the herd size when bargaining is possible (that is, it will not affect the allocation of resources), it will affect the distribution of wealth between ranchers and farmers because it determines who possesses the underlying property right, which is valuable. Clearly, farmers would be better off if the law always required ranchers to pay for crop damage, whereas ranchers would be better off if the law never required them to pay. The assignment of property rights will therefore always have distributional implications, even when the Coase Theorem holds.

---

[4] One test for causation in tort law, called the "but-for test," says that an action by A is the cause of a harm suffered by B if the harm would not have occurred but for A's action. Both farming and ranching obviously satisfy this test given that the removal of either activity would eliminate the harm.

Second, the Coase Theorem establishes that government intervention is not necessarily required to internalize externalities as long as bargaining is possible. The significance of this insight is not that the government has no role to play in dealing with external costs. Rather, as will be emphasized in the next section, it reveals the importance of transaction costs, or other impediments to bargaining, in formulating the best response to an externality. In particular, it allows us to ascertain the conditions under which government intervention in the market is in fact justified. Having recognized the importance of transaction costs, we now turn to a more detailed examination of their role in externality problems.

1.3. The Role of Transaction Costs

The reader may justifiably observe that the Coase Theorem has little practical relevance because in most actual externality settings, the conditions required for it to hold are unlikely to be satisfied. In particular, because externalities often involve a large number of individuals, transactions costs between injurers and victims will generally prevent the sort of bargaining that may be needed to ensure an efficient allocation of resources. In that case, the assignment of legal responsibility for the harm will matter for efficiency as well as for income distribution. In other words, if the parties to an externality cannot bargain with one another, for whatever reason, the prevailing legal rule will determine the final assignment of rights. Thus, the rule needs to be chosen with the goal of efficiency in mind.

To illustrate, suppose in the farmer-rancher case that the crop damage can be entirely eliminated if the farmer "fences in" his crops (or, equivalently, "fences out" the straying cattle) at a cost of $9. Note that when this option is available, the socially optimal herd size is four. This is true because, once the fence is built, the marginal crop damage drops to zero regardless of the herd size. Thus, the total profit from the four steers less the cost of the fence, equal to $5.00 ($14.00 − $9.00), exceeds the net profit from the socially optimal herd of three without the fence: $10.50 − $6.00 = $4.50.

Initially, suppose that the prevailing law holds ranchers strictly liable for crop damage, and that bargaining between the parties is not possible. In this case, the farmer will clearly have no incentive to build the fence because he knows he will be compensated for any crop damage he suffers. The rancher, in reaction to the threat of liability, will therefore reduce his herd to three (as in the earlier example without the fence), which in the current example is inefficient. (The assumption that bargaining is not possible precludes the rancher from simply buying the fence for the farmer's land.)

Now suppose the law is changed so that ranchers are not held liable for crop damage. In this case, the rancher will increase his herd to four so as to maximize his private profit, whereas the farmer, who is no longer compensated for his losses, will find it profitable to build the fence because the $9 cost is less than the $10 in total crop damage. Thus, the outcome is now efficient (though clearly less desirable from the perspective of the farmer).[5]

This example illustrates the important point that, when transaction costs preclude bargaining between the parties, the law matters for efficiency and therefore must be chosen with this goal in mind (Demsetz, 1972). This is a crucial insight because it defines those situations in which government intervention is needed to correct the failure of the market to internalize the externality. The next section expands on this point by introducing the role of enforcement rules.

1.4. Enforcement Rules: The Choice between Property Rules and Liability Rules

The preceding section showed that in the presence of high transaction costs, the assignment of legal responsibility for external costs is important for achieving an efficient allocation of resources. Equally important is the legal rule for enforcing or protecting that assignment. In their seminal analysis of the choice among enforcement rules, Calabresi and Melamed (1972) distinguished between *property rules* and *liability rules*.[6] The difference turns on the conditions under which the protected entitlement can be transferred, and is again best illustrated by means of an example. Suppose that party A wishes to plant a row of trees on his beachfront property, but his neighbor, party B, objects because the trees will block her view of the ocean. Assuming that planting trees is a legal activity, the question is under what conditions B can stop A from exercising that right. If A's right to plant trees is protected by a property rule, B can only stop him by offering to pay an amount of money that A is willing to accept. In other words, B must purchase A's right to plant trees in a consensual transaction. B will therefore only be willing to do so if she values the ocean view more than A values the

---

[5] Under English common law, owners of livestock were traditionally held liable for any damage that they caused. In the American West, however, many states rejected this rule in favor of a so-called open range law, which only entitled victims of animal trespass to collect damages if they had fenced in their land. See Ellickson (1991, pp. 42–48) and Sanchez and Nugent (2000).

[6] For more detailed analyses of property and liability rules, see Polinsky (1980), Kaplow and Shavell (1996), and Ayres and Balkin (1997).

trees. In contrast, if A's right to plant trees is protected by a liability rule, B can go to court to block A from planting the trees without first seeking A's permission, but B must be willing to pay damages, as assessed by the court, for the loss in value suffered by A. In other words, B is able to force a transfer of A's right to plant the trees, without first obtaining A's permission, at a price set by the court.

Property rules, because they necessitate consensual transfers, therefore form the basis for *market* exchanges, whereas liability rules, because they allow non-consensual (court-ordered) transfers, form the basis for *legal* exchanges.[7] The virtue of property rules is that they allow right-holders to refuse any offer deemed unacceptable, thereby ensuring that only value-enhancing (efficient) transactions occur. The drawback of property rules is that, if transaction costs are high, as they often are in externality settings, they will prevent some efficient transfers from going forward, given the need for consent. Thus, property rules will tend to result in too few efficient exchanges. This provides the rationale for liability rules because, by removing the need for a would-be purchaser to obtain the right-holder's consent, they avoid bargaining costs. And as long as the court sets the amount of compensation at the right-holder's true valuation of the right in question, then the transaction is efficient, even though it is forced. The problem, of course, is that if the amount of compensation is *not* correctly set, then the transaction will not generally be efficient. If the amount of compensation is set too high, there will be too few transactions, and if it is set too low (as will more often be the case), there will be too many.

To illustrate, suppose in the previous example that the value of the ocean view to B is $1,000. Then it is only efficient for her to prevent A from planting the trees if A values the trees at less than $1,000. Under a property rule, B will never be able to block the trees if A values them at more than $1,000 because she would never be willing to offer more than $1,000 to do so. Thus, property rule protection of A's right to plant the trees will never result in its being inefficiently transferred. However, B may be unable to block A even if A values the trees at less than $1,000 if the costs of bargaining are high. Thus, as noted, a property rule risks too few transactions. In contrast, a liability rule will only guarantee an efficient outcome if the court sets the damages exactly equal to A's valuation of the trees. If it sets damages below

[7]   Calabresi and Melamed also discuss a third enforcement rule, called an *inalienability rule*, which prevents the transfer of a right under any circumstances. Examples of rights protected by an inalienability rule (called inalienable rights) include the right to vote and the right to free speech. For an economic perspective on inalienable rights, see Lueck and Miceli (2007, pp. 245–249).

that level, B may block the trees too often, and if it sets damages above that level, B may not block the trees often enough. The efficiency of liability rules therefore depends entirely on how accurately the court is able to measure the damages suffered by A.

This example shows that the choice between property rules and liability rules depends on a weighing of the transaction costs between the parties on the one hand against the ability of courts to assess damages on the other. It follows that whenever transaction costs are low, property rules are preferred because then only those exchanges that promise mutual gains will be completed. However, if transaction costs are high and courts are reasonably good at setting damages, then liability rules are preferred in order to allow the completion of efficient exchanges that may otherwise have been foregone due to the cost of bargaining. This prescription, along with the insights gained from the Coase Theorem, form the foundation for the economic approach to property law as described in the next section.

1.5. The General Transaction Structure

One of the important insights gained from the economic analysis of law has been the recognition of the role of the law in facilitating the efficient allocation of resources when markets fail to do so. In this sense, the law acts as a substitute for the market. The preceding discussion of the Coase Theorem, coupled with the Calabresi-Melamed analysis of the choice between property rules and liability rules, suggests a general framework for defining the proper relationship between markets and law in this regard. I will refer to this framework as the *general transaction structure*.[8]

Table 1.2 depicts this structure in the context of the rancher-farmer dispute. It consists of two dimensions: an *assignment* of the legal right in question – in this case, whether the rancher has the right to impose crop damage, or the farmer has the right to be free from crop damage (the horizontal dimension); and an *enforcement rule* to protect that assignment – either a property rule or a liability rule (the vertical dimension). The four cells depict the four possible combinations. In cells I and III, the right is awarded to the rancher, protected by a property rule (cell I) or a liability rule (cell III). The difference between the two is that under the property rule, the farmer has to bargain with the rancher, in the manner described earlier, to reduce the harm, whereas under the liability rule, the farmer can go to court to force the rancher to curtail his operation, but must compensate him for the lost profit (as assessed by the court).

---

[8] This approach is based on Klevorick (1985) and Coleman (1988, chapter 2).

Table 1.2. *The general transaction structure*

		Assignment of the right	
		Rancher	Farmer
Enforcement rule:	Property rule	(I) Rancher is free to impose harm	(II) Farmer can enjoin harm
	Liability rule	(III) Rancher can seek compensation for cost of preventing harm	(IV) Farmer can seek compensation for harm sustained

Likewise, in cells II and IV, the right is awarded to the farmer, protected by a property rule (cell II) or a liability rule (cell IV). Under the property rule, the farmer can enjoin the rancher from imposing harm, which the rancher can only lift by offering the farmer an acceptable payment to allow his cattle to continue to stray. In contrast, under the liability rule, the farmer cannot prevent the rancher from imposing harm, but can only seek compensation for the resulting crop damage. Note that the traditional Pigovian approach to externalities under which the government taxes the "cause" of the damage (in this case, the rancher) corresponds to this last outcome (cell IV). A key insight of the general transaction structure is that this is only one of four possible remedies to the externality problem.

As for the choice among these possible remedies, note that efficiency considerations dictate the choice of the enforcement rule (the vertical dimension) as described in the preceding section. Specifically, a property rule (cell I or II) is preferred when transaction costs are low, and a liability rule (cell III or IV) is preferred when transaction costs are high. As for the assignment of the right, this is primarily a distributional question because it determines who must pay whom in any transaction that involves a transfer of the right. Thus, in cells I and III, the farmer either bears the crop damage himself or pays the rancher to reduce it, whereas in cells II and IV, the rancher either compensates the farmer or curtails the damage at his own expense.

As an illustration of the foregoing framework, consider the famous case of *Spur Industries v. Del E. Webb Development Co.*[9] The case involved a real

[9]   494 P.2d 700 (1972).

estate developer who, in the course of developing land west of Phoenix, Arizona, encroached on a pre-existing cattle feed lot that was legally operating at that location. As a result of the encroachment, the foul odors from the feed lot interfered with the developer's ability to sell further homes, so the developer sued to have the lot shut down.

Note that if the court had taken the traditional Pigovian perspective in deciding this case, it presumably would have identified the feed lot as the "cause" of the harm (considering that it was the source of the odors) and granted the plaintiff's request for a remedy. That is, it would have chosen either cell II or IV, depending on whether it ordered the feed lot to shut down outright (cell II) or required it to pay damages to the developer in order to continue operating (cell IV). In fact, the remedy the court actually imposed was to order the feed lot to shut down or relocate, but it required the developer to pay the feed lot's costs. In other words, it awarded the right to the feed lot and protected it by a liability rule (cell III). In doing so, it essentially reversed the traditional roles of cause and effect, revealing Coase's insight that, at least as regards the efficient resolution of the dispute, the designation of a single cause is arbitrary. Although the feed lot was the physical source of the odors, its activity would have imposed no harm if the development had not encroached on it. In this sense, the developer was as much a cause of the harm as the feed lot.

The court's ruling in this case reflects the common law doctrine of "coming to the nuisance," under which pre-existing uses are awarded rights against newcomers who claim to suffer harm (Wittman, 1980). This doctrine reveals that the law long ago recognized the arbitrariness of causation in externality cases. As for the choice of a liability rule to protect the feed lot's right, this apparently reflected the court's belief that transaction costs between the parties were high, thus requiring the court to set the terms of the transaction rather than leaving it to the parties to determine. [10]

As a final point, the *Spur* decision provides a context for relating the preceding discussion of externalities back to the eminent domain issue. First of all, observe that eminent domain is itself a form of liability rule in the sense that it entitles landowners to seek just compensation (damages) for their land but does not allow them to refuse the transaction. Seen in this light, the remedy in *Spur* in effect allowed the developer to "take" the feed lot's land in return for a payment of compensatory damages. The general transaction structure

---

[10] I will argue later, however (Section 2.7 of Chapter 2), that the assignment of *Spur* to cell III in Table 2.1 was a debatable ruling given that there were only two parties involved in this case (the lot owner and the developer). Thus, bargaining should have been possible under a property rule, suggesting that cell I may have been a better choice.

provides a logical basis for this interpretation by viewing the use of eminent domain (or more generally, forced exchange) within the larger context of an efficient legal and economic environment for exchange. This framework provides the conceptual basis for the remaining chapters of this book.

1.6. Overview of Takings Law

Before commencing with the economic analysis of eminent domain law, it will be useful to survey the legal landscape. I offer here only a brief overview of the extensive case law in this area in an effort to highlight the principal issues to be discussed in subsequent chapters. A more thorough discussion of the key cases will be provided as each topic is introduced.

The law of eminent domain focuses on three main issues: the public use limitation, the definition of just compensation, and the compensability of government actions that regulate land without taking actual physical control of it (the regulatory takings issue). The bulk of the case law on eminent domain concerns the first and third of these issues.

The case law on public use has focused on defining the proper scope of the government's use of its taking power. In particular, it asks whether the use of this power should be limited to truly public projects like highways, airports, or parks, where the acquired land is openly available for public use, or whether it should also be allowed for largely private projects, like those aimed at economic development, that create some discernable public benefits, usually in the form of jobs or taxes. Historically, courts have permitted a fairly expansive interpretation of public use in this regard, going beyond the standard economic definition of a public good by granting entrepreneurs the right to use the takings power for such private enterprises as mill-dam construction, railroads, canals, mining, and urban renewal. Indeed, the Supreme Court's most recent ruling in this area in *Kelo v. New London* (2005) upheld the use of eminent domain for a re-development project whose benefits were largely private, based on the argument that the expected increase in jobs and tax revenues that would flow to the community satisfied the public use requirement. The ruling in this case, however, was viewed by many as an unjustified expansion of the meaning of public use, suggesting that the debate regarding the proper scope of public use is far from settled.

The second requirement for the use of eminent domain is the need to pay just compensation to owners whose land is taken. In theory, this requirement is intended to leave the displaced owner as well off as if the taking had not occurred; in other words, to make the owner whole. In economic terms, this requires that the amount of compensation should reflect what the owner would have demanded in a consensual transaction. The problem is how to determine that amount once the requirement of consent is removed. The usual solution courts have adopted is to award the fair market value of the property, which reflects what a ready and willing buyer would have paid for it. This measure has the advantage of being relatively easy to observe, for example, by looking at the sale price of recently sold comparable properties, but, as will be demonstrated in Chapter 3, it almost certainly undercompensates owners compared to what they would have demanded in a consensual sale. Thus, although it is accepted legal doctrine that the definition of just compensation is fair market value, this measure raises important questions of both fairness and efficiency.

The final major area of case law concerns the applicability of the eminent domain clause to the multifarious government actions that have the effect of reducing the value of a piece of property without actually taking legal title to it. Examples include zoning, environmental and safety regulations, rent controls, wildlife protection laws, and so forth. From an economic perspective, a regulation is merely a partial taking of an owner's property rights, and as such, it differs in degree rather than kind from a full (physical) taking. The law, however, has treated the two types of cases quite differently: Whereas compensation is virtually always required for physical acquisitions, it is rarely awarded for mere regulations. The issue is usually phrased as a threshold question: Specifically, does a regulation ever go so far in reducing the value of a piece of property that it constitutes a taking for which compensation is due (a so-called regulatory taking)? As a general rule, courts have granted the government wide latitude to enact regulations without triggering compensation, based on the government's responsibility to use its police power to protect the public from so-called noxious uses, defined to be those activities that are deemed harmful to health, safety, and welfare, broadly defined.

In fact, courts have historically recognized only two conditions under which compensation is required for a regulation. The first is when the regulation in question involves a physical invasion of private property, as when airplanes fly through the airspace above a piece of property at a low enough level to cause harm or annoyance to people or animals on the ground, or when a cable company installs equipment on a privately owned building. This "physical invasion" test, however, is of little or no relevance for the vast majority of government regulations, which involve no invasion. The second, and more important, situation in which courts have required the payment of compensation is when a regulation "goes too far" in reducing the value of a landowner's property. However, the courts have left the definition of what constitutes "too far" to be decided on a case-by-case basis, thus leaving considerable uncertainty regarding its interpretation.

(The only situation in which compensation is virtually assured is when the regulation deprives the owner of *all* beneficial uses of the regulated property.) The analysis in Chapter 5 focuses on this "threshold" approach to the compensation question and asks, in particular, whether economic theory can give it a firmer basis.

1.7. Plan of the Book

The scholarly literature on eminent domain, like the case law, is extensive. The focus of this book is to assess the contribution that economic theory has made to this issue, which has become especially prominent in the past quarter-century.[11] The book surveys and synthesizes that literature while also seeking to place it within the larger context of an economic theory of the choice between market (voluntary) and legal (involuntary) exchange, as described in previous sections of this chapter.

Chapter 2 begins by examining the first of the two constitutional limitations imposed on the use of eminent domain by the Fifth Amendment, namely, public use. As noted, the issue here is the proper scope of the government's taking power. Specifically, should it be limited to the taking of land for truly public projects – those that meet the traditional economic definition of a public good – or should it also be allowed for projects that are largely private in nature as long as they have some identifiable public component? The answer, I will argue, depends on whether public use is best interpreted in terms of the manner in which the targeted land will be used (the ends), or the manner in which it is, or should be, acquired (the means). In other words, the question is whether eminent domain is justified by the government's role in providing public goods (a demand side problem) or by the need to overcome the holdout problem associated with land assembly (a supply side problem). The plain meaning of the takings clause suggests that it is the former – that is, "public use" equals "public good" – but economic theory reveals that it is more properly seen as the latter. In this sense, economic theory provides support for the *Kelo* decision, though not necessarily for the reasons offered by the Court.

More broadly, we will see that the distinction between the public good and holdout rationales for government intervention in the market provides a general framework for defining the government's role in facilitating economic exchange, whether through the forced sale of land for public use

---

[11] I date the growth in the economics literature on takings to the publication of the seminal paper by Blume, Rubinfeld, and Shapiro (1984). I discuss this article and its implications at length in Chapter 4.

(eminent domain) or the forced purchase of inputs for providing public goods (taxation). Examination of cases from both nuisance and contract law reinforces the economic logic of this framework and illustrates its generality as a theory of the choice between market (consensual) and legal (forced) exchange. As a further illustration, the framework is applied to two recent areas in which the use of eminent domain for largely private purposes has recently been advocated: namely, promoting urban renewal and combating urban sprawl.

As a counterpoint to the "pure" economic theory of public use, which interprets eminent domain primarily as a response to the holdout problem, the chapter offers some commonly advanced reasons, both economic and legal, for limiting the use of eminent domain to truly public projects. The chapter concludes by presenting some empirical evidence based on state-by-state variation in the use of eminent domain for private projects, as well as the political response to the *Kelo* decision.

Chapter 3 turns to the just-compensation requirement for eminent domain. As noted, courts have universally defined the measure of just compensation to be the fair market value of the acquired property, but economists have long recognized the shortcomings of this measure, especially the fact that it almost certainly undercompensates owners compared to what they would have accepted in a consensual sale. In light of this problem, the chapter reviews various demand-revealing schemes that economists have derived to discover owners' true valuations, but concludes that these mechanisms generally are not practical solutions to the measurement problem. Market value thus represents the most workable measure, but this concession to practicality has economic consequences. The most obvious is that the government may have an incentive to convert too much land to public use because it faces less than the full opportunity cost of the land. Chapter 4 takes up this argument in the context of recent economic models of efficient land use.

Possibly offsetting the threat of overacquisition, however, is the suggestion that the market-value measure could serve as an implicit subsidy to private developers who would otherwise *underinvest* in large scale, *Kelo*-type projects that promise substantial external benefits to the community. Although economic theory supports the subsidization of such projects, I will argue that explicit, targeted subsidies would likely accomplish this goal in a more direct and efficient manner than the use of eminent domain, given that the amount that fair market value undercompensates owners will generally bear no relation to a particular project's external benefits.

Another possible inefficiency associated with market-value compensation is the temptation it creates for local governments to use eminent domain to augment their property tax bases. This possibility arises because property tax assessments are also based on market value. Thus, any outside offer to buy a particular piece of property, if accepted by the owner, would necessarily raise the market value of the property, thereby promising the local government increased property tax revenues. In other words, any sales of properties within the jurisdiction benefit the local government by raising its tax base. The problem, however, is that an owner who values his or her property in excess of its market value may find a given offer unacceptable and refuse to sell, thereby depriving the community of the greater tax revenues. Ordinarily, the government has no leverage to intervene in such transactions, but if they are part of a large-scale project, the government might be tempted to use its eminent domain power based on the argument that the enhanced revenues would benefit the public, thus satisfying the public use requirement as defined in *Kelo*. Once again, the crux of the problem is the unobservability of the owner's true valuation, which prevents the government from simply re-assessing the properties in question at that amount. As a remedy (or deterrent) for this "tax-motivated" use of eminent domain, I propose a scheme for re-assessing targeted parcels that avoids (or at least reduces) the risk of inefficient land transfers.

Chapter 3 next turns to an evaluation of other arguments, besides excessive government acquisition of land, for paying compensation, such as providing public insurance for risk-averse landowners against takings risk, and avoiding the so-called demoralization costs of not paying compensation. Chapter 3 also evaluates an oft-made argument *against* paying compensation – namely, that owners who buy land in the face of a regulatory or taking risk pay a discounted price and hence have no claim for compensation if and when the threatened action actually occurs. Although compelling, what this "capitalization" argument ignores is the loss suffered by the owner at the time the threat of government action first materializes. Chapter 3 also discusses grandfather clauses as an alternative to monetary compensation and concludes by drawing the link between the public use and just compensation requirements of the Fifth Amendment. In particular, it argues that the two requirements are intended to work in concert to ensure, to the extent possible, that a forced sale replicates the outcome that would have been achieved under ideal market conditions by a consensual sale.

Chapter 4 takes up the effect of eminent domain on land use incentives. The focus of the analysis continues to be on the amount of compensation, but attention shifts to the impact of compensation on landowner investment decisions. This is perhaps the area in which economists have made the most significant contributions to the literature on eminent domain, especially since the seminal paper by Blume, Rubinfeld, and Shapiro (BRS) (1984). The key insight of the BRS analysis was that compensation acts as a form of insurance against taking risk, thereby creating a moral hazard problem that causes landowners to overinvestment in land that may be suitable for a taking (or regulation) at some future date. BRS showed that lump-sum compensation eliminates this problem, but most of the attention since their article was published has centered on their special case of zero compensation. Not surprisingly, the apparent unfairness of this "no-compensation result," not to mention its incongruity with constitutional law, has generated a large amount of scholarship, most of it aimed at offering counterarguments. Chapter 4 surveys and synthesizes the resulting literature.

As noted earlier, probably the chief argument against a rule of zero compensation is that it creates the risk of excessive takings. This argument is based on the premise that the government makes its takings decisions according to the actual budgetary cost of the taken land rather than a consideration of social welfare. Such a government is said to have "fiscal illusion." Much of the literature since BRS has therefore focused on deriving the optimal compensation rule in the presence of the trade-off between the moral hazard problem associated with full compensation and fiscal illusion problem that would likely emerge under zero compensation.

Another argument advanced for paying compensation arises in a dynamic setting where landowners control not only the amount of investment, but also its timing. In that setting, some amount of positive compensation is generally needed to prevent landowners from developing early in an effort to reduce or pre-empt the risk of a taking or regulation. Finally, Chapter 4 re-examines the insurance and demoralization-cost arguments for compensation in the context of the land use models reviewed in this chapter.

Chapter 5 turns to the issue of regulatory takings, and specifically to the question of whether or when compensation should ever be paid for government actions that reduce the value of a piece of property without physically acquiring it. The question here is whether land use regulations ever rise to the level of a taking. As previously noted, economic theory does not recognize a distinction between partial and full takings in the sense that they lie on a continuum. As a result, the economic analysis of regulations in principle should not be different from that of physical takings. (Indeed, the land use models studied in Chapter 4 generally do not distinguish between physical takings and regulations.) However, the law has historically treated regulations quite differently from physical takings in the sense that courts have rarely awarded compensation for mere regulations. Thus, the challenge for a positive economic theory of regulatory takings is to recognize the underlying theoretical consistency between physical takings and regulations, while at the same time accounting for the dramatically different legal treatment of the two actions.

The solution proposed in this chapter is a "threshold" compensation rule that conditions payment of compensation on the efficiency of the government's regulatory decision. Specifically, the so-called efficient threshold rule says that full compensation should be paid if the government acts inefficiently (overregulates), but no compensation is due if it acts efficiently. Using the insights from the land use models developed in Chapter 4 (and also from the economics of tort law), I first argue that this rule induces efficiency of both the regulatory and land use decisions (that is, it resolves the trade-off between moral hazard and fiscal illusion). I then go on to show that it is also consistent with the existing case law on regulatory takings. In this way, the proposed rule goes a long way toward clarifying what otherwise appears to be a muddled area of law. Chapter 5 also examines the possibility of in-kind compensation for those regulations that provide offsetting benefits by protecting landowners from pervasive neighborhood externalities. Finally, Chapter 5 applies the analysis to various policy areas in which the compensation question has historically arisen.

Chapter 6 concludes the book by summarizing the results of the previous chapters in the form of lessons that economic theory teaches us about eminent domain. The purpose here is to highlight the insights provided by an economic approach to eminent domain, rather than to claim that it offers a complete account of this important and controversial subject.

In an effort to do justice to the recent economic advances in the study of eminent domain without overburdening the general reader with technical details, I have included appendices to each of the substantive chapters (Chapters 2–5) to provide formal demonstrations of most of the key results discussed in the text. (So as not to interrupt the flow of the book, the appendices are all collected at the end.) This material is intended to acquaint interested readers with the state of the art of research in each area, while also attempting, to the extent possible, to present these results within a common theoretical framework. I also provide references to the relevant literature so that interested readers can pursue various topics in more detail. Those readers who have neither the interest nor the background for this material, however, should have no trouble following the non-technical arguments and numerical examples employed in the text. The appendix to this chapter provides a brief review of the key efficiency concepts that will form the basis for the analysis throughout the book.

TWO

Public Use

It's the great equalizer. We don't have large tracts of land. Urban centers are cut up into little parcels. Where do we acquire large parcels of land to attract large economic engines to enable us to compete with suburbia? We can only get it through eminent domain.

Tom Londregan, New London City attorney, cited in Benedict (2009, p. 250)

The first requirement for use of the power of eminent domain is that the acquired land must be put to "public use." Although seemingly straight-forward, this issue continues to evoke debate regarding the proper inter-pretation of the phrase "public use." In cases where the land is targeted for a truly public project like a highway, park, or airport – projects that meet the traditional economic definition of a public good – the use of eminent domain is not controversial. It is when the land is to be used as part of a largely private project, for example in the case of urban renewal, that it raises questions. Still, courts have generally allowed eminent domain to be used in such cases as long as the project in question promises substantial public benefits in the form of job creation, enhanced taxes, or the revitaliza-tion of an urban area. Some have argued, however, that this use of eminent domain – because it involves the transfer of land from one private party to another – renders the public use requirement essentially meaningless.[1]

The purpose of this chapter is to use economic theory to provide a coher-ent interpretation of public use. It does this by examining the proper use of eminent domain within the context of the general transaction structure developed in the previous chapter. First, however, I offer a brief review of the case law in this area.

---

[1] See, for example, Epstein (1985, p. 161), Merrill (1986, p. 61), and Rubenfeld (1993, 1078–1079).

2.1. Case Law on Public Use

As noted, the courts have historically permitted a fairly expansive interpretation of public use. For example, in *Berman v. Parker*,[2] the Supreme
Court allowed the use of eminent domain for a redevelopment plan for
Washington, D.C., that was aimed at eliminating urban blight in the
city. The Court found that all property in the designated area, included
non-blighted property, could be taken as part of the project, given that
redevelopment of the entire area was in the public interest. Similarly, in
Poletown Neighborhood Council v. City of Detroit,[3] the Michigan Supreme
Court allowed the city of Detroit to condemn an entire ethnic neighborhood in order to clear the way for a General Motors assembly plant. In
this case, the Court argued that, although the intended use of the land was
largely private, the public use requirement was satisfied by the new jobs and
tax revenues that the plant promised for the city. Interestingly, in 2004, the
Michigan Supreme Court overturned its ruling in *Poletown* in the case of
County of Wayne v. Hathcock.[4] The Court argued there that the public use
requirement was not satisfied by the mere showing of a general economic
benefit associated with a redevelopment project, and further, that its earlier
ruling in *Poletown* was contrary to the fundamental protection of private
property afforded by the Constitution.[5]

Although the *Hathcock* decision suggested that the public use issue was
not quite a dead letter, the U.S. Supreme Court seemingly put the matter
to rest a year later in the case of *Kelo v. New London* when it invoked the
logic of *Berman* and *Poletown* to allow the use of eminent domain by
the City of New London, Connecticut, for a re-development plan aimed
at revitalizing the distressed downtown and waterfront areas.[6] The plan
authorized the use of eminent domain to acquire the properties of several
unwilling sellers within the proposed area, and then called for the bulk
of the land to be turned over to a large pharmaceutical company for the

---

[2] 348 U.S. 26 (1954).
[3] 304 N.W.2d 455, 410 Mich. 616 (1981). See Fischel (2004) for some interesting background on this case.
[4] 684 N.W.2d 765, 471 Mich. 445 (2004).
[5] The Court nevertheless said that private takings could still take place under the following
conditions: "(1) where 'public necessity of the extreme sort' requires collective action; (2)
where the property remains subject to public oversight after transfer to a private entity;
and (3) where the property is selected because of 'facts of independent public significance,'
rather than the interest of the private entity to which the property is eventually transferred." *County of Wayne v. Hathcock*, 684 N.W.2d 765, 783 (2004).
[6] *Kelo v. New* London, 545 U.S. 469 (2005)

construction of a research facility.[7] The Connecticut Supreme Court had previously found that the city's use of eminent domain was appropriate for this purpose, arguing that the planned development satisfied the public use requirements of both the state and U.S. constitutions. In a controversial 5–4 decision, the U.S. Supreme Court agreed, stating that "[t]he City has carefully formulated an economic development plan that it believes will provide appreciable benefits to the community, including – but by no means limited to – new jobs and increased tax revenue.... Because that plan unquestionably serves a public purpose, the takings challenged here satisfy the public use requirement of the Fifth Amendment."[8] Note the Court's use of the term "public purpose" in place of "public use," thereby apparently justifying the more expansive interpretation of the constitutional requirement.

In her dissenting opinion, however, Justice O'Connor argued that the ruling went beyond previous definitions of public use by allowing the transfer of land from one private party to another "so long as the new use is predicted to generate some secondary benefit to the public – such as increased tax revenue, more jobs, maybe even esthetic pleasure."[9] As a result, she concluded that the standard placed few limits on the government's ability to use eminent domain to acquire private property for supposedly more productive private uses (Kelly, 2006, p. 17). Justice Thomas went even further, saying that "[i]f 'economic development' takings are for a 'public use,' any taking is, and the Court has erased the Public Use Clause from our Constitution..."[10]

Two other notable cases illustrate the extremes to which courts have been willing to go in defining acceptable public uses. In *City of Oakland v. Oakland Raiders*,[11] the California Supreme Court upheld in principle the City of Oakland's right to use eminent domain to condemn the contractual rights associated with the Oakland Raiders football franchise in an effort to prevent the team from relocating to Los Angeles. And in *Hawaii Housing Authority v. Midkiff*,[12] the U.S. Supreme Court upheld the Hawaii Land Reform Act, which allowed the public housing authority to use eminent domain to transfer land from landlords to tenants as a strategy for reducing the high degree of market power in the Hawaiian land market.

---

[7] See Benedict (2009) for an interesting history of the case.
[8] *Kelo v. New London*, 545 U.S. 469, 483–484 (2005).
[9] *Id.*, p. 501.
[10] *Id.*, p. 506.
[11] 32 Cal.3d 60, 646 P.2d 835, 183 Cal. Rptr. 673 (1982)
[12] 467 U.S. 229 (1984). See LaCroix and Rose (1995) for an analysis of this case.

The preceding cases illustrate the general principle that courts have traditionally been very deferential to legislatures in their interpretation of the meaning of public use, to the point where "almost any governmental taking, including a taking involving a private transfer, would qualify as a legitimate public use" (Kelly, 2006, p. 12). The goal of the remainder of this chapter is to see whether economic theory can be used to restore some substance to the public use requirement.

2.2. The Means-Ends Distinction

The starting point for this inquiry is the seminal analysis of the public use issue by Thomas Merrill (1986), which is based on the distinction between the "means" and "ends" of a governmental action. Consider a government-sponsored project that requires the assembly of multiple parcels of land. The means concerns the manner in which the needed land will be acquired, whereas the ends concerns the specific use to which it will actually be put. The literal meaning of the public use limitation suggests that the justification for eminent domain should depend on an analysis of ends – that is, will the land be used for a public purpose? On the other hand, the actual exercise of eminent domain, because it involves a coercive taking of land, concerns the means by which the land is acquired. The distinction between ends and means therefore raises the question of whether the proper justification for eminent domain is the use to which the land will be put (the ends), or the manner in which the land will be acquired, irrespective of its ultimate use (the means). An economic approach to this question turns on the relationship between two potential sources of market failure: the free-rider problem and the holdout problem (Cohen 1991; Miceli 2010).

2.3. The Free-Rider Problem

The free-rider problem arises in the context of public goods, which economists define to be those goods having the characteristic that, once produced, their benefits cannot be denied to any consumers, including those who have not contributed to the cost of provision. Public goods are therefore said to be "non-excludable."[13] Because of this feature, voluntary purchase will generally result in underprovision of public goods (or, in the extreme case, no provision) because each consumer would prefer to have someone else bear the cost. This is what is meant by the free-rider problem.

---

[13] Public goods are also "inexhaustible" in the sense that consumption of the good by one person does not reduce the quantity available for others.

Table 2.1. *Returns for the gardening example*

		Neighbor 2	
		Hard	Easy
Neighbor 1	Hard	50, 50	20, 60
	Easy	60, 20	30, 30

A simple game-theoretic example illustrates the problem. Suppose two neighbors agree to share a vegetable garden, the output of which they will divide equally at the end of the growing season. Total output will depend on how much effort each neighbor devotes to maintenance activities, such as weeding, watering, fertilizing, and the like. To make things simple, let us suppose that each neighbor has two choices, either work "hard" or take it "easy," and that neither is able to monitor the other's effort. Assume that output from the garden depends on the neighbors' efforts as follows: It will be maximized if both work hard, it will be somewhat lower if one works hard while the other takes it easy, and it will be lowest if neither works hard. Finally, assume that both individuals value the output from the garden but are also averse to hard work. Thus, each individual's net return from investing in the joint venture reflects his or her equal share of the resulting output less the cost of whatever amount of effort he or she chooses to devote to it.

Table 2.1 summarizes the resulting returns as a function of the effort choices of the two neighbors. (In each cell, the return for Neighbor 1 is listed first, and the return for Neighbor 2 is listed second.) Thus, when both work hard (upper left cell), they each get a net return of 50, reflecting their equal inputs of effort and equal division of the output. Likewise, when neither works hard (lower right cell), they each get a return of 30. Finally, when one works hard and the other takes it easy (lower left and upper right cells), the hard worker gets only 20 while the "loafer" gets 60. The loafer therefore free-rides on the effort of the hard worker, again, given equal division of the output. Given these payoffs, note that the joint returns are maximized when both neighbors work hard and minimized when neither works hard. The question is, what strategies will each party actually choose?

Consider first Neighbor 1's optimal strategy. If she expects Neighbor 2 to work hard (column one), she will prefer to take it easy because by doing so she will receive a return of 60 rather than 50. (That is, she will get half of the output but avoid the cost of effort.) Similarly, if she expects Neighbor 2 to take it easy (column two), she will again prefer to take it easy because she will receive a return of 30 rather than 20. Thus, Neighbor 1's optimal strategy is to take it easy regardless of what she expects Neighbor 2 to do; we say that taking it easy is Neighbor 1's "dominant strategy." And because the payoffs are symmetric, Neighbor 2's dominant strategy is the same, namely to take it easy.

Readers familiar with game theory will notice that this game has the structure of a prisoner's dilemma.[14] Thus, the Nash equilibrium involves both neighbors taking it easy rather than working hard. This is true despite the fact that both would be better off if they could somehow both agree to work hard. The reason for this suboptimal outcome is that, given equal division of the output, each neighbor hopes to free-ride on the other's effort. And because both neighbors recognize this incentive, each wants to avoid being the "sucker" – that is, to work hard while the other takes it easy. As a result, they both take it easy, and output is correspondingly low.[15]

This simple example illustrates the fundamental problem associated with provision of public goods. Namely, because individuals cannot be denied consumption of the resulting output owing to the good's non-exclusivity, no one has an incentive to contribute to the cost of providing it in the first place. Thus, public goods will be underprovided, or not provided at all, by the private market. As a result, economists generally argue that to achieve the efficient outcome, the government needs to take over the provision of public goods (or to subsidize their provision) and to coerce payment from all consumers in the form of taxes in order to finance the cost. In this way, "forced purchase" replaces market exchange as a way of overcoming the free-rider problem.[16]

---

[14] In the paradigmatic prisoner's dilemma game, two suspects are apprehended for a crime, say armed robbery, but the evidence would only allow them to be convicted of a lesser crime, say burglary. The prosecutor thus separates the suspects and offers each a deal: "If you agree to testify against the other guy, you will receive a reduced sentence (something less than the sentence for burglary)." The jointly optimal strategy is for both to refuse to testify against the other given the lack of evidence, but the dominant strategy (and hence the Nash equilibrium) is for both to testify. See Poundstone (1992) for a history and discussion of the applications of this game.

[15] The example is not a frivolous one. Ellickson (1993, pp. 1338–1339) relates the experience of the Plymouth Colony, which was initially organized communally – that is, all settlers were allowed to share equally in the production of food and other necessities. As a result, agricultural output from the common field was poor. However, when each household was later allocated its own land for cultivation, overall output increased substantially. By assigning private property rights to land rather than leaving it as communal, agricultural production therefore became a private rather than a public good, and the free-rider problem was largely eliminated.

[16] In Chapter 1 we distinguished between externalities and public goods as two different sources of market failure, but the free-rider problem associated with public goods can actually be characterized as a form of beneficial externality. That is, once someone purchases a unit of the public good, others receive some or all of the benefits. Thus, in the

Although this solution can theoretically result in the efficient provision of public goods, it is important to point out that government provision cannot perfectly replicate the outcome that an efficient market would achieve because the government does not know with certainty how much each consumer values the good (that is, it cannot observe individual demand curves). Thus, tax payments cannot generally be matched to benefits, resulting in some individuals being overcharged and some undercharged. For example, taxes to finance public goods are usually assessed based on some observable magnitude, such as a consumer's income or property value, rather than on his or her unobservable valuation of the good. Not only does this prevent the matching of individual contributions to benefits, but it potentially prevents the efficient quantity of the public good from being provided because the determination of that quantity depends on an aggregation of the unobservable individual valuations.

The so-called Lindahl tax scheme for financing public goods shows how both of these problems – that is, matching individual payments to benefits and providing the efficient quantity – can be achieved in theory, but it fails in practice because it relies on the truthful reporting of benefits by all consumers in order to set the individually optimal tax prices. Demand revealing tax schemes can be designed to overcome this problem, but they are generally too complex to implement in practice.[17] (I will review the principles underlying these schemes in Section 3.2 of the next chapter in the context of defining just compensation rules.) Thus, realistic government tax schemes for overcoming the free-rider problem cannot generally achieve the most efficient outcome.

2.4. The Holdout Problem

The second market failure relevant for developing an economic approach to public use is the holdout problem. This problem arises in the context of large-scale development projects, both public and private, that require the assembly of several contiguous and individually owned parcels of land. Examples include highways, airports, parks, and large real estate developments. The problem a land assembler faces in these settings is that once the process of assembly begins, individual sellers realize that they can impose substantial costs on the buyer by refusing to sell. Consequently, sellers

---

garden example, if one neighbor works hard, the other receives a share of the resulting benefits (given equal sharing of the output).

[17] See, for example, Feldman (1980, chapter 6) and Atkinson and Stiglitz (1980, chapter 16)

acquire a kind of monopoly power that allows them to hold out for prices well in excess of their true valuations. The usual result is that the project is either inefficiently delayed or is not completed at all, as in the case of the proverbial "highway to nowhere."

Economists and legal scholars have long recognized the importance of the holdout problem and have characterized it in a variety of ways: as a problem of transaction costs (Cooter, 2000, p. 289), monopoly (Posner, 2003, p. 55), asymmetric information (Strange, 1985; Shavell, 2010), rent seeking (Goldberg, 1985), and anti-commons (Heller, 1999, p. 1170).[18] All may be correct, depending on the particular circumstances. The specific manner in which the problem is conceptualized, however, is not especially important; what is important is that at its base, it is the result of a supply-side externality that impedes efficient assembly of property.[19] A simple example based on the strategic behavior of sellers illustrates the resulting inefficiency.[20]

Consider two identical and individually owned parcels of land located side by side. Let the value of each parcel to its owner be $100,000, reflecting the amount each would accept in a consensual sale. Now suppose a developer wishes to purchase the two parcels in order to construct an office building that would be worth $400,000 when completed. Consolidation of the parcels thus yields a net surplus of $200,000 and therefore represents the efficient use of the land. However, if the owners are aware of the project, they may behave strategically in their dealings with the developer in a way that could impede completion of the project. Notice in particular

[18] Heller (1998) defines the anti-commons problem generally as "a property regime in which multiple owners hold effective rights of exclusion in a scarce resource" (p. 668). Thus, "[u]nlike owners in a private property regime, owners in an anticommons regime must reach some agreement among themselves for the object to be used ..." (p. 670). This description suggests that the anti-commons problem is more general than the holdout problem in the sense that it can encompass both failures of bargaining between a buyer and multiple owners of individual parcels of land (as in the prototypical holdout situation), as well as failures of bargaining among multiple co-owners of a single (undivided) asset like a house or business. The result in both situations is the same; namely, failure to use the asset(s) in question efficiently, but the nature of the cost involved (and hence the optimal remedy) may be quite different. In the first case (the holdout problem), it is a contracting cost, whereas in the second, it may be more usefully characterized as a governance cost. See Coase's (1937) classic discussion of the difference between these two types of costs, which has generated a large literature on the optimal boundary between the firm and the market. Also see the discussion of partition statutes in Section 2.8 in this chapter.

[19] Heller (2008, p. 111) describes the holdout problem as creating a "one-way ratchet" toward greater fragmentation of land. Interestingly, Parisi (2002) likens this tendency to the Second Law of Thermodynamics in physics, which says that in a closed system, the extent of disorder (entropy) will increase over time.

[20] The example is based on the model in Miceli and Segerson (2007). Also see Menezes and Pitchford (2004).

that as soon as one of the owners sells his or her land to the developer, say for $100,000, the value of the second parcel to the developer immediately jumps to $300,000, which is substantially above its average value of $200,000. Recognizing this, each owner would obviously like to wait until the other owner sells before beginning to negotiate with the developer. The timing of sales is thus important in this setting.

To be concrete about the strategic behavior of the sellers, suppose that there are two time periods, "today" and "tomorrow," and that the developer can proceed with the project if he acquires both parcels today, one today and one tomorrow, or both tomorrow. Suppose, however, that there is a cost of delay, equal to $50,000 for each parcel acquired tomorrow. The net value of the project therefore diminishes with time: If both parcels are acquired today, the project is worth $400,000; if one is acquired today and one tomorrow, it is worth $350,000; and if both are acquired tomorrow, it is worth $300,000. After that, assume that the project is worthless and will be abandoned.

For simplicity, suppose that in any successful transaction, the sale price is determined by the buyer's value. In other words, the seller (or sellers) obtain all of the surplus from any transaction. Thus, if both sell today, they split the $400,000, yielding $200,000 each. Likewise, if both sell tomorrow, they each get $300,000/2=$150,000. Finally, if one sells today and the other tomorrow, the one selling today gets $100,000, whereas the one selling tomorrow gets $350,000–$100,000=$250,000.[21] These returns are summarized in Table 2.2.

As in the earlier gardening example, we determine the equilibrium of the sellers' "entry game" by first deriving the optimal strategy for each seller in response to each of the possible strategies for the other seller. Take Seller 1, for instance. If she expects Seller 2 to sell today, it is optimal for her to sell tomorrow because she receives $250,000 rather than $200,000. Likewise, if she expects Seller 2 to sell tomorrow, it is also optimal for her to sell tomorrow because she receives $150,000 rather than $100,000. Thus, the optimal (dominant) strategy for Seller 1 is to sell tomorrow regardless of what Seller 2 does. And considering that the payoffs are symmetric, the optimal strategy for Seller 2 is the same. Thus, the dominant strategy for both sellers is to sell tomorrow. As in the earlier gardening example, this game has the structure of a prisoner's dilemma, and the unique equilibrium is for both

---

[21] The basic results would be the same if the price were determined by bargaining such that both parties expect to receive share of the surplus. This is the case studied by Miceli and Segerson (2007).

Table 2.2. *Returns for the sellers' entry game*

		Seller 2	
		Today	Tomorrow
Seller 1	Today	1: $200,000	1: $100,000
		2: $200,000	2: $250,000
	Tomorrow	1: $250,000	1: $150,000
		2: $100,000	2: $150,000

sellers to sell tomorrow; that is, for both sellers to hold out. Although the office building is eventually built, this only happens after a delay that costs the developer (and society) $100,000.[22]

It is difficult to evaluate the importance of the holdout problem in practice because of the lack of empirical evidence. The previous example suggests that delay is likely, but the extent of the problem is unknown. In an effort to gain some insight into its actual impact, Cadigan et al. (2010) used experimental methods to examine the prevalence of holdouts in bargaining games involving a single buyer and two sellers whose properties exhibit the type of complementarity described earlier. Their results showed that in a multi-period setting with costly delay, holding out is a common strategy on the part of sellers. Further, as the number of periods during which the project could be completed increased, both the buyer and sellers adopted tougher bargaining stances in early periods, thus increasing delay in reaching an agreement. Although the authors found that higher delay costs mitigated the problem, it did not eliminate it. The good news is that bargains were eventually reached in nearly all experiments, reflecting the parties' recognition of the mutual gains from a successful transaction. The results therefore suggest that the principal cost of the holdout problem is delay rather than failure to complete the project altogether. Still, the social costs of such delay can be substantial.

One way to overcome the inefficiency associated with the holdout problem is forced sales. That is, substitute liability rule protection for property rule protection of the land of those sellers who threaten to hold out. In the previous example, suppose that in the first period, the buyer tries to bargain with the sellers to arrange a consensual sale, but he and the sellers all know

---

[22] The costs of delay are actually borne by the sellers themselves because they extract all of the surplus in this example. Thus, their strategic behavior, aimed at increasing their individual payoffs, actually ends up hurting them. This paradoxical conclusion is a characteristic of all prisoner's dilemma games.

Table 2.3. *Returns for the sellers' entry game with the possibility of forced sales in period two*

		Seller 2	
		Today	Tomorrow
Seller 1	Today	1: $200,000	1: $250,000
		2: $200,000	2: $100,000
	Tomorrow	1: $100,000	1: $100,000
		2: $250,000	2: $100,000

that he will have the power to force a sale in period two by any sellers who chose to hold out in period one. Further, suppose that the price for a forced sale is set by a court at $100,000. The revised payoffs for the sellers' entry game in this scenario are shown in Table 2.3.

Note that the payoffs when both sellers sell today (upper left cell) are unaffected, but any seller who sells tomorrow receives only $100,000. Suppose, for example, that Seller 1 sells today while Seller 2 holds out. Because the buyer knows he will be able to acquire Seller 2's land tomorrow for $100,000, Seller 1 can negotiate a price of $250,000=$350,000–$100,000 today (assuming, as before, that the seller extracts all of the surplus). Given these payoffs, it is easy to verify that the equilibrium of this game is for both sellers to sell today. Thus, the mere threat of a forced sale in period two overcomes the holdout problem in this example, and the efficient outcome is thereby achieved.

As with taxation for public goods, however, a forced sale is not a perfect substitute for a market exchange because of the unobservability of individual seller's reservation prices. In the example, we assumed that the price of a forced sale was set by the court at the seller's true valuation ($100,000), but that will not generally be possible because the seller's valuation will be private knowledge. (Recall that this was the disadvantage of liability rules as described in Chapter 1.) Indeed, as we will argue at length in Chapter 3, courts set compensation for government takings at the fair market value of the taken properties, which will generally be systematically less than an owner's true valuation. In addition to concerns about the undercompensation of individual owners (a fairness issue), this creates the risk that too much land will be taken. This last point suggests that the decision to use eminent domain to overcome holdouts involves a trade-off between the risk of too little (or delayed) assembly if it is not used versus the risk of too much assembly if it is used.

2.5. The Relationship between Free-Riders and Holdouts: Toward a General Framework for Public Use

The preceding sections have illustrated the free-rider and holdout problems, as well as the appropriate government responses to them. In particular, we have seen that the free-rider problem is a demand-side externality that can be resolved by forced purchases (taxation), whereas the holdout problem is a supply-side externality that can be resolved by forced sales (takings). The key point is that because these problems are on different sides of the market, they are separable in the sense that the presence of one does not necessarily imply the presence of the other. For example, public goods do not always require land assembly, and projects involving land assembly are not always public goods. Thus, whether it is appropriate to resort to one of the proposed remedies, whether taxes or takings (or both), depends on the particular characteristics of the transaction in question.

Table 2.4 illustrates this idea in the context of a hypothetical transaction by asking whether the transaction involves a free-rider problem (the vertical dimension) or a holdout problem (the horizontal dimension).[23] The four cells depict the possible cases. In Case I, neither problem is present, so neither tax financing to force a purchase nor eminent domain to force a sale is justified. This represents the situation with ordinary market transactions, whether they are between two private individuals or between a private individual and the government. Here, the Invisible Hand Theorem implies that consensual, or market, exchange will achieve the efficient outcome; thus, there is no need for government intervention.

Case IV depicts the other extreme where both a free-rider and a holdout problem are present. This case reflects the prototypical public use situation, where the government needs to assemble land for provision of a large-scale public good like a highway. Here, the use of eminent domain is justified by the means approach, and tax financing to raise the revenue necessary to compensate owners is justified by the ends approach.[24]

Next consider Case III, where a free-rider problem is present, but there is no holdout problem. This situation describes a "mixed" case where the government is providing a public good that does not require land assembly. Here, taxation to finance the good is appropriate to overcome the free-rider problem, but the use of eminent domain to acquire the land (or other

---

[23] The following discussion is based on Miceli (2010).

[24] Ulen's (1992) "dual constraint" approach to eminent domain would limit its use to this case. See Section 2.11 in this chapter. Also see Calabresi and Melamed (1972), who point out the relationship between free-riders and holdouts in this context.

Table 2.4. *General framework for determining the appropriate scope for government intervention in the market*

		Holdout problem?	
		No	Yes
Free-Rider Problem?	No	Case I: No tax financing No eminent domain	Case II: No tax financing Eminent domain
	Yes	Case III: Tax financing No eminent domain	Case IV: Tax financing Eminent domain

inputs) is not justified because there is no holdout problem. For example, the government properly uses taxes to finance the provision of police protection for all of its citizens because deterrence of crime is a public good, but it would not be justifiable to allow the government to use its taking power to conscript police officers,[25] to acquire a fleet of patrol cars, or to take a single parcel of land for a police station. Instead, the government should have to acquire these inputs by means of market transactions, just as a private security firm would. And in fact, Fischel (1995a, p. 74) notes that in most cases, governments do this voluntarily because the transaction costs of using eminent domain in settings where holdouts are not present are generally high enough to deter its overuse. In this sense, Fischel argues, the use of eminent domain in the situation described by Case III is largely "self limiting."

Finally, consider Case II, in which there is no free-rider problem but there is a holdout problem. Most "private takings" cases fall into this category – that is, they involve private developers facing holdout problems. As noted, courts have historically tended to allow the use of eminent domain in such cases, but, as the *Kelo* and *Poletown* cases showed, they nearly always seek to justify this action in terms of ends – that is, the expected public benefits that will flow from the project – rather than means – that is, the need to overcome holdouts (Merrill, 1986, p. 67). The reason for this confusion is the ambiguous meaning of the phrase "public use." As Epstein (1985, p. 166) notes, "The language of public use invites the theory of public goods," by which he means that the plain meaning of the public use limitation suggests that eminent domain should only be used to acquire land that will literally

---

[25] See Fischel (1996), who likens the military draft to eminent domain.

be put to a public use; that is, to provide a public good. However, the above analysis shows that this focus on ends is misguided because it suggests that eminent domain is being used to resolve a demand-side failure, whereas the proper economic justification is the presence of a holdout problem – a supply-side failure. By conflating ends and means, however, courts strain to identify the "public purpose" behind what is largely a private project.

It is nevertheless the case that most large-scale development projects generate *some* spillover benefits to the public, so finding a "public purpose," broadly defined, is nearly always possible. The problem is that the court's propensity to employ such reasoning ultimately places few limits on those situations in which eminent domain will be allowed, which is why many observers have called the public use requirement a "dead letter" (Merrill, 1986, p. 61; Fischel, 2004, p. 934). (And besides, such spillover benefits, if present, would call for a subsidy of the development rather than the use of eminent domain.)[26] If, in deciding public use cases, courts instead focused on the means rather than the ends, they would easily identify the proper economic test for the use of eminent domain – namely, the presence of a holdout problem. As a result, much of the confusion (if not the controversy) surrounding private takings cases would likely vanish.

To summarize the argument in this section, the taxonomy in Table 2.4 prescribes the use of eminent domain to overcome the holdout problem (cases II and IV), and taxation to overcome the free-rider problem (cases III and IV). The important point is that the two dimensions are, in principle, independent of each other in the sense that not all public goods involve holdouts, and some private goods do. Thus, the proper economic justification for the use of eminent domain according to this "pure" theory of public use is, in truth, unrelated to the publicness of the project in question. However, the natural tendency to equate public use with public goods (as described above in terms of the confusion between means and ends) indicates that there is both a risk of overuse (Case III) and underuse (Case II) of eminent domain. The remainder of this chapter both elaborates on and qualifies this argument.

2.6. Bilateral Monopoly

The preceding section highlighted the holdout problem as the principal rationale for eminent domain, but high transaction costs and failed

---

[26] See Section 3.4 in Chapter 3, however, where I suggest that market value compensation might be interpreted as providing such a subsidy.

negotiations can also occur in transactions involving only one buyer and one seller – a situation that economists refer to as a "bilateral monopoly." Suppose, for example, that a particular location is uniquely suited to build an airport or to mine coal, but has little value otherwise. In this case, neither the buyer nor the seller has a good alternative except to deal with the other, but there is a large surplus to be gained if they can reach an agreement. Usually, the potential for mutual gain will induce the parties to reach a deal, but the transaction costs can be quite high as each seeks as large a share of the profit as possible (Posner, 2003, p. 61). In this sense, bilateral monopoly is a close cousin to the holdout problem, and as a result, some argue that it may warrant the use of eminent domain (Bell, 2009, p. 530).

The problem with this rationale for eminent domain, however, is the risk that any two-party transaction could potentially be labeled as a bilateral monopoly, given the unobservability of transaction costs. (At least with the holdout problem, the multiplicity of sellers is evidence that bargaining is likely to fail.) Although we saw above that the high administrative costs of using eminent domain will often discourage the government and private parties alike from seeking to use the power when transaction costs are in fact low, the possible overuse of eminent domain if it were routinely allowed in two-party transactions would seem to be quite high. This suggests that courts should closely scrutinize requests for eminent domain power in such cases, with the burden on the would-be buyer to justify the need.

2.7. Other Examples of Private Takings

One of the strengths of economic theory when applied to law is to recognize fundamental similarities across different, seemingly unrelated areas of law. I will pursue this point in more detail in Chapter 4 (see Section 4.6). Here, I make use of this basic insight to suggest that the difficulty courts seem to have had in justifying private takings (forced sales) in the presence of holdouts is a bit incongruous with the pervasiveness of similar remedies in other areas of the law. This section uses two well-known cases from the law of nuisance and one from the law of contracts to make this point and, in so doing, to illustrate the general applicability of the analysis in the previous section.

The first example is the well-known case of *Boomer v. Atlantic Cement Co.*,[27] which involved a cement factory whose operation caused pollution that imposed harm on several nearby residents. In an effort to avoid the

[27] 26 N.Y.2d 219, 309 N.Y.S.2d 312, 257 N.E.2d 870, Court of Appeals of New York (1970).

harm, the residents filed suit seeking an injunction to have the factory shut down. The court opted instead to allow the factory to continue operating as long as it was willing to pay damages to the residents. That is, the court ruled in favor of the residents, but protected their right to be free from harm with a liability rule rather than a property rule. Notice that in so doing, the court essentially allowed a private taking by the factory of the residents' right to be free from noise and pollution (Fischel, 1995a, pp. 75–77). In other words, the factory was allowed to continue emitting harmful pollution without the residents' consent as long as it was willing to compensate them for the damage it caused.

In terms of the taxonomy in Table 2.4, this ruling therefore belongs to Category II, along with *Kelo* and *Poletown*, given that the factory likely would have faced a type of holdout problem if each resident had been awarded the right to enforce an injunction against it. In particular, the factory would have had to negotiate with each affected resident to obtain permission to continue to operate (i.e., to have the injunction lifted). Recognizing the high transaction costs that this likely would have entailed, the court therefore acted properly to award damages instead. Because from an economic standpoint, the problem facing *Boomer* under an injunction (property rule) would have been analytically the same as that facing a land assembler, the appropriate remedy was the same; namely, a forced sale (liability rule) to overcome the holdout problem.[28]

The second nuisance case, *Spur Industries v. Del E. Webb Development Co.* (494 P.2d 700, 1972), was first discussed in Chapter 1 to illustrate the choice between property rules and liability rules. Recall that the case involved a land developer who encroached upon a pre-existing cattle feed lot and sought to have it shut down due to the foul odors. The court granted the developer's request but ordered him to pay the feed lot owner's re-location costs. In effect, therefore, the court allowed the developer to take the feed lot's land in return for compensatory damages. An important difference between this case and *Boomer*, however, is that there were small numbers involved here. As a result, one suspects that a consensual transaction between the developer and the feed lot owner would have been possible. It therefore seems that a better remedy would have been for the court to have protected the

---

[28] Posner (2003, p. 71) instead refers to the *Boomer* case as an example of a bilateral monopoly owing to the "fewness of the parties," but he still endorses the court's use of a liability rule based on the likely presence of high transaction costs (as discussed in the previous section). Epstein (1985, p. 165, n. 11), in contrast, apparently disagrees with the ruling in *Boomer*, as he approvingly cites the dissenting opinion, which argues for injunctive relief (a property rule) in nuisance cases of this sort.

feed lot's right to operate with a property rule, which would have forced the developer to bargain with the owner over the terms of a buyout rather than having them set by the court.[29] In other words, the court allowed a private taking, but one could argue that it should have encouraged a consensual transaction given the small numbers involved. In terms of the framework in Table 2.4, therefore, the case should have been interpreted as falling under Category I rather than Category II.

As a final illustration, consider the case of *Peevyhouse v. Garland Coal & Mining Co.*,[30] which involved a breach of contract suit between the Peevyhouses, who owned a large tract of undeveloped land, and a mining company that wanted to conduct a strip-mining operation on the land. The contract in part called for the mining company to restore the land to its pre-mining state after completing the mining operation, but the company breached this clause based on its claim that the $29,000 cost of restoration greatly exceeded the mere $300 increase in market value that would have resulted from the restoration work. The court therefore allowed the breach and awarded the Peevyhouses $300 in damages. Again, one can interpret the court's ruling in this case as having authorized a private taking by the mining company. Specifically, it allowed the company to take the Peevyhouses' contractual right to performance of the restoration work in return for compensatory damages equal to the market value of the resulting loss.

Notice, however, that the small numbers involved, and the absence of a holdout problem, suggest that this case is more like *Spur* than *Boomer*. Thus, we would conclude that the court acted improperly to allow the taking. In other words, like *Spur*, this case properly belongs to Category I in Table 2.4, implying that the appropriate resolution of the dispute would have been for the mining company and the Peevyhouses to engage in a consensual transaction regarding the completion of the work. To encourage such a transaction, the court therefore should have ordered the mining company to perform the contract, thereby enforcing the Peevyhouse's property right to their land and setting the stage for the necessary bargaining.[31]

---

[29] Coleman (1988, chapter 2, footnote 5) similarly argues that, given the small numbers involved, the court should have protected the feed lot's entitlement with a property rule.

[30] 382 P.2d 109, *cert. denied*, 375 U.S. 906, Okla. (1962).

[31] See Friedmann (1989) and Ulen (1984) who argue for the superiority of specific performance (a property rule) over money damages (a liability rule) in breach-of-contract cases, given the generally low transaction costs between parties to a contract. Of course, one could argue that both *Spur* and *Peevyhouse* were cases of bilateral monopoly, thereby justifying the use of a liability rule (private taking). As suggested in Section 2.6 in this chapter, however, the presumption in two-party settings should be against the use of forced transactions, absent clear evidence of high transaction costs.

2.8. The Mill Acts and Partition Statutes

Another interesting historical example of private takings cases is provided by the mill acts, which many states passed in the eighteenth and nineteenth centuries to encourage economic development during the early stages of the industrial revolution (Epstein, 1985, pp. 170–175). These acts authorized would-be mill builders to flood upstream land without the owners' consent for purposes of creating mill ponds as a power source, provided that the builder was willing to pay compensation to flooded owners in an amount set by a court. The mill acts thus effectively allowed private takings by mill builders of the upstream owners' land, thereby raising the public use issue.

The reaction of courts to these statutes reflected the same fundamental problem discussed earlier in connection with the means-ends distinction; namely, how to reconcile the benefit of forced exchange to overcome the holdout problem that mill builders almost certainly would have encountered if required to obtain the land by voluntary exchange, against the constitutionally required need to assert a public use justification for the taking. A similar question arose in the context of statutes that allowed mine owners to take land for purposes of building access roads. In one of these mining cases, *Dayton Mining Co. v. Seawell*, the court upheld the statute in question based on the following logic:

In the building of hotels and theaters the location is not necessarily confined to any particular spot, and it is always within the reach of capital to make the proper selection, and never within the power of any one individual, or individuals, however stubborn or unreasonable, to prevent the erection of such buildings. The object for which private property is to be taken must not only be of great public benefit and for the paramount interest of the community, but the necessity must exist for the exercise of the right of eminent domain.[32]

Although the court explicitly recognized the need for eminent domain to overcome holdouts, note that it also felt the necessity of adding the public use language. (Scheiber [1973, p. 246] also emphasizes this point.)

The U.S. Supreme Court adopted a different strategy in evaluating the constitutionality of the mill acts. In the case of *Head v. Amoskeag Mfg. Co.*,[33] for example, the Court attempted to sidestep the public use issue altogether by likening the mill acts, not to takings, but to state partition statutes that allowed a disgruntled joint owner of real estate to force a sale of the property

---

[32]   11 Nev. 394, 411 (1876).
[33]   113 U.S. 9 (1885).

against the wishes of his or her co-owners. Partition statutes were an out-growth of the common law of partition, which allowed joint owners to seek a physical division of the property in question into separate, individually owned parcels (so-called partition-in-kind). The economic logic of this rule is to avoid the anti-commons problem, or the inability of co-owners to agree on the proper use of the land, resulting in its being left idle or otherwise inefficiently used (Heller, 1998, 1999; Miceli and Sirmans, 2000). In some cases, however, it is either impossible or impractical to divide the property physically. Recognizing this, most states therefore enacted statutes that allowed the court to order a forced sale of the land, with proportionate division of the proceeds, in lieu of a physical partition.

As an illustration, suppose a parcel of land that is jointly owned by two individuals is worth $10,000 to a buyer in its undivided state, but if phys-ically divided, each partition would only be worth $4,000. The market therefore attaches a $2,000 premium to the undivided parcel.[34] But suppose that Owner 1 values his one-half share at $3,000 whereas Owner 2 values her share at $6,000. Thus, in the face of an offer of $10,000 for the undi-vided parcel, it is efficient for the parties to sell, with Owner 1 receiving, say $3,500, and Owner 2 receiving $6,500. Ordinarily, the parties would arrive at this mutually beneficial outcome through bargaining. However, if the parties are unable to bargain with each other – let us say the co-owners are involved in a messy divorce – Owner 1 may seek physical partition, even though that is not the efficient course of action. Although a buyer could re-assemble the separate parcels, this would require further transac-tions that could fall prey to the holdout problem. It is therefore appropriate on economic grounds in this case for the court to substitute a forced sale for a physical division. The advantage is that the parcel remains undivided, thereby preserving its maximum value.

The analogy to private takings should be obvious. The court's order of a forced sale in this case actually prevents the inefficient *disassembly* of the parcel, which would have occurred as a result of the breakdown in bargaining. Thus, despite the Supreme Court's effort in *Head* to avoid con-fronting the public use issue directly, its appeal to partition statutes as the legal justification for the mill acts actually succeeds in making the Court's point precisely because partition *is* a private taking that is justifiable on holdout grounds. Still, the mill acts and partition statutes both suffer from the same criticism; namely, they fail to compensate non-consenting owners

---

[34] See Colwell and Munneke (1999), who undertake an empirical analysis of the relationship between land value and parcel size.

for their subjective value. In the previous partition example, for instance, equal division of the proceeds from the forced sale, yielding $5,000 to each owner, would undercompensate Owner 2 by $1,000. Likewise, market value compensation under the mill acts deprives landowners of the amount that they value their land in excess of its assessed value. We pursue this point at length in the next chapter. (See in particular Section 3.1.)

2.9. Urban Renewal and Takings

Recall that the *Kelo* case re-established the legal principle, first laid down in *Berman*, that the public use requirement for eminent domain is satisfied for urban renewal projects based on the external benefits they generate for the public in the form of new jobs, increased tax revenue, and the general eradication of "urban blight."[35] However, the use of eminent domain for this purpose, although consistent with the pure economic theory of public use as described above, provides a further illustration of the confusion over ends versus means in defining the proper scope for the power. To make this point, we first need to understand the economic theory underlying the policy of urban renewal.

The economics of urban renewal is based on the role of the government in correcting a market failure arising from so-called neighborhood externalities. Neighborhood externalities arise from the interconnectedness of property values, especially in densely populated urban areas. The idea is that the market value of any individual property depends not only on the attributes and condition of that property itself, but also on the attributes and condition of surrounding properties. Thus, for example, when an individual owner mows his grass and paints his house, it not only increases the value of his own house, but also of all the other houses in the immediate neighborhood. The result is that individual owners, because they cannot capture the full benefits of these spillover effects, will tend to underinvest in maintenance activities.

This conclusion is once again easily illustrated with a simple two-person game.[36] Consider two adjacent property owners who must decide whether or not to invest in maintenance of their properties. Each owner will make the choice that maximizes the value of his or her individual property. The difficulty arises because, as argued above, the value of Owner 1's property also depends on the decisions made by Owner 2, and vice versa. To be concrete,

---

[35] On eminent domain and urban renewal, see Epstein (1985, pp. 178–180) and O'Flaherty (1994).

[36] This example is based on Davis and Whinston (1961). For a more formal analysis, see Schall (1976).

Table 2.5. *Returns to property owners from the various investment strategies*

| | | Owner 2 | |
		Invest	Not invest
Owner 1	Invest	8, 8	4, 10
	Not invest	10, 4	5, 5

suppose each owner has $1,000, which they can either invest in maintaining their buildings or in some alternative investment, say a government bond. Let us suppose that if both invest in their buildings, they each will get an 8% return, whereas if neither invests in their building (and instead, both invest in the government bond), they each will get a 5% return. Thus, investing in the buildings is the efficient choice. Now suppose Owner 1 invests in her building but Owner 2 does not. Owner 2 is therefore able to get the 5% return on the government bond, plus the spillover benefit from Owner 1's investment in her building, resulting in an overall return of, say, 10%. Owner 1, in contrast, only gets a 4% return, reflecting the positive effect of the investment in her own building, but offset by the negative effect of Owner 2's failure to invest in his.[37] The returns are symmetric when Owner 2 invests but Owner 1 does not. Table 2.5 summarizes the returns from the various strategy combinations.

Using the now familiar approach, we derive the equilibrium for this game by first supposing that Owner 2 chooses to invest. The optimal response for Owner 1 is also not to invest because she gets a return of 10% rather than 8%. Similarly, if Owner 2 chooses not to invest, the optimal response of Owner 1 is again not to invest because she gets a return of 5% rather than 4%. It is therefore optimal for Owner 1 not to invest, regardless of the strategy choice of Owner 2. Given symmetry, Owner 2 reacts the same way. Thus, not investing is the dominant strategy for both owners, implying that neither invests in the Nash equilibrium.

Like the preceding examples of the free-rider and holdout problems, this game has the structure of a prisoner's dilemma, which, as we have seen, has the characteristic that the equilibrium is suboptimal in the sense that the owners could have achieved higher returns if they somehow could have agreed to invest in their buildings. That outcome is not sustainable

---

[37] The magnitude of the spillover effect may seem large, but in actual neighborhoods, it will reflect the cumulative decisions of multiple neighbors.

as an equilibrium, however, because each owner could do better by deviating (i.e., by not investing). The problem stems from the interdependence of the returns, which allows owners to free-ride on the investments made by their neighbors while saving the costs of investing themselves. In this sense, the problem is identical to the free-rider problem in that both involve a demand-side (beneficial) externality.[38]

Schall (1976) has used this logic to explain the existence – and more importantly, the persistence – of slums in inner cities. He thus emphasizes the likelihood that a neighborhood that is revitalized by urban renewal, or some other one-time, government-financed upgrade in neighborhood quality, will likely revert back to the original inefficient equilibrium if the previously mentioned forces are left intact. In other words, simply rebuilding the neighborhood without putting policies in place to address the externalities that caused the deterioration in the first place will not produce a sustainable outcome.

What is the role of eminent domain in this context? In answering this question, it is important to recognize that the decentralized structure of ownership that engendered the neighborhood externalities in the first place also likely gives rise to an assembly problem at the start of a renewal process if that process requires consolidating ownership into the hands of a single entrepreneur (as was the case in both *Poletown* and *Kelo*). In this sense, urban renewal potentially involves a market failure on both the demand side (a neighborhood externality), and on the supply side (a holdout problem). Thus, it falls into Category IV in Table 2.4. Consequently, the use of eminent domain as part of an urban renewal project is justified as a response to the supply-side externality at the onset of the project (the holdout problem), given that consolidation of ownership is part of the renewal strategy. However, the demand-side (neighborhood) externality calls for a different sort of government intervention altogether, such as financial incentives (like subsidies and tax breaks) or direct regulatory controls (like zoning and housing codes) to sustain the desired level of development once the renewal project is completed. In other words, eminent domain is a justifiable *tool* in the urban renewal process, but it is not a solution to the underlying cause of the problem that gave rise to the need for urban renewal in the first place. The situation is similar to the distinction between means and ends.

---

[38] The disincentive to invest arising from the presence of neighborhood externalities is exacerbated in urban neighborhoods by the fact that most residents are renters, which further discourages investment as a consequence of the so-called rental externality. See, for example, Henderson and Ioannides (1983) and Harding, Miceli, and Sirmans (2000).

2.10. Urban Sprawl and Takings

Limiting urban sprawl is another rationale sometimes used to justify the private use of eminent domain. Urban sprawl describes the somewhat vague notion of excessive expansion of land development in and around cities. For example, Galster et al. (2001, p. 685) have defined urban sprawl to be "... a pattern of land use that exhibits low levels of some combination of eight distinct dimensions: density, continuity, concentration, clustering, centrality, nuclearity, mixed uses, and proximity." Nechyba and Walsh (2004, p. 178) offer a somewhat more concise definition: "By sprawl we ... mean the tendency toward lower city densities as city footprints expand."

This last definition reflects the culmination of two trends that have been occurring throughout the twentieth century in the United States: an increasing urban population combined with an outward spatial expansion of urban areas, a process referred to as "suburbanization." To illustrate, the fraction of the overall population living in urban areas has increased from 50% in 1920 to 79% in 2000. At the same time, the fraction of the urban population living in the suburbs increased from 35% in 1950 to 65% in 1990, whereas the amount of land occupied by central cities fell from 40% of all urban land in 1950 to 20% in 1990 (Nechyba and Walsh, 2004).

Urban economists attribute these trends to two primary factors. The first is the steady decline in transportation costs throughout the twentieth century, which has led to the outward spatial expansion of cities, and the second is the flight of higher-income households to the suburbs in search of more and better public services, and to escape the disamenities of city life.[39] Whereas most urban economists would agree that some amount of outward urban growth is a necessary by-product of an efficiently growing economy, the notion of urban sprawl, at least when discussed in a policy context, generally reflects a view that this expansion has become inefficient or excessive.

Brueckner (2000) cites three possible sources of market failure that might have caused or contributed to this inefficiency. First, the price of agricultural land does not reflect its full social value as open space, resulting in excessive development at the urban fringe. Second, commuters ignore the costs of congestion when making their location decisions, resulting in excessively long commutes. Third, developers do not account for the full social cost of development, both in terms of pollution and the loss of open space, also

---

[39] Henderson (1985) (technical) and O'Sullivan (2009) (less technical) examine both issues in the context of standard urban economic models.

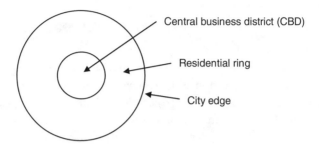

Figure 2.1. The monocentric city model.

causing excessive development. The earlier discussion of the holdout problem suggests that it might represent a fourth source of market failure contributing to the inefficient outward expansion of cities. Drawing the link between the holdout problem and sprawl,[40] however, requires some simple urban economics.

The standard economic model of cities developed by urban economists, referred to as the monocentric city model, consists of a central business district (the CBD) where business firms congregate, surrounded by a residential ring, where workers live (see Figure 2.1). Firms cluster in the CBD to take advantage of so-called agglomeration economies, or cost savings realized by firms that locate near one another. These savings arise from several sources, including the joint use of transportation nodes like truck depots or train stations, joint use of power sources, access to common input suppliers, savings in search costs for prospective workers, economies in research and development (R&D), and transportation savings for multi-stop shoppers. Given the existence and location of the CBD, the residential ring forms around it to minimize the commuting costs of workers. The edge of the city is determined endogenously in the model by the operation of the land market and is defined by the locus of points where the value of land in development equals its value for agricultural use. Over time, the spatial extent of the city expands outward as part of the normal process of economic growth in the urban economy. Specifically, as economic growth occurs, the value of land for development rises, causing the edge of the city to move outward.

A particular implication of the monocentric model is that lot sizes within the residential ring decrease toward the city center. This is true for two reasons: First, increasing land prices toward the city center cause housing developers to substitute capital for land, holding the quantity of housing

---

[40] This link was first made by Miceli and Sirmans (2007).

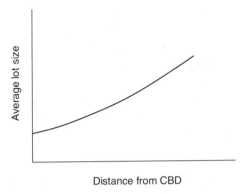

Figure 2.2. Relationship between average lot size and distance from the city center.

fixed (thus resulting in taller buildings closer to the CBD); and second, increasing housing prices toward the city center cause the demand for housing to fall. Together, these factors imply that the lot size per household decreases toward the CBD. The resulting spatial configuration of lot sizes is shown in Figure 2.2, which graphs the average lot size per housing unit as a function of distance from the city center. It follows that ownership of land is more dispersed closer to the CBD.

Now consider a land developer who wishes to assemble a given quantity of land for a large-scale development project within the residential area. In a perfectly functioning land market, the developer will choose where to locate the project based on the spatial distribution of land prices and consumer demands, resulting in an efficient location choice. Given the need for assembly, however, the developer also needs to account for the strategic costs associated with the holdout problem in his calculation. It is reasonable to suppose that these costs increase as the number of owners the buyer must negotiate with increases, therefore the severity of the holdout problem will likely increase as ownership becomes more dispersed, holding all other things equal. As a consequence, the holdout problem will become more severe as the proposed development gets closer to the city center. It follows that the optimal location choices of developers will tend to be systematically distorted away from the CBD and toward the urban fringe where ownership is less dispersed (that is, where average lot sizes are larger). By the same logic, projects situated further from the CBD will use more land, all else equal, because that component of land costs attributable to the holdout problem will be smaller. In the absence of growth controls, these factors will tend to result in a city characterized by inefficient outward growth, or urban sprawl.

We argued earlier that eminent domain is an appropriate response to the holdout problem, so making it available to developers for urban renewal projects represents one solution to the problem of urban sprawl. Other remedies involve policies aimed at increasing the cost of suburban development (for example, by implementing zoning and other regulatory controls, development taxes, and impact fees) in combination with policies aimed at encouraging inner city development (for example, the creation of enterprise zones and the granting of tax breaks for brownfield redevelopment).[41]

2.11. Arguments against the Private Use of Eminent Domain

To this point, the thesis of this chapter has been that eminent domain is best understood as a response to market failure arising from the holdout problem associated with land assembly. A corollary of this thesis is that, because holdouts can threaten private as well as public projects involving assembly, the granting of eminent domain power to private developers facing a holdout problem is justifiable on economic grounds. And even though courts have seemed to follow this logic in practice, for example by permitting the use of eminent domain for urban renewal, railroads, water-powered mills, and other large-scale private projects, they nevertheless struggle to identify public components of those projects in an effort to satisfy the plain language of the public use requirement of the Fifth Amendment. The result is a situation that one might characterize as the "paradox of public use."

Still, some scholars, including some economists, have argued for limiting the use of eminent domain to truly public projects. For example, Ulen's "dual constraint" approach to public use would allow the power to be used "only in circumstances in which the government was likely to encounter high (objective) transaction costs in the course of its efforts to provide a public good" (Ulen, 1992, p. 174). According to this view, the existence of a holdout problem would be a necessary, but not a sufficient, condition for the use of eminent domain. In terms of Table 2.4, the takings power would be limited to those situations described by Category IV.

In relation to the analysis up to this point, what I earlier called the pure economic theory of public use, this approach would seem to represent an overly restrictive use of eminent domain in the sense that it would deprive private land assemblers of the ability to force transactions when they face a holdout problem. Moreover, it commits the error of conflating means and

---

[41] See, for example, Brueckner (2000) and McFarlane (1999). But also see Turnbull (2005) and Nechyba and Walsh (2004) for countervailing arguments.

ends by tying eminent domain to public goods. Despite these criticisms, there are some good economic arguments in support of this perspective that are not captured by the simple framework depicted in Table 2.4.

The first argument for limiting the use of eminent domain to truly public projects is that private developers often have at their disposable several strategies for overcoming holdouts that do not involve the need to resort to forced sales. These include the use of secret buying agents, option agreements, and various other ways of maintaining secrecy about the intent and scope of the project.[42] The law of undisclosed agency facilitates this practice by allowing buyers to conceal the identity of their principal under certain conditions (Parisi, 2002, pp. 617–619). Once the holdout problem is resolved, there is no further justification for the use of eminent domain. This argument, however, naturally raises the question of why the government cannot resort to similar strategies to avoid the need to use eminent domain. The simple answer is that, in a democratic society, the government needs to operate in the open with regard to its spending policies (Merrill, 1986, p. 82; Fischel, 1995a, p. 70). Thus, the maintenance of secrecy in land purchases, especially for very large projects, is neither a practical nor a desirable policy for truly public projects.

A second factor relevant for determining the proper scope of eminent domain concerns the distribution of the gains and losses from those projects in which it is used. Because takings are non-consensual, that distribution will necessarily be different from that which would arise under market acquisition. In particular, as we will argue in the next chapter, the requirement of market value compensation under eminent domain precludes the landowner from negotiating for a share of the surplus from the transaction, and moreover, likely deprives him of the full opportunity cost of his land. As a result, the taker, whether the government or a private party, captures all of the surplus from the transaction, and possibly then some.

This distribution of gains in favor of the buyer has two consequences. The first, as already discussed, is that the taker does not face the full opportunity cost of the land and hence will likely have an incentive to acquire too much.[43] This problem, however, is present regardless of the identity of the taker (assuming that private developers and the government alike are

---

[42] These alternatives have been suggested by many critics of the private use of eminent domain. See, for example, Kelly (2006), Ulen (1992, p. 176), and Merrill (1986, p. 81).

[43] Fischel (2004) notes that this problem was amplified in the *Poletown* case by the fact that the redevelopment project was heavily subsidized by the federal government, thereby further distorting the decision by local officials regarding whether or not to go ahead with the project.

sensitive to the cost of land in deciding how much to acquire), and hence provides no clear guidance regarding the proper scope of eminent domain. In other words, there is no obvious reason to think that this source of inefficiency (excessive takings) will be any more or less severe if the power of eminent domain were granted solely to the government.

The second consequence of the distribution of gains under eminent domain is that the resulting concentration of benefits in the hands of the taker could lead to a problem of rent seeking and political corruption, as various interest groups seek to acquire the power.[44] This threat *would* seem to be especially severe for private projects precisely because the benefits from those projects are concentrated in the hands of a few, in contrast to truly public projects, where the benefits tend to be more dispersed. For this reason, Epstein (1985, pp. 173–174) and Kelly (2006) have urged that the use of eminent domain should be limited to provision of public goods so as to minimize the risk of such activities. We pursue this argument further in Section 3.1 of the next chapter.

A final argument for limiting the use of eminent domain to truly public projects maintains that the Fifth Amendment's takings clause was never intended to advance an economic theory of takings, and thus should not be interpreted in that way. According to this view, the public use requirement should be taken literally as a matter of law, regardless of the economic issues involved.

2.12. Historical Patterns of the Delegation of Eminent Domain to Private Enterprises in the United States

This chapter on public use has been primarily theoretical, but I want to conclude it with some historical and empirical evidence on the extent of the private use of eminent domain in the United States.[45] During the early decades of the Republic, eminent domain policy was largely determined by state courts, and by the 1820s, they had arrived at three guiding principles regarding the use of the power: (1) eminent domain was an inherent right of the state; (2) the power could only be used for a public use or purpose; and (3) just compensation was required. In addition to these basic principles, courts also formulated a set of doctrines that established the actual scope and practice of the power, particularly in regard to the meaning of

---

[44] See, for example, Merrill (1986, p. 86), Somin (2004), and Kelly (2006).

[45] This survey is based largely on Schieber (1973). Also see Friedman (1985, p. 182) and Horwitz (1992, pp. 63–74).

just compensation. One of these was the so-called benefit-offset principle, which allowed the state to reduce the amount of compensation it owed to an owner whose land was only partially taken by deducting the amount that the proposed project increased the value of the untaken portion.[46] Another was to exclude consequential or indirect damages from the meaning of just compensation.[47]

A more important step taken by courts in the early nineteenth century was their willingness, as already noted, to extend the power of eminent domain to certain private enterprises in the interest of promoting general economic development. Naturally, this raised the issue of the meaning of public use. Industries that initially benefited included turnpike, canal, and railroad builders on the grounds that these businesses served essential public purposes because of the importance of transportation to the process of economic growth. But by the 1870s and up to about 1910, eminent domain was widely used to subsidize this or that industry, with little apparent regard for the meaning of public use: Any industry that could be construed as contributing in some way to public welfare was a possible beneficiary. By 1910, however, the situation began to change as many states made changes to their constitutions in an effort to curtail the seemingly unrestricted use of eminent domain.

Fischel (1995a, pp. 88–90) has conjectured that the initial expansion and subsequent curtailment in the private use of eminent domain during this period in American history can be broadly explained by the economic principle of diminishing marginal benefit, as illustrated by Figure 2.3. Specifically, when development projects like railroad construction were in their early stages, the marginal benefit to society was very high relative to the marginal cost, as shown, for example, by point q' in Figure 2.3. Thus, politicians were inclined to subsidize the further development of these industries to ensure that society would receive the fullest possible economic benefits. One way they did this was by adopting a liberal interpretation of the public use and just compensation provisions, such as the benefit-offset principle mentioned earlier. Whatever costs were borne by the few landowners who were asked to sacrifice their property in this cause were seen as a necessary consequence of economic development. Later, however, as continued expansion of railroad or mill construction had reduced the marginal benefit of further construction to the point where it

---

[46] See the further discussion of the benefit-offset principle in Section 3.4 of Chapter 3.

[47] See Epstein (1985, pp. 51–56). Also see the discussion of *Callender v. Marsh* (1 Pick. 417, Mass. 1823) in Section 3.9 of Chapter 3.

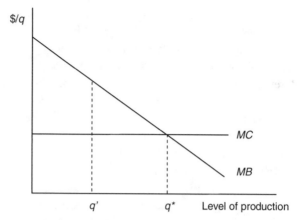

Figure 2.3. Marginal benefit (*MB*) and marginal cost (*MC*) of a government-sponsored project.

approached equality with the marginal cost, as at point q^* in Figure 2.3, courts and legislatures more eagerly acted to curtail the use of eminent domain by interpreting its provisions more strictly.

Fleck and Hanssen (2010) have formalized this argument in a model in which citizens decide whether or not to delegate eminent domain (or other powers) to the government. That power may have a very high social value initially, for example when it promotes the development of a nascent industry, but eventually its value declines based on the principle of diminishing marginal benefit. Courts are charged with the responsibility of monitoring the use of the delegated power, and in particular, they act to limit its overuse when the optimal level of development is reached. The resulting "cycles" in eminent domain use reflect its initial expansion and then contraction in the context of various historical episodes linked to the development of particular industries. In addition to Fischel's example of the railroads, Fleck and Hanssen discuss the use of eminent domain to promote the construction of water-powered mills in eighteenth-century America (as discussed above), mining in the Rocky Mountain states in the nineteenth century, and, most recently, urban renewal in the twentieth century. These examples illustrate the ongoing role of courts in striking a balance between the socially beneficial use and the possible abuse, of eminent domain as a spur of economic growth.

To obtain a broader perspective on the attitude of courts to the public use issue, Merrill (1986) undertook a systematic survey of all state and federal court rulings in public use cases decided between 1954 (the year of *Berman*) and 1985. The resulting sample included 308 cases, 291 decided by state courts and 17 decided by federal appellate courts. Of these cases, 261 (84.7%) found that the government action satisfied public use, whereas 47 (15.3%) did not. Notably, all of the federal cases upheld the proposed use of eminent domain, prompting Merrill to conclude that "state courts are much less deferential to legislative declarations of public use than one would expect in light of *Poletown*, *Oakland Raiders*, and *Midkiff*. In fact, state court enforcement of the public use limitation has generally increased since 1954" (Merrill, 1986, p. 65). A noteworthy recent example, of course, was the Michigan Supreme Court's ruling in *County of Wayne v. Hathcock* (2004), issued only a year before *Kelo*, which overruled its earlier decision in *Poletown*.

2.13. Statistical Analysis of State Use of Private Takings and the Political Response Thereto

A more recent survey of private takings cases, compiled by Berliner (2003) under the auspices of the Castle Coalition,[48] documented all known instances of the actual or threatened use of eminent domain for private projects over the five-year period from 1998 to 2002, categorized by state. This survey differs from Merrill's study in that it describes the willingness of states to delegate the power of eminent domain to private parties, and in that respect, it is more reflective of the political rather than the legal climate in a given state (though of course the two are interrelated). More importantly, the comprehensiveness of the data allows one to undertake a systematic statistical analysis of the factors that affected states' use of private takings for economic development over this period.

Table 2.6 reports the results of a study by Diop et al. (2010) that used regression analysis to determine the factors that affected the number of *filed takings* as reported in Berliner (2003). The explanatory variables used in the study include two measures of the severity of the holdout problem facing would-be developers. The first is the percentage of *urban land* in a state (urban land as a percent of all land), and the second is *urban density* (urban population divided by urban land area). Higher values of both of these variables are associated with more fragmented ownership of land and hence should result in a larger number of takings according to the holdout theory of public use.

---

[48] The Castle Coalition (http://www.castlecoalition.org) was formed by the Institute for Justice (http://www.ij.org), which is a non-profit public-interest law firm located in Washington, D.C.

A second set of explanatory variables is meant to capture the demand for economic development. These include the state's *population* and per capita *disposable income*, both of which should have a positive effect on the demand for development and hence on the number of takings. The growth rate in *gross state product* (GSP) is also included,[49] though the expected sign of this variable is unclear. On one hand, a higher growth rate in GSP should increase the demand for development, implying a positive effect, but on the other, if state officials view eminent domain as a tool for spurring economic growth (as exemplified by *Kelo*), the effect could be negative (i.e., more takings will be used in states with lower growth rates). The *median price* of homes is also included to test whether government officials take account of the opportunity cost of targeted properties. If they do, this variable should be negatively correlated with the number of takings.

The effect of political considerations on the decision to use eminent domain for private development is captured by two variables: the party of the state's governor,[50] and the direction of the state's vote in the presidential election in 2000. Again, there are cross-cutting effects. States that lean democratic should favor policies aimed at revitalizing cities, which are predominantly occupied by the poor and minorities, but they may also be resistant to government actions that would coercively transfer resources from low- and middle-class landowners to wealthy business interests. As for republican-leaning states, one would expect them to favor policies that promote economic development, but also to be wary of the perceived violation of private property rights that is epitomized by the use of eminent domain for private takings. Finally, a Herfindahl index of racial concentration is included to test whether there is a racial bias in the private use of eminent domain.

Table 2.6 reports the results of two models, one that includes all of the previously mentioned explanatory variables (Model 1), and one that excludes the race and the political variables (Model 2). For each model, the table shows the estimated coefficient, reflecting the marginal influence of that variable on the number of filed takings, and the associated p-value. The

---

[49] Specifically, GSP is the ratio of real 1999 gross state product to real 1989 gross state product.

[50] Two states (Maine and Minnesota) had independent governors. Thus, two dummies are used: Dem. Governor =1 if the governor is a democrat and zero otherwise, and Ind. Governor=1 if the governor is independent and zero otherwise. Republican governor is the excluded category.

Table 2.6. *Regression analysis of the determinants of filed private takings by state, 1998–2002*

Independent variable	Dependent variable: Filed Takings			
	Model 1		Model 2	
	Coefficient	p-value	Coefficient	p-value
Constant	−38.4749	.0274	−39.6898	.0052
Urban Land	.2167	.2103	.2327	.0351
Urban Density	1.3267	.1292	1.8014	.0301
Population	1.1084	.0005	.9668	.0001
Disposable Income	2.8202	.1436	3.9314	.0273
GSP Growth	−3.3916	.0018	−2.8284	.0091
Median Price	−1.0640	.3679	−2.1279	.0284
Race	.8792	.2871		
Presidential Election	−.0768	.9311		
Dem. Governor	−.6560	.1210		
Ind. Governor	−.4561	.6411		
Number of observations	50		50	
Adjusted R^2	.5244		.5339	

Notes: The dependent variable is the log of filed private takings in each state for the period January 1, 1998 to December 31, 2002, as compiled by Berliner (2003). The independent variables are also in log form except for Presidential Election, which equals 1 if democratic and 0 if republican, and the two governor variables (republican is the excluded category). Presidential Election indicates how the state voted in the 2000 election; Governor indicates the party of the governor in 2000. The regression results are adapted from Diop, Lanza, Miceli, and Sirmans (2010).

p-value is a measure of the statistical significance of the coefficient, with lower values indicating a higher degree of significance.[51] A p<.10 is usually associated with a statistically significant coefficient. Note that the two measures of the severity of the holdout problem (urban land and urban density) have the predicted positive sign in both models, but they are only significant in Model 2. The two measures of the demand for economic development (population and disposable income) are also positive in both models, but disposable income is not significant in Model 1. Growth of GSP is negative and significant in both models, suggesting that policy makers do indeed use private takings as a spur of economic growth. Median home price is of the predicted sign in both models (negative), reflecting the opportunity cost of land, but it is not significant in Model 1. Finally, the race and political

[51] Specifically, if the null hypothesis is that the coefficient is zero, the p-value is the probability that one would erroneously reject the null hypothesis.

variables are not significant in Model 1. However, when these variables are dropped in Model 2, all of the remaining variables are significant ($p \leq .05$) and are of the predicted sign.

Overall, the results provide fairly strong support for the hypothesis that the use of private takings is driven by economic factors. Specifically, private takings are used to overcome holdouts, and they are more likely to be used as the demand for economic development increases, as the opportunity cost of land decreases, and as part of a state policy to promote economic growth. In contrast, there is no evidence that the use of private takings reflects either a political or a racial bias.

In the wake of the *Kelo* decision, numerous states passed legislation aimed at limiting the use of eminent domain for purely private projects (Castle Coaliton, 2008). Three studies have examined the factors that influenced the political responses (or lack thereof) by the various states. Morriss (2009) focused on those states that responded with some form of legislation, as opposed to a citizen-initiated response.[52] His results showed that a state was more likely to enact a reform that substantively limited the use of eminent domain for private development if the growth rate in population in the state was higher, and if the fraction of republicans in the state legislature was larger. In contrast, a state was less likely to enact a substantive reform if it had a statutory limit on taxes and expenditures, and if it had a republican governor. The results suggest that states with stagnant growth, or with limited ability to tax and spend, were more likely to retain the power to use eminent domain to spur economic development. The political variables suggest a more subtle effect: The positive effect of a republican-dominated legislature reflects the expected ideological opposition to the use of eminent domain for private development by republicans, except when one of their own was governor.

In a similar study, Lopez, Jewel, and Campbell (2009) found that a state was more likely to enact a reform limiting the private use of eminent domain the higher was the value of new home construction, the larger was the number of local governments, and if the state had a past history of using eminent domain for private development. The first and third variables suggest that homeowners sought legislative protection from the use of eminent domain the higher was their property value and the more inclined local governments were to use the power. The impact of the number of local governments likely reflects a free-rider problem – as the number of governments rises, one expects that it would be harder for them to organize to

---

[52] Thus, his analysis excluded Arizona, Nevada, North Dakota, and Oregon.

influence the state legislature to allow them to retain the power to use eminent domain for local development. In contrast to the Morriss study, Lopez et al. found that political factors did not affect state decisions of whether or not to enact reforms, nor did racial diversity. However, states with less income inequality were more likely to impose limits on the use of eminent domain.

The study by Diop et al. (2010) similarly found that state responses to *Kelo* were largely driven by economic rather than political factors. In particular, states with larger residential construction industries were more likely to impose limits on the use of eminent domain, suggesting that state legislatures were sensitive to the interests of residential land users in their competition with commercial users over the limited supply of land. In contrast, more urbanized states were less likely to enact restrictions. As argued earlier, because urbanization measures the extent to which developers are likely to face holdouts in undertaking large-scale development projects, states where this problem is more severe were less likely to deprive local governments of eminent domain as a tool for overcoming it. States with tax and spending limits were also less likely to enact restrictions on the use of eminent domain (as in the Morriss study), and states with a history of using eminent domain for economic development were more likely to enact such restrictions (as in Lopez et al.). In contrast to previous studies, however, Diop et al. found no evidence that political factors or measures of income inequality affected a state's response to *Kelo*.

A final study by Turnbull and Salvino (2009) exploited the varying state responses to the *Kelo* decision for a different purpose – namely, to test the Hobbesian "Leviathan Theory" of government, which asserts that governments behave as if their primary objective is to expand their size (Brennan and Buchanan, 1980). Because the *Kelo* decision effectively eliminated the public use limitation of the federal constitution as a constraint on government expansion, states were left to establish their own policies with regard to the private use of eminent domain. The question then became whether states would use their newly expanded takings powers to increase their tax bases and hence their spending on public services, as predicted by the Leviathan model, or if they would invoke state-level constraints on the use of eminent domain for private development as a way of limiting government growth. The results show that states that allowed local governments to retain broad eminent domain powers for economic development purposes also tended to have large public sectors, thus providing support for the Leviathan hypothesis.

THREE

Just Compensation

It's home to us. It's home to my parents and my family for a hundred years. Simply put, there is nowhere else I would rather be. My mother has lived there her entire life. She's eighty-three years old. I know she wants to die in that house. I don't think that's asking too much.

Matt Dery, plaintiff in Kelo v. New London
quoted in Benedict (2009, p. 256)

The second requirement for the use of eminent domain is that "just compensation" must be paid to the owner whose land is taken.[1] The Constitution is silent about exactly what this requires, but one definition, based on an analogy to the law of torts, is that it represents an amount of money (or possibly an offsetting in-kind benefit) that leaves the owner as well off as if the property had not been taken. Alternatively, given that eminent domain involves a transfer of the land, just compensation could reflect an estimate of the price that the owner would have accepted for the property in a hypothetical market transaction.

Based on this second measure, courts have actually defined just compensation to be the fair market value of the property. I will argue, however, that this amount almost certainly undercompensates landowners compared to what they would have demanded in a consensual sale. This chapter begins by exploring the reasons for this bias, and then evaluates some proposed solutions aimed at inducing owners to reveal their true valuations. Given the impracticality of these schemes, the chapter turns to an examination of the consequences of the market value measure, and also suggests some reasons why full compensation may not be desirable, even if it were feasible.

---

[1] See Treanor (1985) for a discussion of the origins of this requirement.

3.1. Just Compensation Equals Fair Market Value

Because the taking clause does not specify what amount of compensation is required to satisfy the just compensation requirement of the Fifth Amendment, courts have defined it to be fair market value. This represents the value of comparable properties that have recently sold, and is the same measure used by local governments for property tax assessments (a point that will become important for the discussion in Section 3.6 in this chapter). The primary virtue of this measure of compensation is that it is relatively easy to observe. As noted, however, it is almost certainly less than what the owner would have accepted to sell the property in a consensual, or market, transaction for reasons that I now explore.

Several authors have commented on the inadequacy of market value for compensating owners. For example, Merrill (1986) notes that market value

awards the condemnee what he would obtain in an arm's length transaction with a third party, but does not compensate him for the subjective "premium" he might attach to his property above its opportunity cost. In some cases, such as those involving undeveloped land, there may be no subjective value. But in other cases, the premium may be quite large (p. 83).

Ellickson (1973) notes that this "subjective value" component is likely to be especially high for family homes, and that its magnitude will tend to be increasing in the owner's length of tenure. Fischel (1995b) and others (see, for example, Hovenkamp [1991] and Miceli and Minkler [1995]) have attributed the difference between a property's market value and its value to the owner to what they variously call the "offer-ask" disparity, the difference between "willingness-to-accept" and "willingness-to-pay" measures of value, and the "endowment effect."[2] Whatever the label, there is abundant experimental evidence that this difference exists and that it can be substantial. As Judge Oliver Wendell Holmes (whom we shall meet again later) once colorfully observed, "A thing which you have enjoyed and used as your own for a long time, whether property or opinion, takes root in your being and cannot be torn away without your trying to defend yourself" (Holmes, 1897, p. 477).

---

[2] Behavioral economists attribute the observed difference between what one would pay to acquire a good and what one would ask to give it up to the phenomenon of "loss aversion," which maintains that people weigh losses more heavily than gains. See, for example, Jolls, Sunstein, and Thaler (2000).

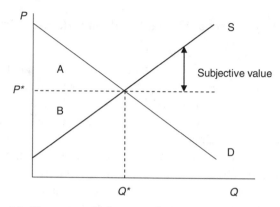

Figure 3.1. Illustration of subjective value in a demand-supply diagram.

The idea behind subjective value is well known to economists and can be illustrated in an ordinary supply-demand diagram as shown in Figure 3.1. Suppose, for concreteness, that this represents the market for land, though the underlying principle is perfectly general. The demand curve in the graph represents the amount that potential buyers are willing to pay for additional units of land, where its negative slope reflects the usual assumption of diminishing marginal benefits. That is, the more one consumes of the good, the less he or she values additional units. The supply curve represents the minimum price owners are willing to accept to sell their land, and thus reflects its value in its current use (what economists refer to as its opportunity cost). The demand curve can therefore be interpreted as a "willingness-to-pay" measure of the land's value, whereas the supply curve can be interpreted as a "willingness-to-accept" measure of its value. Neither measure, however, is separately observable in the market. What is observed is the equilibrium, or market price, P^*, which is determined by the intersection of the supply and demand curves. The market price can be interpreted as the fair market value of a unit of land. Note that at this price, those parcels from 0 to Q^* sell, whereas those beyond Q^* do not.

Consider first the parcels that sell. For these parcels, the market price falls between the buyers' willingness to pay and the sellers' willingness to accept. The triangular area below the demand curve and above the price over this range (labeled area A in Figure 3.1) is called the buyers' (or consumers') surplus and reflects the aggregate gains from trade for buyers. Likewise, the triangular area above the supply curve and below the price (area B) is the sellers' (or producers') surplus and reflects the aggregate gains from trade for sellers.[3] The fact that the equilibrium price is determined by the intersection of the curves ensures that all possible gains from trade are exhausted by the market. This reflects the efficiency of the competitive market as asserted by the Invisible Hand Theorem.

Now consider the parcels to the right of Q^*, which are not sold in the market because the current owners' valuation (willingness to accept) exceeds the amount would-be buyers are willing to pay. Suppose that one such parcel is taken by eminent domain, and the owner is paid its market value, P^*, as the measure of just compensation.[4] Note that, considering that the owner would only have sold the parcel for a price at least as high as the relevant point on the supply curve, he or she suffers a loss equal to the vertical distance between that point and P^*. In other words, the market price undercompensates the owner by this amount, compared to the minimum amount he or she would have required to sell the land voluntarily. This distance is what we have called the owner's subjective value. It is important to emphasize that economists view subjective value (as measured by the supply curve) as a legitimate economic value, despite its unobservability.[5]

In recognition of the undercompensation resulting from the market value measure of compensation for takings, Canada formerly used a "value-to-the-owner" standard for compensation, but had to abandon it given the unobservability of the owner's true value (Knetsch and Borcherding, 1979). This raises the obvious question of why landowners cannot simply be asked how much they value the land and then be paid that amount in compensation. The problem with this approach, of course, is that landowners would have an incentive to misrepresent their valuations. As a result, it would be impossible to distinguish between those owners who refuse to sell at a given price because they truly value their land more than the amount of the offer, from those who are merely holding out in a strategic effort to extract a larger share of the surplus from the transaction (as discussed in Chapter 2).

---

[3] The seller's surplus is roughly equivalent to his or her profit from a sale.

[4] The reason for taking the land in this range may be that the social value of the land, as measured by its marginal social benefit, exceeds the private marginal benefit, as measured by the demand curve. In that case, it would be efficient to take parcels beyond Q^*, up to the point where the marginal social benefit curve intersects the supply curve (see Figure 3.2 later in this chapter). This might be true, for example, if the parcel is to be used to provide a public good.

[5] In contrast, Wyman (2007) argues that subjective value does not merit compensation in takings cases because it may be very expensive, and further, may be "objectionable" and possibly reflective of "existing inequalities" (p. 244).

The reader might wonder why the presence of subjective value does not similarly impede efficient exchange in ordinary markets. Why, for example, does it not prevent exchanges over the range from 0 to Q^* in Figure 3.1, where buyers and sellers are similarly ignorant of each other's valuations? The reason is that, in perfectly competitive markets, sellers are price takers, and only sell if their true value is less than the market price. Thus, there is no bargaining over the posted price, and hence sellers gain no advantage by concealing their value. In markets where buyers and sellers do bargain over price, so-called thin markets like those for real estate and automobiles, it is true that both sides wish to conceal their true valuations, but if a bargaining range exists (that is, if the buyer's willingness to pay exceeds the seller's willingness to accept, as is true for all units up to Q^*), the parties also have a joint interest in reaching a deal. The threat that either can walk away from the transaction thus provides an incentive for them to reach an agreement, but also guarantees that any transaction will be mutually beneficial.[6]

In contrast, when the government can compel a sale at a price set by a third party, as in the case of eminent domain, the conditions for mutual benefit are no longer necessarily present. Thus, although a forced sale has the advantage of avoiding the holdout problem, it has the drawback of potentially allowing inefficient sales, precisely because the seller cannot walk away. The trade-off mirrors that between a property rule and a liability rule as described in Chapter 1.

An issue related to the problem of subjective value is whether court-awarded compensation under the market value standard should reflect any impact that knowledge of the impending public project might have on the market value of the land. Consider, for example, a parcel that has a market value of $100,000 in its current use, reflecting the equilibrium price of comparable properties that have recently sold. Suppose, however, that it becomes public knowledge that the parcel will be taken, along with several others, for use in a public project that will be worth $1.5 million when completed. If, say ten identical parcels will be taken in all, then the pro-rated value of each of the targeted parcels in the proposed project would therefore be $150,000. The question is whether the proper measure of just compensation is the parcel's market value of $100,000 in its current use, or its proportional market value of $150,000 in the proposed public use.

The Supreme Court addressed this issue in the case of *U.S. v. Miller*.[7] The Court said that compensation should *not* reflect the public value, arguing

---

[6] Existence of a bargaining range does not, however, guarantee that a deal will be reached, as in the case of bilateral monopolies (see Section 2.6 of Chapter 2).

[7] 317 U.S. 369 (1943)

that the landowner is only entitled to indemnity for his loss.[8] In effect, this standard denies landowners a share in any surplus created by the public project.[9]

Richard Epstein has taken a different position on this question based on his contention that "the compensation requirement is as much concerned with the distribution of gains and losses between persons as with their aggregate amount" (Epstein, 1985, p. 115). In particular, he argues that limiting compensation to market value, thereby depriving landowners of their subjective value, plus any share in the surplus from the taking,[10] is only justified for those projects whose benefits are widely distributed. The idea is that, when the gains from a forced transaction are dispersed, narrow interests cannot enrich themselves at the expense of a few landowners (the problem of rent seeking described in Section 2.11 of the previous chapter).[11]

In the case where the land is to be used for a true public good, this requirement is easily satisfied because the benefits of public goods are, by definition, broadly distributed. For example, no one person enjoys a disproportionate benefit from the construction of a highway. When eminent domain is used for largely private projects, however, this criterion is less likely to be met because the benefits are generally more concentrated, notwithstanding any spillover benefits. Thus, Epstein (1985, p. 174) urges that a taking is justified in such cases "only when efforts are made to replicate

---

[8] This same issue arose in a somewhat different context in 1963, when the government took title to various personal possessions of Lee Harvey Oswald as part of its evidence collection following the assassination of President Kennedy. The statute authorizing this action called for just compensation to be paid to Oswald's widow, but there was a dispute about how to measure the market value of the items. The district court awarded $3,000 based on the value of items "similar in kind" to those taken, but, in a ruling contrary to the principle in *Miller*, the appeals court increased the award to $17,000, reflecting the value of the items as enhanced by their connection to the notorious crime. (See *Porter v. United States*, 473 F.2d 1329, 5th Cir., 1973; and Adelstein (1974).) Similarly, in 1997, the government took possession of the famous Zapruder film of the assassination, declaring it a public record, and a three-judge panel awarded the Zapruder family $16 million in compensation, again reflecting the film's value as enhanced by the event in question.

[9] See the related discussion of the benefit-offset principle in Section 3.4 in this chapter.

[10] Fennell (2004) argues that the "uncompensated increment" created by the market value measure consists of the two components just noted – namely, the owner's subjective value plus a share of the surplus from the transaction – but also includes the value associated with "the autonomy of choosing for oneself when to sell" (p. 958). In essence, she argues that this third element is a fundamental component of having property rule rather than liability rule protection of one's property. In other words, it is the right to refuse a sale on any grounds, even if compensation is "full."

[11] But on the other hand, Levinson (2000, p. 375) argues that when the gains from a project are dispersed but the costs are concentrated, losers might be able to organize and exert disproportionate political influence, resulting in *too few*, rather than too many, takings.

in the transfer situation the same distribution of costs and benefits that is found with normal public goods." In other words, the taking victim is entitled to a share of the benefits from the transaction.

To illustrate his point, Epstein (1985, pp. 170–175) uses the example of the mill acts, which we discussed in the previous chapter as an example of private takings. Recall that these acts allowed mill builders to flood upstream land without the owner's consent provided that the builders paid compensation as set by the court, usually in an amount equal to the landowners' losses. However, an interesting exception, cited approvingly by Epstein, was the New Hampshire Mill Act, which required mill builders to pay flooded owners the market value of their property *plus a 50 percent premium*. Thus, the act authorized a private taking, but by setting compensation substantially above market value, it prevented mill builders from capturing all of the surplus from the transaction. In this way, the transaction involved a distribution of costs and benefits that more closely approximated what would have arisen under a consensual sale; that is, where sellers are compensated for their subjective values and can also bargain for a share of the surplus. Of course, the 50 percent premium is arbitrary (as any fixed premium would be) and hence does not assure full compensation for all owners, given the natural variation in subjective values. In some cases it would overcompensate owners and in others it would undercompensate them. Still, given the systematic bias inherent in market value, it is at least a move in the right direction, and as a result, confronts the taking party with a cost that is most likely closer to the full opportunity cost of the targeted land.

Krier and Serkin (2004) propose an alternative approach that would set compensation at the traditional fair market value measure for true public uses (public goods) but would award victims of private takings the value of the land as enhanced by the government action (in contrast to the principle in *Miller*). Fennell (2004) similarly argues for enhanced compensation for private takings, but further proposes that the threshold separating public and private uses should be determined by a balancing test like that used to judge when a government regulation crosses the threshold and becomes a regulatory taking (see Chapter 5). Specifically, if the proposed taking meets the test for an uncompensated regulation, then fair market value would be sufficient compensation, but if it is judged a compensable regulation, then some amount of enhanced compensation would be required.

3.2. Schemes for Revealing Sellers' True Valuations

One possible solution to the problem of undercompensation caused by market value is to find a way of inducing sellers to reveal their true valuations.

Such "demand revealing" schemes have been proposed for determining optimal tax shares for provision of public goods,[12] and they can in principle be used to reveal sellers' true valuations. A review of the principles underlying these schemes, however, shows the difficulties of applying them in practice.

Recall from the discussion of the free-rider problem in Chapter 2 that the main impediment to designing an efficient tax scheme for public goods is that individual demands are unobservable, and that individuals will generally be unwilling to reveal their demands in hopes of consuming the public good without contributing to its costs (i.e., free-riding). The trick, therefore, is to design a tax scheme that eliminates the incentive for individuals to misrepresent their valuations. The key insight in this quest was provided by Vickrey's (1961) analysis of sealed-bid auctions.

Vickrey compared two formats: a "first-price" auction, in which the winning bidder pays his or her own bid, and a "second-price" auction, in which the winning bidder pays the amount bid by the second highest bidder. In the first-price auction, bidders do not have an incentive to bid their true valuations because they fear they may end up paying a price substantially above the minimum amount that would have won the auction. For example, suppose bidder A truly values the good in question at \$1,000 whereas bidder B values it at \$500, but neither knows the other's value. Obviously, if A knew B's value, he would bid \$501 because this would allow him to win the auction while enjoying a surplus of \$499. However, because he does not know B's value, his optimal bid will balance his probability of winning against his desire to pay the lowest possible price. Generally, this will entail a bid somewhere between \$500 and \$1,000. Thus, the first-price, sealed-bid auction systematically understates the true value of the good to the winner.

Now consider the second-price auction. Because the winner pays the second highest bid, he no longer has an incentive to bid anything less than his actual valuation. This is true because now, an individual's bid only determines his probability of winning, not the amount he will actually have to pay if he wins. Thus, there is no longer an advantage to bidding less than one's true valuation.[13] Several authors have used the insights from Vickrey's analysis of second-price auctions to design demand-revealing tax schemes for public goods. The common feature of all of them is that they sever the link between the valuation that an individual reports as his or her true valuation and the amount that he or she has to pay in taxes.

---

[12]   See, for example, Atkinson and Stiglitz (1980, pp. 513–517).

[13]   Nor is there a gain from bidding more than one's valuation. Suppose, for example, that bidder B (who values the good at \$500) strategically bids \$1,100 whereas A bids \$1,000. B therefore wins the auction but has to pay \$1,000, which is well above his true valuation.

Plassmann and Tideman (2008) have applied this logic to the problem of ascertaining a landowner's true valuation for purposes of determining just compensation for a taking. In particular, they propose a self-assessment scheme in which landowners announce a value for their property that will be used both as a base for property taxation and as a measure of compensation in the event of a taking.[14] Such a mechanism balances the incentives of landowners to overstate their valuation for purposes of compensation (the standard objection to a value-to-the-owner standard for just compensation) against their incentive to understate it for purposes of taxation. One can prove that these effects just offset, and owners report their values truthfully, if a certain condition is met; namely, that the property tax rate equals the probability of a taking.

An example illustrates this result. Suppose an owner whose true valuation is $100,000 reports a valuation of x under the proposed scheme. She is then assessed a property tax of tx, where t is the tax rate. Assume that she has to pay the tax before the taking decision is made, but if her land is subsequently taken, she receives compensation of x. The landowner's realized net wealth under this scheme is therefore $x-tx$ if the land is taken and $100,000-tx$ if it is not. Now let p be the probability of a taking, which the landowner knows. We can then compute the expected value of the landowner's property at the time she reports her valuation to be

$$p(x-tx) + (1-p)(\$100,000-tx) = (1-p)(\$100,000) + (p-t)\,x. \qquad (3.1)$$

Now observe that if $p = t$, the final term in this expression vanishes, in which case the landowner's expected value is simply $(1-p)(\$100,000)$, which is independent of her reported valuation, x. Thus, she has no incentive either to underreport or overreport her valuation.

The principal objection to this scheme in terms of its practical application is the requirement that the probability of a taking must equal the property tax rate. Actually, there is a limited sense in which this equality must hold; namely, if all parcels are identical and if the tax revenue raised from the property tax is used exclusively to pay compensation to takings victims.[15] This can be seen as follows. Suppose in the previous example that there are 1,000 identical parcels, ten of which will be taken at random for public use. Thus, landowners compute the probability of a taking to be $p = 10/1,000 = .01$. If each owner reports a valuation of x, then the total

---

[14] Colwell (1990) proposed a similar scheme.
[15] A similar argument is made in the next chapter in the context of constitutional choice models for the design of efficient compensation rules. (See Section 4.3.)

amount of revenue that will have to be raised to compensate the ten owners whose land is taken is $10x$. Because x is also the base for taxation, the total revenue collected from the 1,000 landowners will be $(1,000)tx$. Under the assumption that compensation is the only budgetary expense, a balanced budget requires that revenue equals costs, or $(1,000)tx = 10x$. It follows that $t = 10/1,000 = .01 = p$, which proves the claim.[16]

In actuality, of course, the probability of a taking will not generally equal the property tax rate. This is true primarily because compensation for takings is only a minute portion of most local budgets. Thus, if compensation is financed out of general revenues, the tax rate will generally have to exceed the probability of a taking, most likely by a substantial amount.[17] Because this will make the final term in (3.1) negative (given that $p < t$), the proposed self-assessment scheme will give landowners an incentive to systematically understate the value of their property. Intuitively, owners will perceive the tax cost of reporting a given value as outweighing the expected compensation.

Shapiro and Pincus (2007) have proposed an alternative value-revealing scheme that depends on an auction of the assembled land, referred to as the "assembly district," to the highest bidder, where the assembly district would constitute a pre-determined set of parcels within the area designated for re-development.[18] To ensure that owners within the district receive at least their individual reservation prices as compensation in the event of a taking, each would be asked to announce a minimally acceptable price for the district as a whole. The actual reserve price would then be set at the maximum of these reported prices. In the event of a successful bid by the developer (i.e., a bid greater than or equal to the actual reserve price), each owner would receive a pre-determined share of the winning bid. Shapiro and Pincus show that in this setting, the optimal strategy of each owner is to reveal his or her true valuation.

---

[16] Note that this result does not depend on the assumption that taxes are assessed before the taking decision is made. Suppose that only those landowners whose land is not taken are taxed. In that case, expression (3.1) – the expected wealth of landowners – would be $(1-p)(\$100,000-tx) + px = (1-p)(\$100,000) + x(p-t(1-p))$, which induces truth telling if $t = p/(1-p)$. Now observe that the balanced budget in this case requires $(990)tx = 10x$, or $t = 10/990 = p/(1-p)$.

[17] This problem could be avoided by imposing a separate tax dedicated to raising revenue for financing takings claims and using the self-assessment scheme solely for collecting this tax.

[18] The idea of an assembly district was first proposed by Heller and Hills (2008) as a solution to the assembly problem (also see Heller [2008, pp. 118–121]). Under the proposal, residents within the district would organize a kind of homeowners' association that would decide collectively whether or not to accept a buy-out offer from any would-be developers.

As with the self-assessment scheme, this scheme works because individual owners have nothing to gain by overstating or understating their true valuations. If an individual overstates her true value, she runs the risk of preventing a sale that would have yielded a surplus, whereas if she understates it, she runs the risk of allowing a sale that would cause a loss. The chief drawback of the scheme is that it may prevent some otherwise efficient projects from going forward. This is true because the maximum of the announced reserve prices could be higher than the sum of the individual valuations, given that the pre-determined shares cannot be conditioned on the unobservable distribution of owner valuations. Thus, some bids that exceed the sum of the true valuations will fail, resulting in too little assembly.[19] The bias inherent in the Shapiro-Pincus auction scheme is therefore in the opposite direction from that in the Plassmann-Tideman self-assessment scheme, which, recall, tended to result in underassessment by owners (and thus too much assembly).

The preceding examples illustrate the fundamental difficulty in eliciting the true valuation of landowners in a non-market setting. The problem stems from the removal of consent, which deprives sellers of the ability to walk away from any transaction that does not promise a net gain. As a practical matter, therefore, the constitutional requirement of "just" compensation will not generally coincide with the economic meaning of "full" compensation.

3.3. Estimation of Actual Compensation Paid in Eminent Domain Cases

The acceptance of fair market value as the *legal* standard for just compensation, however, does not necessarily ensure that landowners will *actually*

---

[19] To illustrate, suppose that there are three owners whose true valuations are $200, $300, and $500. Thus, if an assembler values the consolidated land at more than $1,000 (the sum of the individual valuations), the assembly is efficient. Suppose initially that the announced shares for the three owners are proportional to their true valuations; that is, they are 0.2, 0.3, and 0.5, respectively. In this case, the optimal strategy for each owner under the proposed scheme is to announce $1,000 as the overall reserve price for the consolidated parcel, which is the efficient amount (i.e., $200/0.2 = $300/0.3 = $500/0.5 = $1,000). But suppose instead that the announced shares are based on a different distribution of market values, say 0.3, 0.3, and 0.4. In that case, the maximum announced reserve price would be $1,250=$500/0.4 by Owner 3, given that his share is less than proportional to his true valuation. As a result, if the highest bidder valued the consolidated parcel at an amount between $1,000 and $1,250, he would fail to win the auction even though the transaction is efficient. It should be easy to see that this problem will arise whenever the announced shares are not strictly proportional to owners' true valuations.

receive that amount in eminent domain cases. In a classic study, Munch (1976) found that in fact they generally did not. Using data on condemnations from three large urban renewal projects undertaken in Chicago between 1962 and 1970, she compared the compensation amounts paid for the acquired properties to market value estimates of comparable properties sold in similar Chicago neighborhoods over the same time period. Her results showed "that low-valued properties receive[d] less than market value and high-valued properties receive[d] more than market value." More specifically, "a $7,000 parcel receive[d] about $5,000, a $13,000 property [broke] even, and a $40,000 property may [have gotten] two to three times market value" (Munch, 1976, p. 488). Finally, she found that court-awarded damages tended to be more "regressive" compared to cases that settled out of court. That is, courts awarded less than settlement amounts for low-valued properties, but more than settlement amounts for high-valued properties (Munch, 1976, p. 493).

After pointing out several shortcomings in Munch's study, Chang reported the results of his own estimation of the amount of compensation paid in eminent domain cases in New York City based on data from cases that settled out of court between 1990 and 2002 (Chang, 2010a), and from court-adjudicated cases decided between 1990 and 2003 (Chang, 2010b). First, for the settled cases (of which there were 430 during the sample period), Chang found that less than 10 percent of landowners received fair market value, whereas the rest received either above- or below-market value. Indeed, about one-half of condemnees received "extreme" compensation – either 50 percent above or 50 percent below market value.[20] Further, the deviations from fair market value could not be explained by any observable characteristics of the properties (Chang, 2010a, p. 239).

The court-adjudicated sample consisted of only twenty-seven cases decided over the sample period. In contrast to the settled cases, the results here revealed a systematic upward bias in compensation amounts compared to fair market value, though the awards more closely tracked the offers made by condemnors than the claims made by landowners (perhaps reflecting the court's belief that condemnors were more realistic in their assessments of a property's market value) (Chang, 2010b). Taken together, these studies suggest that actual compensation awards in eminent domain cases do not closely track the fair market value standard.

---

[20] The conclusions were similar for all categories of land, whether residential, commercial, or vacant.

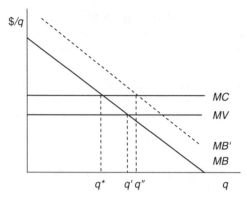

Figure 3.2. Overacquisition of land under market-value compensation.

3.4. Eminent Domain as a Subsidy to Developers

The next three sections examine the allocative consequences of the market value measure of compensation. Subsequent sections then turn to different aspects of the compensation requirement.

As has been noted, the most obvious consequence of market value compensation is that the government, in making its takings decisions, may be induced to take too much land because it does not face the full opportunity cost of the land. Indeed, many commentators have argued that the primary reason for requiring the government to pay compensation at all, at least in terms of efficiency, is to restrain it from transferring an excessive amount of land from private to public use (see, for example, Johnson, 1977). Figure 3.2 illustrates the point graphically. In the figure, the *MB* curve represents the marginal social benefit of converting land to public use, whereas the *MC* curve represents the marginal social cost of such a conversion, reflecting the true value of the land in private use to its current owners. (The MC curve thus corresponds to the supply curve in Figure 3.1; it is drawn here as horizontal merely for simplicity.)[21]

Because the *MC* curve is unobservable, however, the government sets compensation at the market value of the land, measured by the *MV* curve, which, for reasons emphasized earlier, is shown as lying below the *MC* curve for all landowners. The efficient amount of land to be acquired for the proposed project is determined by the intersection of the *MB* and *MC*

---

[21] The *MB* curve, in contrast, will not generally coincide with the demand curve in Figure 3.1. Rather, it will likely be above the demand curve, reflecting the social benefits of the land as reflected in the public project.

curves, or q^* parcels. In contrast, the actual amount of land that the government will take if compensation is set at MV will be q', the point where the MB and MV curves intersect. Thus, the government takes too much land. A government that acts in this way is sometimes said to have "fiscal illusion," reflecting its concern for the budgetary cost of its actions rather than their true social cost (Blume, Rubinfeld, and Shapiro, 1984). (If the government automatically took the efficient amount of land, there would be no need for it to pay any compensation on efficiency grounds.)

There is, however, a possibly offsetting efficiency justification for setting compensation below the full opportunity cost of the land, even if that amount is observable. As discussed in the previous chapter, courts have often sought to justify the use of eminent domain for largely private development projects based on the spillover, or external, benefits that they create. Such benefits often do exist. For example, construction of a new shopping center may cause nearby property values to rise as demand to live in the community increases, and existing businesses may experience an increase in profit from the greater customer traffic generated by the new development.[22] Similarly, construction of a railroad or highway will increase the value of land along the route.

To illustrate, return to Figure 3.2 and suppose that the MB curve is the marginal private benefit of a proposed project as perceived by the developer. That is, it reflects the gains that he can fully capture through the market. The marginal *social* benefit is shown by the curve labeled MB', which is above MB, where the vertical distance between the two curves is the amount of the spillover benefit per unit of land. In this case, the socially optimal acquisition of land for the project, which occurs at the intersection of MB' and MC, is q''. Notice that the amount of land the developer will actually acquire under market value compensation, which occurs at the intersection of the MB and MV curves (given by q'), is closer to the social optimum, q'', than is the amount he would acquire if compensation were full (q^*). The reason is that market value compensation provides an implicit subsidy, equal to the vertical distance between the MC and MV curves, thereby inducing the landowner to internalize at least some of the external benefits created by the project.

---

[22] Indeed, the large and growing economic literature on shopping centers is based on the existence of such spillover benefits from one business to another. See, for example, Brueckner (1993) and Miceli and Sirmans (1995). Of course, some offsetting external costs will also be created by the development, such as pollution and traffic congestion. For current purposes, we assume that the net effect is a spillover benefit, for otherwise the government presumably would not authorize the use of eminent domain for the project, and might in fact adopt measures to block it altogether.

Although this argument has some appeal, several caveats are necessary. First and most obviously, there is no way to ensure that the implicit subsidy associated with market value compensation will equal the external benefit; that is, there is no way to ensure that the vertical distance between *MC* and *MV* will equal the vertical distance between *MB* and *MB'*. In the case shown in Figure 3.2, the subsidy is less than would be required for efficiency. Thus, the developer acquires less than the efficient amount of land (though more than he would have under "full" compensation). Consequently, a true subsidy that is precisely chosen would be a better instrument for accomplishing the desired scale of the project.

Second, the cost of the implicit subsidy would fall entirely on those citizens whose land is taken, whereas the cost of an actual subsidy, financed by taxes, could be spread across all citizens, or better still, targeted to those who would benefit most from the development. For these reasons, it does not make sense to use market value compensation as a means of subsidizing private development projects. As for public projects, there should be no need for a subsidy at all because the government should, in principle, internalize the full social benefits of the project.[23]

As noted in Chapter 2 (Section 2.12), eminent domain has been used historically to subsidize economic development through the application of the so-called benefit-offset principle (Fischel, 1995a, pp. 80–84). Most commonly invoked by state courts to assist railroads in acquiring land in the early nineteenth century, this principle established that if only a portion of an individual's land was taken for a public project (for example, a right of way for the railroad), full compensation was required for the portion taken, but that amount could be reduced by any increase in the value of the untaken portion. Suppose, for example, that the railroad needed half of owner A's land, valued at $50,000, for its track, but the value of the remaining half was increased by $40,000 as a result of the railroad's construction. Compensation for the taken land would then be set at $10,000.[24]

The economic logic behind this practice is sound. As Fischel (1995a, p. 83) notes, "railroads, even the most gouging, unregulated of them, could not appropriate all of the benefits their construction entailed. Railroads created substantial agglomeration economies that are reflected at least in

---

[23] This may not be true if the benefits spilled over into a different governmental jurisdiction, for example, across a municipal or state boundary. In that case, a higher-level government that encompasses the full extent of the project's benefits would possibly have to oversee construction (see Ellickson, 1979). More pointedly, Levinson (2000) asks why it is appropriate to assume that the government internalizes the social benefits of public projects.

[24] Apparently, this logic never was extended to the point where a landowner had to *pay* the railroad.

part by increased land values." Thus, it was an appropriate policy to subsidize them, as it would have been for any business that produced external benefits. The problem, once again, is that eminent domain is an overly blunt instrument for accomplishing this purpose in an efficient manner. In the case of the benefit-offset principle, it most likely provided *too little* of a subsidy to railroads because it only applied to individuals whose land was taken. Specifically, although the railroad only took land from landowner A, it presumably also provided benefits to owners B, C, D, and others whose land was not taken, but they were not required to pay anything.[25] Once again, a better approach for internalizing all of the spillover benefits from a private development would have been a direct subsidy, financed by an assessment levied on all affected landowners. In this way, the amount of the subsidy could have been efficiently set and the costs thereby spread among all beneficiaries, rather than falling on just a few.

3.5. Exit as a Source of Government Discipline

Besides compensation, a different force exists to restrain excessive government behavior, at least at the state and local level. That force is the option that developers, or other landowners subject to the threat of a taking or regulation, have to exit their current jurisdiction and relocate to one with a more favorable regulatory climate. According to the Tiebout (1956) model, local governments, whether at the state or municipal level, "compete" with one another for residents, much as competitive firms compete for customers. The resulting Tiebout equilibrium therefore involves an efficient array of jurisdictions with varying tax, regulatory, and spending policies tailored to the preferences of their residents. Efficiency is maintained in this system by the ability of residents to exit a jurisdiction, or to "vote with their feet," if they become dissatisfied with their particular government's policies.

Within this multi-jurisdictional setting, governments will, in principle, be restrained from excessive regulations without the need for a compensation requirement (Been, 1991). If, for example, a local government sought to impose inefficient regulations on businesses located within its boundaries, those businesses could exercise their option to move to a jurisdiction with less onerous regulations. Such a threat would therefore forestall inefficient regulations to the extent that businesses are mobile and local governments value them for their tax bases and employment opportunities.[26]

---

[25] Levinson (2002) expands on this point in regard to the appropriate definition (or "framing") of the transaction for purposes of calculating net benefits.

[26] See Ghosh (1997) for a formal model of this process.

Of course, exit is not always an option because some landowners value certain locations over others. Also, a landowner seeking to exit in the face of a taking or regulatory threat may bear a cost in the form of a reduction in the value of his or her property equal to the capitalized cost of the government action as perceived by the buyer. I will return to this issue in greater detail in Section 3.9 in this chapter.

3.6. Market Value Compensation and Tax-Motivated Takings

The undercompensation inherent in the fair market value measure creates the risk of a different sort of governmental abuse of eminent domain that is connected with the collection of property taxes by local governments. As already pointed out, property is assessed for tax purposes at the local level based on its fair market value. As a result, the owner's subjective value is in some sense "exempted" from taxation because it is not observable to the tax authority. Thus, for example, in Figure 3.1, parcels to the right of Q^* are assessed at P^* rather than the owners' true valuations along the supply curve. The only way that local governments can tax subjective value is when it is converted to market value by a consensual sale of the parcel to a buyer offering more than the seller's willingness to accept. The property can then be re-assessed at this higher market value (as would be the case, for example, of parcels between 0 and Q^* in Figure 3.1). In the absence of a sale, however, the subjective component of the owner's valuation remains effectively untaxable.

But now suppose that a buyer arrives who offers more than the market value for a given property, but the owner refuses to sell. This could be because the offer, even though above the property's market value, is less that the owner's true valuation (that is, it falls between P^* and the supply curve for parcels to the right of Q^*), in which case the parcel should not be sold because the current owner truly values it more than the buyer. Alternatively, the owner could value the property less than the buyer, in which case the sale is efficient, but the owner is holding out in a strategic effort to extract a larger share of the surplus from the transaction. In either case, however, – that is, whether or not the proposed transaction is efficient – the government stands to gain from the sale in the form of higher tax revenues from the property, and thus would like to see it go through.

In this light, recall that one of the arguments advanced in *Kelo*, and previously in *Poletown*, for allowing private takings was that the proposed project would increase the tax revenues that would be available to the community for financing public services. This rationale apparently authorizes a local government to use its takings power to force a sale whenever the proposed project would enhance its tax base, regardless of whether the project is an efficient use of the targeted land or not. Indeed, the majority opinion in *Kelo* recognized that such a threat exists: "[W]ithout a bright line rule [preventing the use of eminent domain for private projects,] nothing would stop a city from transferring citizen A's property to citizen B for the sole reason that citizen B will put the property to a more productive use and thus pay more taxes."[27]

I will refer to this use (or abuse) of eminent domain as a "tax motivated taking" (Miceli, Segerson, and Sirmans, 2008). Although this type of action is apparently justified by *Kelo*, it can lead to inefficient transfers of land as a consequence of the divergence between the assessed value of a property and its true value to the owner.

To illustrate this possible inefficiency, consider two identical properties, each assessed at $100,000, and suppose that the local property tax rate is 3 percent. Thus, the tax revenue generated by the two properties in their current use as individual residences, say, is $6,000. Now suppose a developer seeks to buy the two properties for a commercial development that would be worth $300,000. The new project would therefore generate $9,000 in taxes (an increase of $3,000), which means that the local government, representing the majority of taxpayers in the jurisdiction, would like to see the transaction go through. In most cases, if the sale is truly efficient, it would occur through the market with no need for government intervention, simply because the buyer and sellers, recognizing the joint gains, would complete the transactions on mutually acceptable terms. As suggested above, however, there are two possible reasons why the sale might not take place through the ordinary market mechanism. The first is the holdout problem: Even if the properties are more valuable to the buyer (that is, even if the transactions are efficient), individual sellers may strategically refuse to sell in hopes of extracting a larger share of the gains from trade. As we argued in the previous chapter, eminent domain is an appropriate response to this source of market failure, regardless of whether the intended use of the land is public or private.

Alternatively, the sellers may refuse to sell simply because they value the land more than the buyer, a possibility that arises when assessed values understate owners' true values. To see this, suppose that, in the previous example, each of the owners truly values his or her land at $175,000 in the sense that neither would sell for a lower price. In that case, the land is in fact

[27] *Kelo v. New London*, 545 U.S. 469, 486–487 (2005).

more valuable in its current use than it is to the developer. That is, it is worth $350,000 in aggregate to the current owners, compared to $300,000 to the buyer. However, because $75,000 of each owner's value is unobserved, it is effectively exempted from taxation, and the local government therefore foregoes $2,250 ($= .03 \times \$75,000$) in potential taxes from each parcel. However, if it uses eminent domain to force the sale, the local government can gain additional revenue of $1,500 ($= .03 \times \$50,000$) from each parcel, thereby capturing at least some of the subjective value. And apparently, such an action is justified by the *Kelo* decision as serving a legitimate public purpose.

One might counter that the risk of such an abuse of eminent domain is remote because local governments have alternative, less drastic strategies for obtaining the desired revenue, given that the government's interest is in the taxes from the land rather than the land itself. Two such strategies are, first, to reassess the targeted properties to capture the subjective value, and second, to raise the tax rate. The first strategy, however, requires the government either to be able to observe subjective values, which we have assumed that it cannot, or to use some arbitrary measure to identify "underassessed" parcels. The second strategy – simply raising the tax rate – would uniformly burden all property owners in the jurisdiction, which would be politically unpopular and inconsistent with the presumed motives of a majoritarian government. For these reasons, the threat of tax motivated takings looms as a possibility.

As it turns out, there exists a reassessment scheme that ensures that only efficient transactions will occur while forestalling the government's use of eminent domain purely for tax purposes. The proposed scheme would work as follows: If a landowner turns down a legitimate offer to buy his or her property, the government will reassess the property at the amount of the offer.[28] The details of the scheme, and the proof of its efficiency (along with various qualifications), are provided in the Appendix to this chapter. Intuitively, the scheme results in only efficient transfers because it eliminates the implicit tax subsidy enjoyed by landowners relative to would-be buyers, which arises from the exemption of owners' subjective values from taxation. (This implicit subsidy actually results in too few transactions occurring, absent the use of eminent domain.)

Perhaps more importantly, the scheme removes the government's incentive to take land purely for tax purposes because the amount of revenue

---

[28] This scheme was proposed by Miceli, Segerson, and Sirmans (2008). Note that it resembles the self-assessment scheme proposed by Plassmann and Tideman (2008), which we discussed in Section 3.2 in this chapter.

the government will receive under the scheme will be the same whether or not the proposed transaction occurs. In the earlier example, for instance, if the buyer offers $150,000 per parcel and the owners turn the offers down for any reason, their tax assessments will rise to $150,000. Thus, the combined tax revenues from the parcels will increase to $9,000, which is the same amount the developer would have paid had the transactions occurred. Thus, the government is indifferent as to whether or not the sale occurs and therefore has no incentive to force it. At the same time, the landowners will have a reduced incentive to turn down a truly efficient sale because of the threatened increase in tax liability.

One might object that the proposed scheme would potentially place a disproportionate financial burden on landowners whose properties are reassessed. However, those owners are at least no worse off than if their land had been targeted for a taking. Further, as noted, only "legitimate" offers would trigger the risk of reassessment, where to qualify as legitimate, the project in question would presumably be subject to a similar level of scrutiny as would be required for a proposed use of eminent domain under the public use doctrine.

3.7. Compensation as Insurance

So far, I have concentrated on the role of compensation in restraining excessive government behavior, but a different efficiency justification for paying compensation is to provide risk-averse landowners with insurance against a takings risk. This rationale is based on the argument that, from the perspective of landowners, takings are random events, and risk-averse individuals benefit from insurance against such events. This is why, for example, most homeowners buy fire or flood insurance.

The idea of risk aversion, and the value of insurance in general, can be illustrated with a simple example. Suppose that for a particular house, the probability of a fire in a given year is .001, or one in a thousand. Also, suppose that the cost of rebuilding the house would be $100,000. Thus, the expected cost of a fire in a given year is $.001 \times \$100,000 = \$100$. This is sometimes referred to as the actuarially fair cost of the fire risk. A person who is risk averse would in fact be willing to pay something *more* than this actuarially fair cost per year, say $120, to purchase an insurance policy that would fully cover the loss from the fire. The extra $20 reflects the amount homeowners are willing to pay simply to avoid the risk of a large one-time expense. This amount is also what allows the insurance company to cover its administrative costs and still expect to earn a profit from selling the policy.

As an alternative to market insurance, the homeowner could deal with this risk by self-insuring, which would involve, for example, setting aside some amount of money each year (at least $100) to establish a fund that could be used to rebuild the house in the event of a fire. The problem with self-insurance, of course, is timing; that is, the fire could occur long before the fund has accumulated the necessary amount to rebuild the house. Thus, although people often self-insure to deal with the risk of small losses (like losing a cheap watch), most buy market insurance to cover large losses like a house or car. The insurance company addresses this timing problem by selling enough policies that the number of claims in a given year becomes fairly predictable, and thus, its premium revenue will generally be sufficient to cover any claims. For example, if the company sells 1,000 of such policies to identical landowners, its total revenue per year will be $120,000, and it will expect to have one fire per year, costing $100,000 in claims. Thus, the company will expect to earn a profit of $20,000.[29]

In view of the preceding argument, Blume and Rubinfeld (1984, 1987) have argued that an important economic justification for paying compensation for takings is to provide risk-averse landowners with insurance against the risk of such an event.[30] They argue that the reason the government needs to provide this insurance is that market insurance against takings is generally not available. This, they suggest, is likely a consequence of three sources of market failure that often plague insurance markets in general. The first is the moral hazard problem, which in this context means that landowners who are insured against a government taking will be less inclined to participate in the political process in which the taking decision is made. As a result, properties that are insured will have a slightly higher probability of being taken.

A second and related source of market failure is adverse selection. This problem arises if landowners have better knowledge than the insurance company about the probability that their land will be targeted for a taking, prompting those with higher probabilities disproportionately to buy insurance. Finally, because takings are rare events, the insurance company will have a hard time estimating the probability of a taking, thus preventing it from setting the appropriate premium. Such a problem often prevents insurance companies from selling insurance against rare events like takings.

---

[29] Predictability of costs is a consequence of the law of large numbers and the fact that the risks from the various policies are uncorrelated. In other words, the occurrence of a fire in one house does not affect the probability of a fire in any other house.

[30] Also see Rose-Ackerman (1992), who argues that an efficient takings policy should account for moral hazard, fiscal illusion, and insurance against taking risk (see Chapter 4).

The absence of private insurance against takings, coupled with landowner risk aversion, suggests that there may be substantial economic benefits of government-provided insurance. Of course, the same sort of problems that preclude the emergence of private insurance markets would plague government insurance if it were structured in the traditional way. For example, if the government were the primary insurer against takings, it might be inclined to favor those projects that involve the taking of uninsured parcels, or it might even refuse to insure those parcels that it plans to take. For these reasons, Blume and Rubinfeld argue that insurance against takings must be mandatory; that is, it must be dictated by a rule that precludes strategic government behavior. The constitutional requirement of just compensation, financed by general property tax revenues, fulfills this prescription.

To be sure, this solution is not perfect, principally because it creates another source of moral hazard; namely, that landowners will tend to overinvest in land that is subject to a taking risk. Kaplow (1986) has claimed that this problem represents an important argument against mandatory compensation for a taking (or indeed for any government action that reduces property value). Kaplow's argument implies that, when owners are risk averse, there will generally exist a trade-off between the insurance benefits of paying compensation (as previously described) and the incentive advantages of not paying compensation. I will return to this issue in more detail in the next chapter, which highlights the impact of compensation on land use incentives. (See especially Section 4.7 on the trade-off between moral hazard and insurance.)

3.8. Demoralization Costs: The Costs of Not Paying Compensation

In a highly influential article on takings, Frank Michelman (1967) proposed a utilitarian standard for determining when compensation should be paid. We will examine this standard in more detail in Chapters 4 and 5 (see, in particular, Sections 4.8 and 5.2); here we focus on the various social costs of not paying compensation, which Michelman lumped together under the heading of "demoralization costs." He defined these costs as follows:

"Demoralization costs" are defined as the total of (1) the dollar value necessary to offset disutilities which accrue to losers and their sympathizers from the realization that no compensation is offered, and (2) the present capitalized value of lost production (reflecting either impaired incentives or social unrest) caused by demoralization of uncompensated losers, their sympathizers, and other observers disturbed by the thought that they themselves may be subjected to similar treatment on some other occasion (p. 1214).

The question of interest here is whether, in introducing these costs, Michelman was making an insurance argument, an excessive government argument, or a fairness argument for paying compensation. As his further discussion makes clear, Michelman wished to distinguish between losses that arise as a result of random events such as accidents or natural disasters, and those that arise from strategic or political behavior. The crucial difference is that individuals can deal with the random risk through the purchase of insurance (though, as the preceding section pointed out, this may not always be possible in the absence of perfect insurance markets), but they have a much more difficult time dealing with strategic risk (Fischel, 1995a, p. 149). Based on this distinction, the payment of compensation can be seen as reducing demoralization costs along two routes: first, by serving as a potential curb on political excess such as fiscal illusion (strategic risk), and second, by providing a form of government insurance, in lieu of private insurance, for takings.

Beyond these factors, however, Michelman recognized that compensation is not only about efficiency; it is also about fairness:

Many observers, though they may admit that the question of compensability can logically be viewed as a question of efficiency, will insist that it can also be viewed as a question of justice to be decided without regard to the effect of the decision on the net social product (p. 1219).[31]

The most common notion of fairness employed in welfare economics is referred to as horizontal equity, which requires that people who are alike in all relevant respects should be treated the same (Atkinson and Stiglitz, 1980, p. 353). Of course, this definition begs the question of what respects are "relevant" for purposes of applying the standard. The simple answer is that it depends on the situation. For example, it is acceptable to treat people differently based on gender in some contexts (for example, in the setting of car insurance rates), but not in others (for example, in hiring and firing decisions).

In the context of takings, one interpretation of horizontal equity is that individual landowners cannot be "singled out" to bear a disproportionate burden of the cost of public projects by being forced to give up their land in return for zero (or insufficient) compensation. As Justice Black said, it is

---

[31] Ulen (1992, p. 176) likewise notes that just compensation is also about fairness and distributional justice.

the "Fifth Amendment's guarantee to bar government from forcing some people alone to bear public burdens which, in all fairness and justice, should be borne by the public as a whole."[32]

Although this seems to be an argument for routinely paying full compensation, Michelman goes on to assert that in some cases, it can also be consistent with non-payment of compensation. In particular, he says that:

A decision not to compensate is not unfair as long as the disappointed claimant ought to be able to appreciate how such decisions might fit into a consistent practice which holds forth a lesser long-run risk to people like him than would any consistent practice which is naturally suggested by the opposite decision (p. 1223).

Such a view reflects a Rawlsian "veil-of-ignorance" notion of fairness that is based on equality of *expectations* across landowners rather than equality of *outcomes*. We will return to this idea in Chapter 5 in the context of in-kind compensation for government regulations. (See Section 5.9.)

Behavioral economists argue that people define fairness in market contexts in relation to certain benchmarks. Specifically, they "judge outcomes to be 'unfair' if they depart substantially from the terms of a 'reference transaction' – a transaction that defines the benchmark for the parties' interactions" (Jolls, Susntein, and Thaler, 2000, p. 26). In the case of takings, the obvious reference transaction is a consensual purchase of the land, which suggests that an amount of compensation that is substantially less than what the owner would have willingly accepted will be seen as unfair.

In contrast, Kaplow (1986, pp. 576–581) argues that fairness concerns can be understood largely in terms of risk aversion. In particular, he maintains that the costs and benefits suggested by consideration of that factor, as discussed above, are sufficient to address the compensation question without the need to appeal to alternative, and often subjective, notions of fairness.

Finally, Ghosh (1997) suggests that it may be possible to ignore demoralization costs as long as landowners who are subject to government regulation or seizure have the option to exit the jurisdiction. As argued above, exit offers an alternative to compensation as a restraint on inefficient government behavior. For it to be effective in this regard, however, there must exist other jurisdictions with more favorable regulatory environments, and mobility cannot be too costly. Even so, the exit option only mitigates that component of demoralization costs associated with excessive or arbitrary government actions.

---

[32] *Armstrong v. United States*, 364 U.S. 40, 49 (1960).

3.9. Capitalization and Compensation

Michelman (1967) describes a second situation in which compensation should not be paid, namely when a landowner buys a piece of land at a price that is discounted by the (known) probability that the land will be taken (or regulated) in the future. In such a case, we say that the expected cost of a taking has been "capitalized" into the value of the land. Thus, if the taking actually occurs, one can argue that the landowner has already been implicitly compensated. Notice that this is a sort of insurance argument in the sense that the buyer receives a discounted price at the time of purchase reflecting the risk of a taking, and he or she can, in essence, use that savings to self-insure against the possible future loss.

This is a persuasive argument that has actually been employed by courts to reject compensation claims. For example, in *H.F.H Ltd. v. Superior Court*,[33] the court denied relief to a landowner whose commercial property was re-zoned to be residential, thereby reducing its value. Citing Michelman's article, the court said that: "The long settled state of zoning law renders the possibility of change in zoning clearly foreseeable to land speculators and other purchasers of property, who discount their estimate of its value by the probability of such a change."[34]

However, courts apparently understood this idea long before it was advanced by Michelman. For example, in *Callender v. Marsh* (1823), the plaintiff sought compensation from the City of Boston for costs incurred when the streets adjoining his residence were altered. The court denied compensation, arguing that: "Those who purchase house lots bordering upon streets are supposed to calculate the chance of such [alterations] as the increasing population of a city may require ... and as their purchase is always voluntary, they may indemnify themselves in the price of the lot which they buy."[35]

A simple numerical example illustrates the point. Suppose an undeveloped piece of property is worth \$400,000 in commercial use, as permitted under current zoning laws. However, a proposal is made to re-zone the area for residential use, which, if enacted, would reduce the value of the property to \$50,000. Further, suppose that the likelihood of the re-zoning is estimated to be 0.5. The most that a potential buyer would now pay for the land in the presence of the possible zoning change is $\$225,000 = (0.5)(\$400,000) + (0.5)$ (\$50,000), where the \$175,000 discount reflects the expected cost of the

---

[33] 542 P.2d 237 (1975).
[34] *Id.*, p. 246.
[35] 1 Pick. 417 (1823).

rezoning risk. If a buyer purchased the land at this price and the regulation was actually imposed, his or her claim for compensation would be a weak one; Michelman likened it to demanding a refund for a losing lottery ticket (Michelman, 1967, p. 1238).[36]

Although the logic of this argument is compelling, Epstein (1985) and Fischel and Shapiro (1988) have pointed out that it ignores the loss suffered by the owner *at the instant that the threat of a taking or regulation first materializes*. The facts of *H.F.H.* are illustrative. The plaintiff in that case had first purchased the land well before the re-zoning had taken place, and there was no evidence that the threat of re-zoning was "in the air" at the time (Fischel, 1995a, p. 195). If it had been, the price would have reflected that risk, thereby compensating the buyer, but then the *prior* owner would have suffered an uncompensated loss. The point is that the capitalization argument only works back to the point in time where the possibility of a regulation first arose. In the above example, note that the owner at the time the possibility of re-zoning is first announced suffers an immediate capital loss of $175,000.

The Supreme Court seemed to recognize this point in *Palazzola v. Rhode Island*,[37] which involved a claim for compensation by a landowner who was denied the right to develop waterfront land in Rhode Island by the state supreme court because his application was filed after the enactment of a regulation prohibiting wetland development.[38] The state court's ruling reflected the above notice argument against compensation, but the U.S. Supreme Court rejected this logic, stating that: "Were we to accept the State's rule, the postenactment transfer of title would absolve the State of its obligation to defend any action restricting land use, no matter how extreme or unreasonable. A State would be allowed, in effect, to put an expiration date on the Takings Clause."[39]

One way to offset the loss to the original owner in this situation is to promise full compensation for all regulations. If compensation were always required, the value of the land would not be discounted at the time the regulatory threat first arose because the buyer, knowing he could seek

---

[36] Also see Mandelker (1987).

[37] 533 U.S. 606 (2001).

[38] In fact, the claimant was effectively the owner both before and after the enactment of the regulation. Before the regulation, he was the sole shareholder of the corporation that owned the land, but after the regulation was enacted, the corporation's charter was revoked for failure to pay corporate taxes, and ownership passed to the claimant. Thus, practically (if not legally), the claimant's ownership *did* predate the regulation, and he had filed multiple applications to develop, all of which were denied, prior to that time.

[39] *Palazzola v. Rhode Island*, 533 U.S. 606, 622–623 (2001).

compensation for any future loss caused by the regulation, would have been willing to pay the full value of the land in commercial use. In this way, the land market passes the expected compensation back to the original owner, thereby fully protecting his pre-regulation land value.

Note that under this rule, the buyer in effect purchases a bundled asset that consists of the undeveloped land, whose expected value is $225,000 in the previous example, plus a possible takings claim that would award him full compensation in the event of the zoning change, and no compensation otherwise.[40] At the time of the purchase, the value of this "unripe" claim is therefore $175,000 = (0.5)($350,000), which makes the overall value of the land-plus-takings-claim $400,000. Thus, the original owner is fully compensated by the sale.

An alternative approach to this problem, suggested by Stein (2000), is to allow the seller to assert the takings claim *at the time of the sale* based on the capital loss that he suffered as a result of the regulatory threat. His claim would thus be for $175,000, which is the difference between the initial value of the land, $400,000, and its expected value after the regulatory threat was announced, $225,000.[41] The buyer would then purchase the land for $225,000 and would have no subsequent takings claim if and when the zoning change is enacted.

In theory, these two approaches to the problem of land sales in the presence of a regulatory threat are equivalent. Under both, the original owner's value is fully insured against any capital loss, and the buyer pays a purchase price that is commensurate with the risk he is taking on. Legal obstacles aside,[42] the difference therefore hinges on which party is better able

---

[40] For purposes of illustration, I assume here that the takings claim would result in full compensation with certainty, but this is by no means assured in the case of regulations. See the discussion in Chapter 5.

[41] Stein (2000, p. 131) refers to the proposed takings claim for the original owner as a "sale ripened" claim to distinguish it from traditional takings claims (such as that purchased by the buyer under the above rule), which only ripens upon the actual enactment of the zoning regulation prohibiting commercial development.

[42] The legal obstacles include the willingness of courts to define a new type of takings claim, and the fact that the likelihood of winning the claim may differ under the two rules. (I have assumed that success is certain under both rules.) For example, as discussed in Chapter 5, the success of a claim for lost value as a result of a regulation may depend upon the magnitude of the loss suffered by the claimant (the so-called diminution of value test – see Section 5.1 of Chapter 5). Suppose this is the test courts apply. Then, under the rule where the buyer acquires the takings claim, the loss at the time the regulation is actually enacted is $350,000, or 87.5 percent, whereas under the rule where the original owner asserts a claim at the time of sale (the sale-ripened claim), the loss is $175,000, or only 43.75 percent. Thus, the likelihood of a successful claim is presumably much higher under the first rule (Stein, 2000, p. 151).

to estimate the risk of enactment of the regulation and/or which is better suited to pursuing the takings claim.

3.10. Grandfathering versus Compensation

Another way to offset the loss suffered by individuals whose ownership predates notice of an impending regulation is through the use of grandfather provisions that exempt pre-existing investments from the regulation. From the landowner's perspective, grandfathering is at least as good as monetary compensation because it avoids the risk of undercompensation, but from a social perspective it is inferior because it allows the harmful effects of the exempted land use to continue (Kaplow, 1986, pp. 585–586).

Grandfather provisions, like compensation, may also have distortionary effects on the investment incentives of landowners. As the next chapter will show, the promise of full compensation creates a moral hazard problem that causes landowners to overinvest in land that may be valuable for public use, or that may cause an externality, in the future. Grandfathering prior investments will create the same inefficient incentives. In addition, grandfathering may distort the timing of investment decisions by causing landowners to invest sooner than they otherwise would have (and sooner than is efficient) in an effort to establish a safe haven against future uncompensated regulations. (See Section 4.5 in Chapter 4 for a more detailed analysis of this issue.)

As a general proposition, therefore, grandfather provisions may have some advantage over compensation in terms of fairness or insurance considerations (in the sense that they are more likely to leave the landowner whole), but the downside is that they distort land use decisions and leave inefficient uses in place.

3.11. Conclusion: Public Use and Just Compensation Are Two Sides of the Same Coin

The analysis in this and the previous chapters has evaluated the two constitutional limits on eminent domain: public use, which defines the proper scope for takings, and just compensation, which ensures that individuals whose land is taken are not forced to bear disproportionate costs of public projects. I wish to conclude this chapter by noting that, from an economic perspective, these two requirements are best understood as acting in concert to ensure, to the extent possible in a non-market setting, that only efficient transfers occur.[43] This claim is based by the view that market transactions represent the benchmark for efficient exchange and therefore should serve as the standard by which forced transactions are evaluated.

In Chapter 2 we argued that the proper economic interpretation of public use is to permit only those uses of eminent domain aimed at overcoming the holdout problem, given that the threat of such strategic behavior on the part of sellers, in the presence of interdependencies in their land values, can prevent otherwise efficient projects from going forward. The substitution of a forced transfer for a consensual one, however, removes an important source of discipline on the part of the prospective buyer; namely, the seller's right to refuse the sale. In place of consent is substituted the requirement of just compensation, which in an ideal world ensures that the seller can expect equal (or greater) value in return for surrendering his or her land, thus replicating the outcome of a consensual exchange and guaranteeing that only efficient exchanges will occur. The problem, as emphasized in this chapter, is that the accepted measure of just compensation – fair market value – is known to undercompensate most landowners, thereby creating a systematic bias in the direction of allowing too many takings.

The problem of undercompensation is ultimately why the public use requirement matters (Krier and Serkin, 2004). Given that forced exchange under eminent domain cannot perfectly replicate market exchange, the role of courts in establishing the proper limit on the use of this power entails a balancing of the risk of too few transfers if it is not made expansive enough to overcome market failures, against the risk of too many if it is allowed to become too expansive. At bottom, the problem is the lack of a workable method for measuring owners' true valuations, but that is the unavoidable cost of substituting a court-ordered transaction for a consensual one.

---

[43] Epstein (1985, pp. 332–333) expresses a similar point of view.

FOUR

Land Use Incentives

I look forward to a time when the part played by history in the explanation of dogma shall be very small, and instead of ingenious research we shall spend our energy on a study of the ends sought to be attained and the reasons for desiring them. As a step towards that ideal it seems to me that every lawyer ought to seek an understanding of economics.

Oliver Wendell Holmes, Jr., "The Path of the Law" (1897, p. 474)

The preceding chapter focused on various aspects of the just compensation requirement, including its impact on fairness, its insurance function, and its role in creating proper government incentives. Recent economic literature on takings, however, has highlighted a different aspect of compensation, namely its impact on the investment incentives of landowners who face the risk of a taking. This line of research began with the seminal paper by Blume, Rubinfeld, and Shapiro (1984) (hereafter, BRS), which showed that compensation for takings creates a potential moral hazard problem that causes landowners to overinvest in land that is potentially suitable for a taking. The most famous (or rather, infamous) implication of this research was the so-called no-compensation result, which demonstrated that zero compensation is consistent with efficient investment incentives.

The BRS analysis was actually more subtle than this conclusion suggests, but the no-compensation result has nevertheless provided a convenient straw man for stimulating subsequent research, much of it aimed at providing countervailing arguments. As a consequence, the literature has been very productive in both prescribing efficient compensation rules and understanding actual takings decisions, especially, as will be emphasized in Chapter 5, in the area of regulatory takings.

This chapter, which is primarily conceptual, summarizes the recent economic research on land use incentives in the face of takings risk. In so doing, it will not distinguish between physical takings and regulations because, as has already been emphasized, economic theory does not recognize the need for such a distinction (given that a regulation is merely a partial taking). The next chapter, however, takes up the specific challenge of providing an explanation, within the context of the approach developed in this chapter, for the differential legal treatment of the two types of cases.

4.1. Moral Hazard and the No-Compensation Result

When it was first published, the BRS no-compensation result caused something of a stir, principally because it seemed grossly unfair and also flew in the face of the constitutional requirement of just compensation. From a purely economic perspective, however, the result is not a particularly surprising one considering that it is a simple application of well-known results from the economics of insurance. In particular, it is an example of the moral hazard problem, alluded to in the previous chapter, which arises when individuals are fully insured against a risk and hence have little or no incentive to avoid that risk or to mitigate the resulting loss.

To demonstrate this conclusion more formally, we will consider the problem facing the owner of a parcel of vacant land who is contemplating developing it for commercial use. The data for the example are summarized in Table 4.1. Suppose the developer can choose between two possible projects: *Project 1*, which requires an initial, non-salvageable investment of $25,000 and yields a gross return of $200,000; and *Project 2*, which requires an initial investment of $100,000 and yields a gross return of $300,000. Project 2 thus promises a higher net return, as shown by the third column in Table 4.1. A profit-maximizing developer will therefore choose Project 2, and, absent other considerations, this is also the socially efficient use of the land.

But now suppose that the land in question lies along a route that is being considered for the construction of a new highway. Suppose, in particular, that two routes are being considered, one of which goes though the developer's land, and at a known future date the government will decide which route to follow. If it decides on the route through the developer's land, it will take the land by eminent domain, and the resulting (pro-rated) social value of the land will be $500,000. Thus, after if it is taken, the land is more valuable in public than in private use, regardless of which of the two projects the developer had initially chosen. Finally, suppose that at the time the developer must make his project choice (that is, at the time he must make the non-salvageable investment), it is commonly known that each route will be chosen with probability 0.5. Thus, there is an equal chance that the

Table 4.1. *Data for the land development example*

	Initial investment	Gross private return	Net private return	Net expected social return
Project 1	$25,000	$200,000	$175,000	$325,000
Project 2	$100,000	$300,000	$200,000	$300,000

developer's land will and will not be taken. (If it turns out that the land is not taken now, I assume that there is no further risk that it will be taken in the future.)

The timing of events is crucial. In particular, I assume that the developer must make the capital investment decision *before* the taking decision is made. (Obviously, if he could wait, he would do so and then only invest if the land were *not* taken.) This assumption is not as restrictive as it sounds, however, because it reflects the fact that new public projects are continually being proposed, and that private property is therefore perpetually at risk of being taken. Finally, assume that if the land is taken, any existing capital improvements on the land must be demolished in order to clear the way for the highway. Thus, the developer's initial investment is completely lost, though the basic conclusions would be unaffected if the capital were partially salvageable.

Given these assumptions, let us first consider the socially optimal land use in the presence of the taking risk. This amounts to asking which project maximizes the expected social value of the land at the time the landowner must make his initial investment decision, taking account of the possibility that the land might be taken for construction of the highway at a later date. Using the presented data, we first calculate the expected value of Project 1 to be

$$(0.5)(\$200{,}000) + (0.5)(\$500{,}000) - \$25{,}000 = \$325{,}000. \qquad (4.1)$$

The first two terms reflect the fact that with equal probability, the land will remain in private use, yielding the gross return of $200,000, or be taken for the highway, yielding a gross return of $500,000. The expected value of the land, net of the initial investment, is therefore $325,000. Likewise, the expected value of Project 2 is

$$(0.5)(\$300{,}000) + (0.5)(\$500{,}000) - \$100{,}000 = \$300{,}000. \qquad (4.2)$$

Because Project 1 offers the higher net return in this case, it is the socially optimal choice (see column 4 in Table 4.1). The reason for the difference here compared to the case where there was no takings risk (column 3) is that the private return is now only realized with probability 0.5. Thus, the extra invest-ment of $75,000 required for Project 2 yields an expected incremental return of only $50,000, which is the difference between the gross returns under the two projects, multiplied by 0.5. The expected public value of $250,000 = (0.5) ($500,000), in contrast, is independent of the landowner's initial investment and thus has no effect on the choice between the two projects.

The preceding example shows that the presence of a taking risk can change the socially optimal use of the land. The next question concerns the choice that the developer will actually make. This is where the rule deter-mining the amount of compensation to be paid in the event of a taking may matter.

Suppose initially that compensation is full, as required by the Constitution. That is, if the developer's land is taken, the government must fully reim-burse him for the foregone private value of the land. Thus, if the developer chooses Project 1 and the land is taken, he will receive compensation of $200,000, whereas if he chooses Project 2 and the land is taken, he will receive $300,000. Full compensation therefore leaves the developer indif-ferent as to whether or not the taking occurs (at least as regards his nominal income from the land).[1]

To see the impact of this compensation rule, suppose first that the devel-oper chooses Project 1. Because he will be fully compensated in the event of a taking, his expected return will be $175,000, which is the same return as if there were no risk of a taking. Likewise, if the landowner undertakes Project 2, he will again be fully compensated in the event of a taking, and his expected return will be $200,000. Thus, as was the case when there was no risk of a taking, he prefers Project 2. And because we showed earlier that the socially optimal choice is Project 1, the developer overinvests – that is, he inefficiently chooses Project 2. This represents the moral hazard problem associated with a rule promising full compensation.

This result raises the question of whether there exists a compensation rule that will induce the developer to make the socially optimal investment decision. One possibility, suggested earlier, is zero compensation. To see the effect of this rule, we re-calculate the developer's expected returns under the two projects as follows:

$$\text{Project 1:} \quad (0.5)(\$200,000) - \$25,000 = \$75,000 \qquad (4.3)$$
$$\text{Project 2:} \quad (0.5)(\$300,000) - \$100,000 = \$50,000 \qquad (4.4)$$

---

[1] In examining the impact of compensation on land use incentives in this chapter, I do not distinguish between subjective and market value.

In this case, the developer receives zero return in the event of a taking, and so he now opts for Project 1, the efficient choice. The key thing to notice is that the difference between the two returns here, $25,000, is exactly the same as the difference between the social returns as calculated in (4.1) and (4.2) above. This is a perfectly general result and is the reason that the developer makes the efficient choice under a rule of zero compensation.

Observe in particular that the social returns for the two projects in (4.1) and (4.2) differ from corresponding returns in (4.3) and (4.4) by a constant amount, equal to the expected social value of the land, $250,000 = (0.5) ($500,000). And as we saw earlier, this expected value is independent of the developer's initial investment so it will not affect the relative returns between the two projects. Thus, the private and social choices will necessarily coincide. In contrast, under a rule of full compensation, the amount of compensation *will* generally depend on the developer's choice between the projects because that choice determines the gross returns. The resulting distortion of the developer's choice away from the socially optimal choice is the essence of the moral hazard problem under full compensation.

The preceding example showed that zero compensation induces the developer to make the efficient land use decision, but BRS actually derived a more general result, from which zero compensation emerged as a special case. What they in fact showed was that any rule under which compensation is independent of the amount of the landowner's initial investment will induce the efficient land use decision. In other words, any fixed, or *lump-sum* amount of compensation will be efficient (with zero compensation being one extreme case). The preceding example shows why this result must be true. In particular, adding any fixed amount to both (4.3) and (4.4) will not change the difference between them, and hence will not distort the developer's choice.

Despite this more general conclusion, the no-compensation result of BRS has understandably attracted the most attention. In subsequent sections, I therefore examine several counterarguments that have been advanced in favor of paying some amount of positive compensation.

4.2. Efficiency of the Taking Decision

Although it is efficient in terms of land use decisions, the no-compensation result is unappealing both in terms of fairness and because it is inconsistent with actual law (at least regarding physical takings). As a result, several arguments have been advanced to justify the payment of compensation. The first and most obvious concerns the taking decision. As has been emphasized throughout this book, the most common justification for the constitutional requirement of just compensation is to restrain the government from taking too much land for public use. This concern did not arise in the previously presented model because we assumed that the taking decision occurred randomly, but a more realistic approach explicitly considers the incentives of the government when deciding on how much (or which) land to take for public use. Obviously, introducing this issue requires us to make some specific assumption regarding the motivation of the government. There is no consensus on how to do this, so I consider two alternatives: a benevolent government, and a non-benevolent government.

Benevolent government. A benevolent government is defined here to be one that makes its takings decisions solely to maximize social welfare.[2] In the current context, this means that it only takes land whose value in public use exceeds its private value to the current landowner, whether or not compensation of the landowner is required. In terms of the earlier example, the developer must make his investment decision before the government makes its decision about whether or not to build the highway through the developer's land.

I assumed earlier that the value of the highway, if approved, was fixed at $500,000. (In other words, the developer's land was definitely more valuable in public than in private use.) I now complicate the model by supposing that the social worth of the developers' land as part of the highway can take one of three values: $5,000, $250,000, or $500,000, and that each value can occur with probability equal to 1/3. The government is benevolent, so it will only take the land if the realized value of the highway exceeds its private value; that is, if the taking is socially efficient. Referring back to Table 4.1, if the developer chooses Project 1, the private value of the land will be $200,000. Thus, the government will take the land if the realized value of the highway turns out to be $250,000 or $500,000, but will not take it if the value of the highway turns out to be $5,000. In contrast, if the developer chooses Project 2, the private value of the land will be $300,000. In this case, the government will only take the land if the realized value of the highway is $500,000. Notice, therefore, that the developer's land use choice now affects the probability of a taking. In particular, the probability of a taking is 2/3 if the developer chooses Project 1, but only 1/3 if he chooses Project 2.

As before, we first derive the socially optimal land use. Given the government's taking criterion and the resulting probability of a taking (which

---

[2]   Fischel and Shapiro (1989) also refer to such a government as "Pigovian" in the sense that it considers the social costs and benefits of its actions.

are, by assumption, socially optimal, given the developer's prior land use decision), we proceed in the same way as previously described to calculate the expected social value of the land under Project 1 as follows:

$$\text{Project 1: } (1/3)(\$200,000) + (1/3)(\$250,000)$$
$$+ (1/3)(\$500,000) - \$25,000 = \$291,667. \qquad (4.5)$$

Note that the land remains in private use when the realized value of the public use is $5,000, but it is taken and converted to public use when the realized value is either $250,000 or $500,000. Similarly, the expected social value under Project 2 is

$$\text{Project 2: } (2/3)(\$300,000) + (1/3)(\$500,000)$$
$$- \$100,000 = \$266,667. \qquad (4.6)$$

In this case the land is only taken when the realized value of the land in public use is $500,000. The expected value of the land is higher under Project 1, thus it is the socially optimal land use.

Let us now consider the landowner's actual choice, assuming initially (based on the results from the previous section) that compensation is zero. The landowner's expected private return from each of the two projects in this case is calculated as follows:

$$\text{Project 1: } (1/3)(\$200,000) - \$25,000 = \$41,667 \qquad (4.7)$$
$$\text{Project 2: } (2/3)(\$300,000) - \$100,000 = \$100,000. \qquad (4.8)$$

Thus, the landowner inefficiently opts for Project 2! As a result, zero compensation does *not* yield the optimal land use choice in this case. What accounts for this different conclusion? The problem, as previously suggested, is that the landowner recognizes that, given the government's taking criterion, his land use decision will affect the probability of a taking. In particular, he realizes that by investing more in his land (i.e., by choosing Project 2) he can reduce the probability that it will be taken and that no compensation will be paid. As a result, his expected private return is higher under Project 2. The fact that the landowner's project choice affects the probability of a taking in this example has actually introduced a second source of landowner moral hazard under a rule of zero compensation – namely that the developer will overinvest in order to reduce the probability of an uncompensated taking by the benevolent government.

Thus, we now have two sources of moral hazard on the part of the landowner: one associated with full compensation (the original BRS moral hazard), and one associated with zero compensation. It turns out, however, that both problems can be eliminated by a rule that promises some positive compensation, but the amount of compensation must be specified in a particular way. That is, it must be set equal to the full value of the land *at the efficient level of investment*. In the current example, this means that compensation must be set at $200,000, because that is the private value of the land under Project 1, which we showed earlier to be the socially efficient choice. Note that this measure of compensation satisfies the lump-sum requirement because this amount will be paid regardless of which project the landowner actually chooses. Thus, it will eliminate the first source of moral hazard.

As to the second source, the probability of a taking will still be different under the two projects (because the benevolent government continues to base its decision on the social value of the land compared to its actual private value), but the fact that compensation in the event of a taking is fixed at $200,000, even when Project 2 is chosen, sufficiently reduces the value of that project to the developer that it becomes less profitable compared to Project 1. To illustrate, we re-calculate the expected private returns from the two projects. Under Project 1, we have

$$(1/3)(\$200,000) + (2/3)(\$200,000) - \$25,000 = \$175,000, \qquad (4.9)$$

whereas under Project 2, we have

$$(2/3)(\$300,000) + (1/3)(\$200,000) - \$100,000 = \$166,667. \qquad (4.10)$$

Comparing the two returns verifies that the developer efficiently opts for Project 1.

In a more general setting, one can show that any lesser amount of compensation would result in the landowner's overinvesting in order to reduce the probability of a taking (given that compensation is "too low"), whereas any larger amount would actually result in his underinvesting to increase the probability of a taking (given that compensation is overly generous).[3] Thus, the efficient amount of compensation is uniquely determined by the value of the land in the efficient use.[4]

---

[3] The formal proof of these and the other claims associated with this rule are provided in the Appendix to this chapter. Miceli (1991) first examined this rule. Also see Giammarino and Nosal (2005). Cooter (1985) derived a similar result in the context of breach of contract remedies.

[4] Cooter (1985) describes a slightly different compensation rule under which the government acquires an option from the landowner that allows it to take the land at any point over some specified time horizon for a pre-specified price. (This is referred to as a "call" option – see Ayres and Balkin [1997].) The distinguishing feature of this rule is that it

The compensation rule just described, although efficient in terms of land use incentives, presents some practical difficulties given the need for the court to be able to calculate the value of the land in its efficient use rather than its actual use. In the current context, this requires the court to be able to determine, after the fact, what the efficient level of investment in the land would have been, given the taking risk. Fischel (1985, Chapter 8) suggests the use of community norms (what he calls "normal behavior") as one approach to this problem. I will pursue Fischel's argument in greater depth, including its practicality, in the context of regulatory takings in Chapter 5 (see Section 5.2).

It turns out, however, that the efficient lump-sum compensation rule as just described is not the only one that will induce efficient land use under the assumption of a benevolent government. Hermalin (1995) has proposed two others. The first requires the government to pay the landowner compensation equal to the full (pro-rated) value of the public project in the event of a taking. Under this "gain-based" rule, the landowner automatically internalizes the full social value of his land because his private returns from the two projects exactly coincide with the social returns in (4.5) and (4.6). Thus, he necessarily makes the efficient investment choice. The main drawback of this rule is that it awards the entire surplus from the public project to the landowner(s) in the form of compensation, which may strike some as distributionally unfair, especially if the individuals whose land is taken are small in number compared to those who benefit from the project, as would be true, for example, if the land were taken for construction of a highway or a park. (Notice that this is the flip side of Epstein's argument, discussed in Section 3.1 of Chapter 3, that it is unjust for the *beneficiaries* of the project to receive all of the surplus created by the taking.)

The second rule proposed by Hermalin sets compensation for landowners equal to zero, but allows them to block any proposed takings by *paying the government* the social value of the land. In other words, whenever the government initiates a taking, landowners have the option either to let the taking proceed (in which case no compensation would be paid) or to "buy back" their land at a price equal to its social value (which the benevolent

allows the landowner to participate in the determination of the price before the actual taking decision occurs rather than leaving it to the court to decide at the time of the taking. Mathematically, the analysis of this rule is virtually the same as that for the lump-sum rule, and the conclusion is the same. That is, efficiency requires the option price to be set equal to the value of the land evaluated at its efficient level of investment (see the Appendix to this chapter for a proof). Finally, note the similarity of this rule to the Plassmann and Tideman (2008) scheme discussed in Section 3.2 of Chapter 3.

government will correctly reveal). In other words, landowners can pay the government *not* to take their land.

Whether or not the landowner will exercise this buy-back option to block the taking in the previous example depends on which project he initially chooses. If he chooses Project 1 (with a gross value of $200,000) and the government initiates the taking, he will only buy back his land if the public project turns out to be worth $5,000, but if he chooses Project 2 (with a gross return of $300,000), he will buy back his land if the public project turns out to be worth $5,000 or $250,000. Note that this reflects the efficient decision regarding whether or not to convert the land to public use, conditional on the project choice. To see that the landowner also makes the efficient choice between projects, we calculate his expected returns under the buy-back rule as follows:

$$\text{Project 1: } (1/3)(\$200,000-\$5,000) - \$25,000 = \$40,000 \tag{4.11}$$

$$\text{Project 2: } (1/3)(\$200,000-\$5,000) + (1/3)(\$300,000-\$250,000)$$
$$- \$100,000 = -\$18,333 \tag{4.12}$$

Thus, he chooses Project 1, which is the efficient choice. (Although the net return from Project 2 is negative, it is the best the landowner can do under that project.)

Both rules proposed by Hermalin – the gain-based rule and the buy-back rule – therefore achieve efficient land use decisions, but they differ dramatically in their distributional implications. Under the first rule, the government, representing users of the public project, pays to acquire the resources needed to produce it, whereas under the second rule, the landowner pays to withhold the necessary resources. The fact that both rules are efficient reflects the economic equivalence between out-of-pocket costs and opportunity costs. Hermalin (1995) characterizes the difference between the two rules in terms of the assignment of property rights: "In an externality setting – which essentially is what a takings problem is – the property right can reside with the citizen [the landowner], so she is compensated for what is taken; or the property right can reside with the state, so the citizen pays for the privilege of enjoying her benefit" (p. 66). Note that this conclusion reflects our analysis of the general transaction structure in Chapter 1, which demonstrated that alternative assignments of property rights, reflecting different distributions of wealth, are consistent with efficiency.[5]

---

[5] It also anticipates the logic of the "harm-benefit" rule for determining the compensability of regulatory takings, as discussed in the next chapter. (See Section 5.2.)

Non-benevolent government. The assumption of a benevolent government that always acts to promote social welfare is perhaps overly naïve. More realistic models suppose instead that the government acts in the interests of the majority of landowners, subject to budgetary constraints. As discussed in Chapter 3, such governments are sometimes described as having "fiscal illusion," meaning that they act as if the costs of their actions are the budgetary costs (dollar outlays) rather than the true opportunity costs. Early economic arguments for requiring compensation for takings are based on this logic (Johnson, 1977).

A government with fiscal illusion will take a piece of land if its value in public use (which the government is assumed to internalize) exceeds the amount of compensation that it must pay.[6] This logic suggests that a rule requiring full compensation (i.e., compensation equal to the full value of the land in private use) would be necessary to ensure efficiency of the taking decision. The obvious problem with this criterion, however, is that it sets up a potential trade-off between fiscal illusion on the one hand and the moral hazard problem associated with full compensation on the other.[7] The trick is to design a compensation rule that simultaneously addresses both problems.

Fortunately, it turns out that all three rules examined in the previous section accomplish this objective. First consider the efficient lump-sum rule, which, recall, sets compensation equal to the value of the land at the efficient level of investment. As shown earlier, this measure of compensation, because it is a lump-sum amount, induces the efficient level of investment by the landowner. Moreover, because it requires the government to pay full compensation in the efficient equilibrium, it will also induce a government with fiscal illusion to make the correct taking decision (Miceli, 1991a). To illustrate, recall that in the earlier example, efficient compensation equals the value of the land under Project 1, or $200,000. Thus, a government with fiscal illusion will take the land if and only if the value of the public project exceeds this amount. It will therefore only take the land if that value turns out to be $250,000 or $500,000, which is the efficient decision.

---

6 Levinson (2000, p. 350) asks the following rather obvious question: "If government does not fully internalize the costs of takings unless it must spend its revenues to pay compensation, then why should we expect government to fully internalize the benefits of takings when it does not receive them in the form of revenues?" The economic models address this question with ad hoc theories of government behavior – for example, that the majority of citizens control the government.

7 See Cooter (1985, pp. 3–5), who characterizes the problem of simultaneously achieving efficient behavior by both the government and the landowner with a single compensation rule as the "paradox of compensation." As we note in Section 4.6 in this chapter, this problem also arises in economic models of torts, contracts, and property.

Consider next the two rules proposed by Hermalin. We have seen that both induce efficient land use, therefore we can focus on whether they also induce the efficient taking decision by the government. Recall that the gain-based rule requires the government to pay landowners the full social value of the land in the event of a taking. As a result, this rule will actually leave a government characterized by fiscal illusion indifferent between taking the land and not taking it, regardless of the realized value of the public project. The landowner, however, will only want the taking to occur if the value of the land in public use (which will also be the amount of his compensation) exceeds its value in private use. Thus, if the government, when indifferent, acts in accord with the preferences of landowners, then it will make the efficient taking decision. (That is, it will only take the land when its value in public use exceeds its value in private use.) In this sense, we can conclude that the gain-based compensation rule is "weakly" efficient regarding the taking decision.

Finally, consider the buy-back rule, which, recall, sets compensation at zero but allows the landowner to prevent a taking by paying the government the value of his land in public use. Note that under this rule, a government with fiscal illusion will, in theory, initiate a taking for any public project with positive value because its budgetary costs are zero. However, the land-owner will pay to retain ownership – that is, to block the taking – whenever the private value of the land exceeds its social value, given the initial invest-ment. The landowner therefore in effect makes both the investment and taking decisions under this rule. And, as previously shown, he will make both decisions efficiently because he internalizes the full value of the land in public use.

I conclude this section by noting that there exists a fourth compensation rule that simultaneously induces efficient land use and takings decisions in the presence of moral hazard and fiscal illusion. I will refer to this as the efficient "threshold rule." However, I will defer discussion of it to the next chapter, as it is most relevant in the context of regulatory takings. (See Section 5.3 in Chapter 5.)

4.3. Constitutional Choice Models

A different class of models of the land use and takings decisions is referred to as "constitutional choice" models. These models are based on the notion that the government is not a distinct entity with a separate objective func-tion but is merely the vehicle or agent by which the citizens in a given juris-diction act collectively to govern themselves, including deciding on how much land to devote to public use and how to finance the cost of acquiring that land. Models of this sort envision a two-stage process in which citizens in the first stage hold a hypothetical constitutional convention at which they choose the compensation rule for takings from behind a veil of ignorance regarding which particular parcels will be taken.[8] Then, in a second stage, they make their land use and takings decisions subject to that rule. In this context, landowners realize that they are all potential takings victims, given that it will be efficient to devote some amount of land to public use, but they also recognize that any compensation that must be paid to those citizens whose land is taken must ultimately be financed out of taxes that will be assessed on the remaining citizens. Thus, in designing the compensation rule, rational individuals will presumably take account of both sides of the public ledger and will therefore not be overly stingy with regard to compensation (in case it is their land that will be taken) nor overly generous (to limit their liability as taxpayers).

The first paper to use this approach to derive the optimal compensation rule for takings was by Fischel and Shapiro (1989) (hereafter, FS). In their model, citizens first choose the compensation rule, which is specified as a fraction of the land's market value. In making this choice, they are assumed to be ignorant of their eventual position in society in the sense that they do not know whether their land will be taken for public use. They do know, however, that any compensation required by the rule that they choose must be financed out of taxes assessed on all owners whose land is not taken. In this initial position, all individuals are identical and therefore unanimously agree to institute a compensation rule that maximizes the aggregate wealth of society (which amounts to maximizing each individual's expected net wealth), including consumption of public services. Once the compensation rule is in place, the second stage of the model begins. This stage follows the original BRS formulation, where landowners make irreversible capital investments in their land, and then the "government" makes its taking decision.

The compensation rule that emerges from this framework turns out to depend on two key factors. The first is the assumption regarding the government's behavior, and the second is the manner in which taxes are assessed. Regarding the first, FS consider three cases, corresponding to the three models of government previously discussed. In the first, the government

---

[8] See Rawls (1971), who derived his theory of a just society by imagining what social arrangements people would construct from behind a veil of ignorance about their actual position in that society.

behaves "inexorably" in the sense that it takes land randomly (the original BRS assumption); in the second, it maximizes social welfare (the benevolent, or Pigovian government); and in the third, it maximizes the welfare of the majority of landowners (the non-benevolent, or majoritarian government). Regarding the financing of compensation, FS treat taxes as lump sum in all cases.[9] For now, I will retain that assumption, but later I will consider a more realistic tax assessment rule.

Consider first the case of the inexorable government. Here, the compensation rule plays no role in the taking decision, so only the original BRS moral hazard problem is present. Thus, because compensation is constrained to be a proportion of market value, only zero compensation is efficient. More generally, though, any amount of lump-sum compensation would be efficient, as we argued earlier.

Consider next the case where the government is benevolent. In this case, compensation is unnecessary to restrain excessive takings, but, as we showed earlier, if the landowner perceives that his investment choice will affect the probability that his land will be taken, positive compensation would be required to induce efficient investment (i.e., to avoid the second form of landowner moral hazard). In their model, however, FS avoid this problem by assuming that individual landowners view the probability of a taking as fixed (i.e., independent of their land use decision). Thus, zero compensation is again efficient, and as a result, both the inexorable and benevolent government versions of the FS model yield the same conclusion regarding the efficient compensation rule.

The final, and most interesting, case is that of the non-benevolent government. FS characterize the government in this case as majoritarian in the sense that it maximizes the welfare of the majority of voters. This is equivalent to the so-called median voter model of government, which is assumed to enact those policies that please the majority of voters so as to maximize its chances of re-election.[10] In the context of takings, this essentially involves the government's acting to maximize the welfare of those citizens whose land is *not* taken, assuming that they constitute the majority of landowners. The role of compensation here, as chosen by citizens from behind the veil of ignorance, is therefore to prevent the excessive expropriation of land from the minority of landowners for use by the majority.

The primary result emerging from this version of the FS model is that compensation should be partial, falling somewhere between zero and full

---

[9] By "lump sum" here I mean that taxes are independent of property values. They could therefore be income, wealth, or head taxes.
[10] See, for example, Atkinson and Stiglitz (1980, pp. 299–302).

compensation. Intuitively, partial compensation balances the moral hazard and fiscal illusion problems. On the one hand, compensation cannot be full or it will cause landowners to overinvest, but on the other hand, it cannot be zero or it will cause the government to take too much land. The resulting optimum is second-best, however, because neither choice is made efficiently. In addition, the result fails to explain actual takings law, which typically involves either full or zero compensation. For these reasons, the proposed rule lacks a certain appeal.

It is important to emphasize, however, that FS's partial compensation result is actually an artifact of two key assumptions in their model. The first is that the compensation rule is constrained to be a fraction of market value. As we showed earlier, however, several other forms of compensation can achieve first-best efficiency with regard to both the land use and the takings decisions when the government is non-benevolent, but the FS model explicitly eschews these various efficient rules on grounds that they would be too costly for the court to implement (Fischel and Shapiro, 1989, p. 118).

The second key assumption underlying the FS partial compensation result is that taxes are treated as lump sum and hence have no incentive effects on either the land use or takings decisions.[11] Generally speaking, lump-sum taxes are economically desirable precisely because they do not distort these decisions, but they are generally thought to be impractical or unfair. (Regarding their impracticality, one might therefore argue that there is an inconsistency in allowing taxes to be lump sum but not compensation.) It turns out, however, that in the current setting, where there is already a distortion built into the model by the assumption of a proportional compensation rule, the introduction of a distortionary property tax can actually improve efficiency.[12]

To see this, suppose that instead of being lump sum, taxes are assessed as a proportion of property values.[13] This, of course, is the way most taxes are actually collected at the local level. If we also retain the assumption of a proportional compensation rule, then the landowner faces two distortions in making his investment choice. The first is the usual (BRS) moral hazard problem associated with compensation, which we have seen will tend to make the landowner *over*invest as compensation rises above zero, whereas

---

[11] The balanced budget is achieved by calculating the tax based on the equilibrium (as opposed to the actual) investment level of the representative landowner.

[12] This reflects the theory of second-best, which says that when there exists one distortion in an economic system, adding a second does not necessarily worsen efficiency. See generally Atkinson and Stiglitz (1980, p. 358)

[13] See Miceli (2008) and Nosal (2001).

the second is the distortion from the proportional property tax, which will tend to make the landowner *under*invest as the tax rate on property value increases. The distortions therefore work in opposite directions because compensation and taxes must rise together to maintain a balanced budget. In fact, in the special case where the sole purpose of the tax is to finance compensation, we can prove the following striking result: *the compensation and tax distortions will exactly offset each other under the requirement that the public budget must be balanced.*[14] As a result, the landowner's investment decision will be efficient, regardless of how stingy or generous the compensation rule is.[15] Another way to say this is that the amount of compensation is irrelevant with respect to the landowner's investment decision, which will be efficient. (The formal proof of this proposition, which was first derived by Miceli [2008], is provided in the Appendix to this chapter.)

This same approach can be applied to the choice of how much land the government takes for public use, if we assume (or require) that citizens also make this choice from behind the veil of ignorance. Realistically, decisions about which specific parcels will be taken cannot be made until after the veil is lifted and actual economic outcomes are revealed, but general guidelines, such as what fraction of private property to devote to public use, presumably could be established beforehand. In other words, citizens would authorize the amount of land to take in the same way that they chose the compensation rule, namely to maximize aggregate expected wealth (rather than to maximize the wealth of the majority). Under these conditions, one can show, based on the same logic as presented earlier, that citizens will authorize the efficient amount of land to be taken, regardless of the amount of compensation (Miceli, 2008). Again, the reason for this surprising result

---

[14] This result is similar to the macroeconomic concept of Ricardian Equivalence. See Bernheim and Bagwell (1988). Obviously, if the cost of compensation is financed, along with other public services, out of general property tax revenues, then the equivalence no longer holds.

[15] Miceli (2008) shows that this result hinges on the assumption that all landowners are identical. If landowners vary, for example, in the marginal valuation of their investments, then the compensation rule is no longer irrelevant. The reason is that, given uniform tax assessments, the budget-balancing property tax will vary, depending on which parcels are taken. For example, if low-valued property is taken, the tax rate needed to finance compensation will be lower than if high-valued property is taken. Thus, owners of low-valued property will tend to underinvest, whereas owners of high-valued property will tend to overinvest. Although the compensation and tax distortions must continue to cancel *on average*, they will no longer cancel for individual owners. Consequently, the only compensation rule that ensures efficient investment by all landowners, given proportional compensation and taxation, is zero compensation, because only in that case are all distortions eliminated from the capital market.

is that citizens will account for their dual roles as taxpayers and potential takings victims through the balanced budget requirement, and will therefore make the efficient taking decision no matter how generous or stingy the compensation rule is.

To be sure, it is a debatable point as to whether citizens can realistically pre-commit to the amount of land they will devote to public use in the same way that they can pre-commit (via the constitution) to a compensation rule.[16] The point here is simply to show that the same logic that led to the irrelevance of the compensation rule with regard to the land use decision also applies, in principle, to the taking decision.

As a final point, the analysis of constitutional choice models in this section highlights the importance of accounting for the tax consequences of paying compensation. In particular, this approach shows that the impact of various compensation rules on land use decisions cannot be judged independently from the impact of the taxes used to finance them, given the link between the two through the public budget constraint. For example, a proportional compensation rule, when viewed in isolation, is inefficient due to the moral hazard problem. Likewise, a proportional property tax, when viewed in isolation, is distortionary. However, when the two are paired through the balanced budget, the distortions will necessarily offset, thereby restoring efficient land use incentives.[17]

4.4. Market Value Compensation and the Epstein-Fischel Conjecture

The irrelevance of the compensation rule as derived in the previous section sheds light on the controversial assertion by Richard Epstein that taxes and takings are equivalent in the sense that both represent non-consensual seizures of private property for public use (Epstein, 1985, p. 196). Whereas takings are explicit seizures of land for public use as a highway or park, taxes are seizures of wealth to be used to finance other forms of public spending like education or police protection. In a society where citizens value

---

[16] See the discussion of this point in Fischel (1995a, pp. 204–205).

[17] In a different context, Hamilton (1975) similarly showed that in the Tiebout (1956) model of local public good provision, property taxes will not distort the choice of housing consumption, or the provision of local public services, provided that households sort themselves into homogeneous communities. The reason is that the requirement of a balanced budget in each community effectively transforms the property tax into a benefit tax. Hamilton notes, however, that zoning will generally be needed to maintain homogeneity in such a system, given the tendency for low-income households to follow the rich in an effort to free-ride on their higher tax base.

public spending, they must therefore implicitly consent to both of these forms of coercive government action – namely takings and taxes – given the general failure of the private market to provide these sorts of public goods efficiently. The veil of ignorance, or constitutional choice framework, highlights this implicit consent. It does this by envisioning a hypothetical social contract whereby citizens expect greater welfare overall in return for granting certain powers to the government, even though they know they will sometimes be on the losing end as circumstances actually unfold.

Within this framework, William Fischel has conjectured that market value emerged as the legal measure of just compensation as constitution writers wrestled with the question of how best to balance the demand for public goods on the one hand against the need to prevent the exploitation of a minority of landowners by the majority who might covet their land for collective use on the other hand. Although we argued in Chapter 3 that market value almost certainly undercompensates owners for their true value, thereby possibly inviting excessive takings, the offsetting consideration is that a more generous compensation rule would impose a greater burden on taxpayers. As Fischel (1995a) notes: "… [P]roperty owners were in a position to realize that undercompensation for takings would be borne by themselves or by people with whom they had some natural empathy. But they were also in a position to realize that the burdens of overcompensation would be borne by themselves and their class by virtue of higher taxes or foregoing wealth-enhancing public works" (p. 211). I will refer to this argument in defense of market value compensation as the Epstein-Fischel conjecture.

The constitutional choice model examined in the previous section provides a formal means for evaluating this conjecture because it explicitly asks what compensation rule citizens would choose from a hypothetical position in which they would account for their roles as both taxpayers and potential takings victims. Although that model showed that market value compensation does not in fact emerge as the uniquely optimal rule (the amount of compensation was in fact indeterminate), it nevertheless validated the basic insight from which the conjecture arose, namely that landowners would recognize the fundamental equivalence of taxes and takings (through the public budget) with respect to their impacts on land use incentives, and also potentially on the taking decision.[18] In truth, it is likely that the market-value

---

[18] Miceli (2008) makes this point. Using a similar approach, Nosal (2001) shows that market value compensation is efficient. However, he assumes this form for the compensation rule and shows that it yields an efficient equilibrium. Thus, his result is a special case of the more general irrelevance result in Miceli (2008).

measure was chosen primarily for practical reasons – that is, given a general desire to pay some amount of compensation for fairness or other objectives, courts settled on the measure that was easiest to calculate.

4.5. The Timing of Development

Our discussion of land use incentives to this point has been based on a static model of land use in the sense that the timing of the landowner's investment was not an issue. In particular, the investment decision had no effect on the feasibility of the government's taking decision. In many contexts, this assumption may not be warranted. For example, in the case of physical takings, if the government has more than one suitable location for a public project (like the multiple possible highway routes in the earlier example), it may prefer to take land that is undeveloped in order to avoid the cost of clearing away existing improvements. And in the case of regulations, investments by the landowner may actually render certain regulations irrelevant, as when the owner of a stand of timber harvests the lumber for fear that an endangered species will be discovered living there, or a when a developer fills in a wetland in order to pre-empt an impending ban on development. The problem these situations create is that the threatened taking or regulation may induce the landowner to develop prematurely in order to forestall or reduce the chances of the government action.[19]

The reader may note that the problem here is similar to the previously discussed case where the benevolent government based its taking decision on a comparison of the private and social values of the land. Recall that the landowner there was able to affect the probability of a taking by his investment choice. In particular, we showed that he had an incentive to overinvest if he expected less than full compensation, thereby reducing the probability of a taking. The lesson was that positive compensation may be necessary to restore the correct incentives. The same principle carries over to the current setting with regard to the timing of the investment decision.

We can illustrate this conclusion with the following example. Suppose that the owner of a piece of vacant land has two options: invest now, which yields a net present value of $250,000, or wait and invest later, which yields a net present value of $300,000. In the absence of other considerations, the landowner would therefore prefer to wait. This is like the owner of the stand of timber whose privately optimal harvest time is some point in the future.

---

[19] For formal analyses of this timing problem, see Miceli and Segerson (1996, chapter 8), Innes (1997), Riddiough (1997), Turnbull (2002), and Lueck and Michael (2003).

Suppose, however, that if the landowner leaves the land undeveloped (i.e., chooses to wait), there is a chance that the land will be taken for use as a park or wildlife habitat. Specifically, suppose that with probability 0.5, the land, if left vacant, will turn out to be worth $400,000 in public use. However, if the landowner develops now, the land will have no public use value, now or in the future, and hence it will not be taken. The resulting social returns from the landowner's two options are given as follows:

Invest now: $250,000   (4.13)

Wait: $(0.5)(\$300,000) + (0.5)(\$400,000) = \$350,000$ (4.14)

Thus, from a social perspective, it is also optimal for the landowner to leave the land undeveloped (i.e., to wait) so as to preserve the possibility of the future public use.

The actual decision of the landowner will, of course, depend on what amount of compensation, if any, she expects to receive in the event of a taking. If, for example, compensation were zero, it would no longer be privately optimal for the landowner to wait to develop because that would yield an expected private return of $150,000 = (0.5)($300,000), which is less than the $250,000 return from investing now.[20] In other words, the landowner finds it optimal to invest now in order to avoid the risk of an uncompensated taking. Obviously, one rule that induces the correct decision is to pay the landowner the full value of the public project, or $400,000, if she waits and the land is taken, for in this case, the landowner's expected return coincides with the social return. (Note that this coincides with Hermalin's gain-based rule.) As previously argued, however, this rule is probably not acceptable on distributional grounds because it awards all of the surplus from the public project to the landowner. A lesser amount of compensation will also work in this case as long as it induces the landowner to wait. In the example, any amount greater than $200,000 will increase the expected private return from waiting above the certain return of $250,000 from investing now.[21]

Alternatively, landowners who invest prematurely can be assessed a tax equal to the expected present value of their land in public use. In the example, this would involve assessing a tax of $200,000 ($= 0.5 \times \$400,000$) on all landowners who choose to invest now. Given this tax, the landowner's

---

[20] As discussed in Section 3.10 of the previous chapter, grandfather provisions that protect pre-existing investments from regulation, coupled with zero compensation, will also create an incentive to develop early.

[21] Specifically, if compensation equals $200,000, the expected private return from waiting is $(0.5)(\$300,000) + (0.5)(\$200,000) = \$250,000$.

return from investing now would become $50,000 = $250,000 – $200,000, while the return from waiting would be $150,000, yielding the same relative returns as in (4.13) and (4.14). Thus, the developer would prefer to wait.

The preceding proposals once again illustrate the symmetry between compensation and taxation in creating the incentives for efficient land use. There is, however, a fundamental asymmetry in implementing the tax as compared to compensation, owing to the fact that it is not clear how one would distinguish between "investing now" and "waiting," given that all land is potentially valuable in public use at some future time. In other words, a landowner's decision to develop at *any* time could be interpreted as developing "now" in relation to some hypothetical future public use of the land. Thus, all development would theoretically be subject to the proposed tax. In contrast, the payment of compensation would only be triggered by a specific government action prohibiting development. In this sense, compensation would seem to involve lower administrative costs. On the other hand, the tax would generate revenue for the government, as opposed to entailing an outlay, so a government with fiscal illusion would likely prefer the tax approach.

4.6. A Digression on Unity in Torts, Contracts, and Takings

An important contribution of the economic approach to law is to reveal unifying principles across disparate areas of law. The seminal reference in this context is Cooter (1985), who used a single economic model – the so-called model of precaution – to demonstrate an underlying unity in torts, contracts, and property law. At this point, it is worth noting how the analysis of land use and takings incentives as surveyed so far in this chapter fits into this unifying framework.[22]

The model of precaution was first developed by Brown (1973) in the context of tort law to compare the efficiency of various liability rules with regard to the minimization of accident costs. According to this model, potential injurers and victims (e.g., drivers and pedestrians) take actions aimed at reducing the probability and severity of an accident. For example, drivers adhere to speed limits and invest in periodic maintenance of their cars, whereas pedestrians wear bright clothing and only cross at crosswalks. Because these actions are costly, however, it is not generally efficient (or possible) to invest in them to the point where the risk of accidents is

---

[22] Readers uninterested in this correspondence can skip this section without affecting the continuity of the argument.

eliminated. (In the case of driver-pedestrian accidents, this would probably require an outright ban on driving or walking.) Rather, efficiency dictates that both parties should invest in precaution up to the point where the marginal cost of an additional unit of care equals the marginal reduction in expected accident losses.[23]

Using this model, Brown (1973) showed that a rule of strict liability – that is, a rule requiring injurers to fully compensate victims for their losses in the event of an accident – will not generally lead to an efficient outcome. Whereas such a rule will induce injurers to invest in efficient precaution because it forces them to internalize the full social costs of their actions, it will result in too little precaution by victims because, by fully insuring them against their losses, it allows them to act as if there were no risk of an accident. In other words, strict liability creates a moral hazard problem for victims. Conversely, if injurers were never held liable for the victims' losses (a rule of no liability), victims would have an incentive to take efficient precaution because they would fully bear their own costs, but injurers would take too little (or no) precaution because they are insulated from the risk. Thus, no liability creates a moral hazard problem for injurers.[24]

The analogy to takings is easily seen by viewing the landowner as a potential "victim" of a taking and interpreting his initial investment as his "precaution" in the sense that a lower investment reduces the loss in value (the "damages") that would be caused by a taking. The "cost" of this precaution is the foregone value of the investment in land if a taking does not occur. Correspondingly, the government can be viewed as the "injurer," and its "precaution" is the amount of land it takes, where the more it takes (i.e., the lower is its precaution), the higher will be the expected loss for individual landowners. As we have seen, when compensation is full (corresponding to strict liability), the landowner will take too little precaution (i.e., overinvest in his land), but the government will take the efficient amount of land. Conversely, when compensation is zero (corresponding to no liability) the landowner will invest efficiently, but the government will underinvest (take too much land). Mathematically, the analogy between torts and takings is exact, as shown in Cooter (1985) (and replicated in the Appendix to this chapter).

---

[23] This standard is epitomized in the law of torts by the Hand rule for negligence, to be discussed in Section 5.4 in the next chapter.

[24] Obviously, this simple model ignores the possibility that some losses cannot be compensated, as well as the transaction costs involved in collecting compensation. Even when these factors are accounted for, however, strict liability still leads to less than efficient precaution by victims, and symmetrically, no liability leads to less than efficient precaution by injurers.

Similar reasoning can be applied to contract law, where Cooter (1985) interprets the "accident" to be the breach of a contractual (legally enforceable) promise. Thus, the "injurer" is the party breaching the contract (called the promisor), and the "victim" is the party to whom performance is owed (called the promisee). The action of the promisor is whether (or when) to breach the contract, and the action of the promisee is how much to invest in reliance on performance. The analogy to the takings situation is again exact: The promisor's breach decision corresponds to the government's taking decision, and the promisee's reliance choice corresponds to the landowner's initial investment decision.

In actual contract law, the usual remedy for breach of contract is expectation damages, which is defined to be an amount of money that leaves the promisee as well off after the breach as if the contract had been performed (Shavell, 1980, 1984). In other words, like strict liability, it is designed to fully compensate the promisee (the victim of breach). Cooter (1985) shows that, while this measure of damages results in the efficient breach decision by the promisor (because she fully internalizes the cost of breach), it causes the promisee to overrely on performance of the contract (due to moral hazard). In contrast, zero damages results in excessive breach by the promisor but efficient reliance by the promisee.[25]

Given the mathematical equivalence of the economic models of torts, contracts, and takings, any of the efficient compensation rules proposed earlier in this chapter for the case of takings would also work in the areas of torts and contracts. In other words, it is possible to design rules that will simultaneously induce efficient care by both injurers and victims in accident settings, and efficient breach and reliance in contract settings. Actual legal rules in these areas generally differ in their apparent form as compared to the proposed takings rules, but economic theory shows that the underlying principles are often the same. In this sense, the law in these different areas has converged on similar solutions (though often in outwardly different forms) to a common set of economic problems.[26]

---

[25] This is not strictly true. Because the promisee anticipates that the promisor will breach too often, she actually underinvests in reliance relative to the first-best outcome. However, her reliance is efficient conditional on the probability of breach. The same effects arise in the tort context. See the Appendix for a formal analysis.

[26] In addition to Cooter (1985), see Posner (2003), Shavell (2004), and Miceli (2009a) for textbook treatments of law and economics that emphasize these unifying principles. Interestingly, there is a corresponding concept in evolutionary biology, referred to as "convergent evolution," which describes the independent emergence of certain adaptive forms or traits (Gould, 1985, pp. 411–412).

Where did this underlying unity in the law come from? This is a central question in the positive economic theory of law, which asserts that the common law displays an inherent economic logic. Originally, Richard Posner attributed this underlying logic to the decision making of judges, who he claimed actively promote efficiency because they "cannot do much … to alter the slices of the pie that various groups in society receive, [so] they might as well concentrate on increasing its size" (Posner, 2003, p. 252). More recent theories, however, have attempted to show that efficiency can emerge without the conscious help of judges based on the argument that the common law, like the competitive market, is driven by invisible-hand type forces that propel it in the direction of efficiency. A large literature has arisen to evaluate the merits of this argument.[27]

4.7. Insurance and Incentives

The previous chapter discussed the role of compensation as providing a form of public insurance against takings risk when landowners are risk averse. The conclusion there was that full compensation is efficient given the general lack of private insurance for this particular risk. That result, however, was derived without regard for the effect that compensation would have on the owner's land use incentives. As we have emphasized in this chapter, however, full compensation will generally cause the landowner to overinvest in his or her property due to the moral hazard problem. Combining the insurance benefits of compensation with the risk of moral hazard suggests that there is a likely trade-off between risk sharing and incentives. In other words, full compensation is efficient for insurance purposes but inefficient in terms of its effect on land use decisions.

This trade-off is a pervasive one in economics. Most obviously, it arises in private insurance markets where, for example, full accident or fire insurance protects drivers and homeowners against the risk of catastrophic loss but at the same time reduces their incentives to invest in precaution against these events. This moral hazard problem is well known to insurance companies. One way that they deal with it is by providing only partial coverage, usually in the form of deductibles, which requires the insured party to cover the first, say, $500 of any claim. Such a provision creates at least some incentive for the insured party to invest in precaution, thereby balancing the competing goals of insurance and incentives. (Specifically, a higher deductible improves incentives but reduces insurance.)

---

[27] See, for example, Rubin (1977), Priest (1977), Gennaioli and Shleifer (2007), and Miceli (2009b).

A similar problem also arises in employment relationships when a worker's output is dependent on his or her effort, but also on random factors. For example, a salesperson can exert maximal effort but still produce few sales if market conditions are unfavorable. Similarly, a tenant farmer can work hard but still produce a poor harvest if weather conditions are adverse. In these settings, consideration of risk alone suggests that risk-averse workers or tenant farmers should be paid a salary that is independent of their output in order to insure them against the risk of income fluctuations arising from purely random factors.[28] Such an arrangement, however, provides little or no incentive for the worker to exert optimal effort. In contrast, if insurance were not a consideration, compensation would be based purely on its incentive effect – for example, a salesperson would be paid solely on commission and a tenant farmer would be compensated by receiving a share of the harvest. In these cases, the workers would have an incentive to work hard, but they would be subject to income uncertainty (indeed, it is this risk that provides them with the incentive to exert effort). When both risk sharing and incentives matter, employers often seek to balance these offsetting factors, for example by paying workers a fixed salary supplemented by a bonus tied to some measure of performance.[29]

In the context of takings, one solution to the trade-off between insurance and incentives is to pay lump-sum compensation in an amount equal to the full value of the land at its efficient level of investment. As argued earlier, any amount of lump-sum compensation is consistent with efficient investment incentives (because compensation does not vary with the landowner's actual investment choice), whereas paying "full" compensation insures the landowner. This solution therefore achieves the first-best outcome – namely, it attains both efficient incentives and risk sharing. As noted earlier, however, the problem with this proposal is that it requires the court to be able to determine the efficient level of investment, which may be difficult.

An alternative solution is to pay partial compensation. Like the use of deductibles in insurance, this approach balances the competing objectives of insurance and incentives, though the outcome is necessarily second-best (Kaplow, 1986, p. 603). It is interesting to note that this argument for partial compensation provides another possible rationale for use of the market-value measure of just compensation, given the assertion in Chapter 3 that market value generally undercompensates owners relative to their true valuations. It is unlikely, however, that market value will coincide

---

[28] This assumes that employers and landowners are risk neutral, and hence suffer no cost from bearing all of the risk of random output fluctuations.

[29] See, generally, Holmstrom (1979) and Shavell (1979).

with the optimal second-best measure, given that subjective value (which determines the extent of undercompensation) and risk aversion (which determines the optimal amount of undercompensation) have no necessary relationship and will therefore vary unsystematically across owners.

4.8. Michelman's Standard Revisited

Earlier we discussed Michelman's (1967) wide-ranging and influential article on the takings issue. This article is of interest to economists because, among other things, it articulates a utilitarian standard for determining when compensation for takings should be paid.[30] Michelman's standard consists of three factors: (1) efficiency gains, (2) demoralization costs, and (3) settlement costs. Efficiency gains are defined to be "the excess of benefits produced by a [government] measure over the losses inflicted by it" (Michelman, 1967, p. 1214). Symbolically, this factor can be represented by $B–C$, where B is the gross benefit of the proposed project and C is the opportunity cost of the resources that must be acquired (including the taken land). Positive efficiency gains, or $B–C>0$, are therefore a necessary condition for the project under consideration to go forward, and would also be a sufficient condition under a straightforward cost-benefit analysis. However, they are not sufficient under Michelman's standard because they do not account for either the demoralization or the settlement costs.

Demoralization costs (denoted by D) were first introduced in Chapter 3 (Section 3.8). To reiterate, they represent all of those costs suffered by actual losers and their sympathizers when compensation is not paid. Offsetting these are settlement costs (denoted by S), which are defined to be the costs of actually paying compensation. Specifically, these consist of "the dollar value of the time, effort, and resources which would be required in order to reach compensation settlements adequate to avoid demoralization costs" (Michelman, 1967, p. 1214).

By combining these factors, Michelman's standard offers a two-step approach for determining which projects should go forward and when compensation should be paid to losers. The first step involves comparing the demoralization and settlement costs for a proposed project to answer the compensation question, assuming that the project will go forward. Specifically, it says that if demoralization costs exceed settlement costs $(D>S)$, then compensation should be paid, but if settlement costs exceed demoralization costs $(S>D)$, then compensation should not be paid. The

---

[30] See especially pp. 1214–1218 of this lengthy article.

second step then asks whether the project should go forward, given the outcome of the first step. Specifically, if the efficiency gains of the project exceed the minimum of the demoralization and settlement costs, the project should proceed; otherwise, it should not. Symbolically, the project should be undertaken if and only if $B-C > \min(D,S)$. Note that this criterion blocks some projects with positive efficiency gains if the gains are not sufficient to cover the costs associated with the compensation decision.[31]

We will return again to Michelman's standard in the next chapter in the context of deciding when compensation should be paid for government regulations (see Section 5.2). We conclude this chapter on compensation and land use incentives by relating his standard to the economic models on this issue as reviewed herein.[32] In this regard, it will be useful to divide Michelman's settlement costs into two components. The first are the transaction costs (including legal fees) of actually condemning property and determining the proper amount of compensation to be paid. Although not explicitly included in the previously discussed models, these costs can be substantial, especially considering that landowners typically resist the action. Indeed, as we noted in Chapter 2 (Section 2.5), these costs are often large enough to discourage governments from resorting to eminent domain when market acquisition offers a viable alternative (for example, when the holdout problem is not too severe). The second component of settlement costs is actually the cost associated with moral hazard. Moral hazard falls under settlement costs rather than demoralization costs (as one might have expected) because moral hazard arises in reaction to the promised payment of compensation, not the denial of it.

Turning to demoralization costs, we noted in Chapter 3 (Section 3.8) that they arise from several possible sources, including the fear of government excess (i.e., the case of a non-benevolent government), the absence of market insurance for takings, and a desire for a fair distribution of costs and benefits. The problem of designing a compensation rule that balances any or all of these factors against the problem of landowner moral hazard, as depicted in much of the economic literature on takings since BRS, was

---

[31] Fischel and Shapiro (1988) therefore note that Michelman's criterion falls between the Pareto and Kaldor-Hicks criteria in terms of what projects will be permitted (see the Appendix to Chapter 1). Because Pareto requires that no one can be made worse off by the project, compensation must be paid. Thus, Pareto would only permit those projects for which $B-C > S$, whereas Michelman would permit projects for which $S > B-C > D$. In this sense, Michelman's standard is more permissive than Pareto. In contrast, Kaldor-Hicks would permit any project for which $B-C > 0$, which makes Kaldor-Hicks more permissive that Michelman, given that $\min(D,S) > 0$.

[32] This discussion is based on Fischel and Shapiro (1988).

therefore anticipated in a general way by Michelman's standard through the comparison between demoralization and settlement costs.

4.9. A Proviso on Informational Requirements

I conclude this chapter by noting that several of the compensation rules discussed in this chapter have depended on the efficiency of the proposed government project, or of the landowner's investment choice, which obviously raises the question of how the court acquires the information needed to make the requisite calculations. (In a market setting, efficiency is achieved through decentralized transactions, so no central authority needs to undertake such a calculation.) Most of the models reviewed here simply assume that the court has the necessary information without worrying about how it acquired it. This is an important shortcoming of the existing literature on efficient compensation rules, for it offers little guidance on how courts would apply the rules in practice.[33]

Chapter 3 addressed one dimension of this problem in describing methods for accurately estimating the true valuation of landowners (Section 3.2), but in addition to being impractical, these methods do not address the problem of determining whether a landowner, faced with a threat of a taking or regulation, invested efficiently, or whether the government acted efficiently to take or regulate a piece of land. Sections 5.2 and 5.4 in the next chapter discuss some methods by which courts can (and do) attempt to deal with these problems, both in the takings context and in other areas of law. None of these responses, however, is completely satisfactory. In the end, all we can say is that some residual inefficiencies are the unavoidable cost of relying on non-market allocation mechanisms that require information that the government or the courts cannot easily obtain.

[33] Perry Shapiro emphasized this point to me in a personal communication.

FIVE

Regulatory Takings

The general rule at least is that while property may be regulated to a certain extent, if regulation goes too far it will be recognized as a taking.
Oliver Wendell Holmes, Jr. (Majority opinion,
Pennsylvania Coal v. Mahon, 1922)

Every restriction upon the use of property imposed in the exercise of police power deprives the owner of some right theretofore enjoyed.... But restriction imposed to protect the public health, safety or morals from dangers threatened is not a taking.
Louis Brandeis (Dissenting opinion, *Pennsylvania Coal v. Mahon*, 1922)

To this point in the book, our discussion of eminent domain has focused primarily on government acquisitions, or condemnations, of property. Much more common, however, are government regulations that restrict the use of property without actually seizing title to it. Examples include zoning, environmental and safety regulations, historic landmark designation, rules requiring equal accommodation for the disabled, and so on.[1] I have also emphasized, however, that from an economic perspective, regulations that reduce the value of private property are not fundamentally different from outright takings; the difference is one of degree rather than of kind. This is true because neither economists nor lawyers view property as a single entity, but rather as a bundle of rights or entitlements, each of which has some value.[2] Thus, any deprivation or restriction of a particular right reduces the value of the property proportionately. A physical taking, which deprives the owner of all rights, is simply one end of a continuum.

[1] See Miceli and Segerson (1996) and Meltz et al. (1999) for a detailed examination of several of these regulations within the context of takings law. Section 5.11 reviews some of these applications in light of the theory to be developed in this chapter.
[2] Economists have developed empirical techniques, referred to as hedonic regressions, for estimating the implicit value of these individual components. See, for example, Rosen (1974).

Given this analytical equivalence between seizures and regulations, a separate treatment of the two types of actions does not appear to be warranted by economic theory. Everything we have said to this point about physical seizures should in principle apply to regulations, with appropriate adjustment to reflect the extent of the taking. As noted, most of the recent economic literature on takings, as surveyed in the previous chapter, has not in fact distinguished between the two types of cases. Yet the fact remains that courts have treated them quite differently: Whereas compensation is virtually always required for seizures, it is rarely awarded for regulations. Indeed, courts have historically granted the government broad police powers to enact regulations in the public interest without the need to compensate property owners for lost value. Usually, this is justified by the stifling effect that a universal requirement of compensation would have on the everyday operation of the government. (Though it is not clear why a rule requiring the government to pay for the resources it uses is regarded as an undue restriction.) Still, in some few cases, courts have ruled that if a regulation goes "too far" in restricting private property, it will be ruled a "regulatory taking," and compensation will be due. The question, therefore, is where the dividing line is (or should be) between compensable and non-compensable regulations.

There exists a considerable body of case law and legal scholarship aimed at answering this "compensation question."[3] A review of the various tests that have emerged from this investigation illustrates the range of perspectives that have been brought to bear on this debate, and also reflects the apparent lack of consensus on an adequate answer. The goal of this chapter is therefore to provide a unifying theory based on economic principles developed in the preceding chapters (especially Chapter 4). As a prelude, I provide brief reviews of the case law and legal literature in this area.

5.1. Legal Tests for Compensation

Nearly all courts have agreed that any government action that involves some sort of physical invasion of a landowner's property, even when it does not literally seize title, constitutes a compensable taking. For example, in *Pumpelly v. Green Bay Co.*,[4] the Supreme Court ruled that the state's building of a dam that caused permanent flooding of the claimant's property was a taking

---

[3] More generally, the question of whether or not to compensate the victim of a regulation confronts the larger issue of how to distribute the economic gains and losses caused by any unanticipated change in an existing legal regime. For a review and economic theory of these so-called legal transitions, see Kaplow (1986, 1992).

[4] 80 U.S. (13 Wall.) 166 (1871).

for which compensation was due. Likewise, in *Loretto v. Teleprompter*,[5] the Court held that a state law allowing cable television providers to install wires and other equipment on a private building was a taking. The invasion need not even involve a "physical" occupation of land. In *United States v. Causby*,[6] for example, the Supreme Court found that airplane flights less than 100 feet above a piece of property, the noise from which caused disturbance to the landowner (and killed some of his chickens), constituted a physical invasion of the airspace above the property and hence required compensation for the resulting loss.[7]

Although the *physical invasion test* is well established in takings law, it is of limited usefulness for most regulatory takings because it offers no guidance for the vast majority of government actions, like zoning and environmental regulations, that involve no invasion. The remaining legal tests concern these sorts of cases.

An important early test was established in the case of *Mugler v. Kansas*,[8] which concerned a law passed by the state of Kansas, pursuant to a prohibition amendment to the Kansas constitution, forbidding the operation of breweries. The owner of a brewery sued for compensation on the grounds that the law constituted a taking of his property, but the U.S. Supreme Court denied the claim on the grounds that the state had the right to regulate, without compensation, those activities that are deemed "to be injurious to the health, morals, or safety of the community"[9]: so-called noxious uses. This ruling, which we will henceforth refer to as the *noxious use doctrine*, recognized that the government has broad regulatory powers to prevent land uses seen as potentially harmful to the public. According to this test, the relevant factor in determining the compensability of a regulation is its intended purpose – that is, is it designed to protect the public from harm (however that is defined)? If so, compensation is not due. The impact of the regulation on the landowner's property value apparently has no bearing on the compensation question under this doctrine.

---

[5]   458 U.S. 419 (1982).

[6]   328 U.S. 256 (1946).

[7]   The ruling thus recognized the claimant's ownership of "as much space above the ground as he can occupy and use in connection with the land," but it also held that "[t]he airspace, apart from the immediate reaches above the land, is the public domain" (*United States v. Causby*, 328 U.S. 256, 264, 266, 1946). In so ruling, the Court effectively overturned the traditional *ad coelum* rule that had granted the owner of a piece of land rights to the column of space extending indefinitely above the land (literally "to the sky"). See Baxter and Altree (1972).

[8]   123 U.S. 623 (1887).

[9]   *Id.*, p. 668.

That view changed in 1922 when the Supreme Court decided the famous case of *Pennsylvania Coal v. Mahon.*[10] The case concerned a law passed by the State of Pennsylvania, called the Kohler Act, whose purpose was to protect the safety of surface owners against the risk of cave-ins (or subsidence) by requiring that coal companies leave enough coal in the ground to support the surface. The Pennsylvania Coal Company brought suit seeking compensation on the grounds that the regulation was a taking of its legal right to mine all of the coal under the surface. (Under a common legal arrangement, the mining company had sold the surface rights but had retained the mineral rights to the subsurface coal.) Although the case seemed to be an easy one under the noxious use doctrine given that the Kohler Act clearly met the standard of protecting the safety of the surface owners, the Court ruled that compensation was due.

Writing for the majority, Justice Oliver Wendell Holmes, Jr. began by acknowledging the government's right to impose some regulations without compensation because, as he said, "Government could hardly go on if to some extent values incident to property could not be diminished without paying for every such change in the law." Still, he argued, there must be a limit to that power on the grounds that, if the government were unrestrained, it would overreach until "at last, private property disappear[ed]." That limit, he said, is embodied in the impact of the regulation on the landowner: "One fact for consideration in determining such limits is the extent of the diminution [in the landowner's value]. When it reaches a certain magnitude, in most if not all cases there must be an exercise of eminent domain and compensation to sustain the act."[11]

This argument forms the basis for the *diminution of value test* for compensation, which says that compensation is due if the loss to the landowner as a result of a regulation is sufficiently large. Of course, this begs the question of what amount of loss is large enough to meet the compensation threshold. Holmes only said that "if regulation goes too far it will be recognized as a taking."[12] He was therefore left it to future courts to decide on a case-by-case basis what constitutes "too far."

A related question concerns how, in computing the diminution of value, the property as a whole is to be defined. Surely the intention is to measure the proportional loss in value, and to award compensation if that proportion is sufficiently close to 100 percent. But a question arises as to how to measure the denominator in this proportion: Is it the entire holding of the

[10]   260 U.S. 393 (1922).
[11]   *Id.*, p. 413.
[12]   *Id.*, p. 415.

landowner or some fraction thereof? Obviously, this "parceling problem" (as it is called) is crucial in determining the magnitude of the diminution (Michelman, 1967, pp. 1192–1193; Rubenfeld, 1993, pp. 1090–1091), but again, the case is silent about how to proceed. These practical questions aside, the larger point is that the diminution of value test introduced the impact of the regulation on the landowner as a relevant consideration, along with its intent, in answering the compensation question.

It is interesting to note that many observers have viewed the decision in *Pennsylvania Coal* as an apparent watershed in takings law in recognition of its departure from the prevailing law (Friedman, 1986). For example, Justice Louis Brandeis, in his dissenting opinion to Holmes's ruling in *Pennsylvania Coal*, pointed out that:

Every restriction upon the use of property imposed in the exercise of the police power deprives the owner of some right theretofore enjoyed, and is, in that sense, an abridgement by the States of rights in property without making compensation. But restriction imposed to protect public health, safety or morals from dangers is not a taking. The restriction here in question [the Kohler Act] is merely the prohibition of a noxious use.[13]

Rubenfeld (1993, p. 1088) likewise observed that, "[t]o put it bluntly, a diminution of value test cannot be squared with the harm principle in the *Mugler* line of cases." We will return to this seeming "irreconcilability" between the decisions in *Pennsylvania Coal* and *Mugler* later in this chapter.

The need to balance the factors raised in these earlier cases – namely, the intent of the regulation and its impact on the landowner's property value – was made explicit in the case of *Penn Central Transportation Co. v. City of New York*.[14] This case arose out of the city's decision to designate the Grand Central Terminal as a historic landmark, thereby limiting the sort of alterations that the owners could make. Thus, when the Landmark Preservation Commission turned down a proposal by Penn Central to build a multistory office building above the terminal, the owners sued, claiming a taking of their right to develop. In deciding against compensation, the Supreme Court advanced a three-part test for determining whether or not a compensable taking has occurred. The relevant factors were: (1) the character of the government action, (2) whether or not the regulation interfered with "investment-backed expectations," and (3) the extent of the diminution of value. The first and third of these factors clearly identified the importance of both the noxious use doctrine and the diminution of value test, though

[13] *Id.*, p. 417.
[14] 438 U.S. 104 (1978).

once again there was no explicit guidance on how to balance one against the other, leaving it instead to "ad hoc factual inquiries."[15]

The second factor, emphasizing the importance of investment-backed expectations, captures the idea that any loss suffered by the landowner must have been based on reasonable expectations, backed up by actual investments (Fischel, 1995a, p. 50). In other words, an owner could not claim to have been denied uses that he never would have contemplated, or that would not have been allowed by law, in the absence of the regulation. Thus, as a necessary condition for compensation, a claimant would have to show evidence that he had in fact planned to undertake the prohibited development. (This requirement reflects the logic of the capitalization argument against compensation discussed in Section 3.9 of Chapter 3.)

In his dissenting opinion to the *Penn Central* ruling, Judge William Rehnquist added a further consideration when he stated that "a taking does not take place if the prohibition applies across a broad cross section of land and thereby 'secure[s] an average reciprocity of advantage.'"[16] The phrase "average reciprocity of advantage," first used by Holmes in his *Pennsylvania Coal* opinion, suggests that monetary compensation need not be paid if a regulation restricts all landowners equally, thereby spreading both the benefits and the costs of the regulation. The Supreme Court employed similar logic in the case of *Agins v. Tiburon* when it held that a landowner subject to a zoning restriction "will share with other owners the benefits and burdens of the city's exercise of its police power. In assessing the fairness of zoning ordinances, these benefits must be considered along with any diminution in market value that the appellants might suffer."[17] This logic resembles Michelman's fairness standard as discussed in Section 3.8 of Chapter 3, and will be further elaborated on in Section 5.9 in this chapter.

The final legal test I will discuss here by way of introduction emerged from the case of *Lucas v. South Carolina Coastal Council*.[18] The case involved a land developer, David Lucas, who purchased two beachfront lots in South Carolina with the intention of developing them for residential use. Such a use seemed perfectly reasonable at the time of purchase, given that several similarly situated neighboring lots had already been developed. However, after Lucas's purchase, but before he commenced with the development, the South Carolina legislature passed a law prohibiting further beachfront development in the area in an effort to control coastal erosion. Because the

---

[15] *Id.*, p. 124.
[16] *Id.*, p. 147.
[17] 157 Cal.Rptr. 373, 1979; affirmed 447 U.S. 255, 262 (1980).
[18] 505 U.S. 1003 (1992).

regulation rendered the lots essentially valueless, Lucas sued, claiming a taking. A trial court found in his favor and awarded full compensation. However, the South Carolina Supreme Court reversed the ruling, despite the nearly complete diminution of value, relying instead on the regulation's stated purpose of preventing harm to the public – the old noxious use doctrine.

The U.S. Supreme Court, in turn, reversed the South Carolina Supreme Court and said that compensation was due based on the fact that the regulation denied "all beneficial or productive use of land."[19] Clearly, the regulation in question met the *Pennsylvania Coal* standard of going "too far" by depriving the landowner of *all* value. Still, the Court left open the possibility that the state could avoid paying compensation, despite the total loss, if it could show that the harm prevented by the regulation constituted a nuisance under the state's common law. This standard, known as the *nuisance exception*, provides an objective basis, founded in the common law (as opposed to a simple legislative declaration of harm), for determining what constitutes a noxious use. The appeal to the common law as a source for the definition of harm is attractive because of its apolitical nature; that is, the common-law definition of a nuisance has arisen as a by-product of the resolution of countless legal disputes over time rather than through a particular legislative action. For this reason, we will argue later in this chapter that it makes good economic sense as a basis for determining compensability.

One question not clarified by the *Lucas* decision, however, was what extent of diminution of value was necessary to trigger automatic compensation. The regulation at issue in *Lucas* clearly met any standard the court could have applied because it caused a virtual total loss (the nuisance exception aside). The question therefore remained whether something short of full diminution would also qualify. In *Palazzolo v. Rhode Island*,[20] the Supreme Court revisited this issue in the context of the petition of a landowner who, like Lucas, sought compensation when he was denied permission to develop waterfront property under a wetlands preservation law passed by the state of Rhode Island. The landowner claimed that the regulation met the requirement for compensation under *Lucas* because it denied him "all economically beneficial use" of the land, but the Court found that the regulation in fact left the owner with developable land worth $200,000, compared to his claimed loss of $3.15 million (a 94 percent diminution). It

---

[19] *Id.*, p. 1015.
[20] 533 U.S. 606 (2001).

thus remanded the case for review under the *Penn Central* balancing test. Apparently, therefore, a diminution of at least 95 percent is required to constitute a "total" deprivation under *Lucas*.[21] Later in this chapter I propose a less ad hoc standard for determining what amount of diminution is sufficient.

To summarize this overview, the case law reveals that compensation is determined by a balancing of two fundamental factors: the legitimate interests of the government in preventing harm to the public (however that is defined), and the need to protect private property rights. In a fundamental sense, this trade-off reflects the essence of an economic approach to the regulatory takings issue. The theory to be derived below proposes a rule for balancing these factors in an efficient and objective way.

5.2. Other Tests for Compensation

Before turning to the economic analysis, however, I want to describe several other tests for compensation that have been proposed in the scholarly literature on takings. As will be seen, these tests vary in their economic content and logical consistency.

Two influential tests were proposed by Joseph Sax in a pair of law review articles. In the first (Sax, 1964), he argues that the government owes compensation when it acquires property rights for use in its enterprise capacity, such as when it provides a public good; but it does not owe compensation when it acts as a disinterested arbitrator in a private dispute, such as when it prevents one private party from imposing external costs on other private parties.[22] This test seems to account for the disparate treatment of physical takings and regulations, given that provision of public goods generally requires the physical acquisition of land whereas the arbitration of disputes only involves regulation, but it does not really offer an explanation for the distinction. Instead, it merely restates it.

In a second article, Sax (1971) argues that the government does not owe compensation for any actions that it undertakes to regulate external costs. Daniel Bromley adopts a similar perspective in arguing that paying compensation for such regulations would represent "... indemnification for an inability to continue to impose unwanted costs on others" (Bromley, 1993, p. 677). According to this view, which echoes the noxious use doctrine, the

---

[21] The claimant sought to separate the upland (unregulated) parcel from the wetland portion in an effort to argue that the loss in value of the latter was total, reflecting the parceling problem in computing the diminution of value. However, the Court did not accept this argument.

[22] Rose (1983) makes a similar argument.

law does not (and should not) protect the right of landowners to engage in activities that impose harm on others. However, the difficulty with this test, as noted by Fischel (1985, p. 153), is that it offers "no workable distinction ... between land uses that create spillovers and those that do not. *Every* economic activity can be argued to affect someone else" [emphasis in original].

A similar delineation of property rights underlies the so-called *harm-benefit rule*, which says that no compensation is due for regulations that prevent a landowner from imposing a harm on others (e.g., a regulation against pollution), but compensation is due for regulations that compel the landowner to bestow a benefit on the public (e.g., a regulation preventing development in order to preserve open space). Although this rule has some intuitive appeal, it is not consistent with economic theory in the sense that a prevented harm can always be defined as a benefit, and a forgone benefit can be defined as a harm (Fischel, 1985, p. 158).

Rubenfeld (1993) offers a test that echoes Sax's (1964) distinction between government use of property (which is a taking) and a mere regulation of it (which is not). Based on a literal interpretation of the public use requirement of the takings clause, Rubenfeld says that a taking occurs when the government takes property for some productive use – a so-called using – as opposed to merely depriving the owner of its use. Thus, for example, the regulation in *Mugler* was not a compensable taking under Rubenfeld's test because, although it denied the brewery owner the right to continue operation, it did not enlist the property for an explicit state use. In contrast, the Kohler Act in *Pennsylvania Coal* did involve a compensable taking because it took the coal company's property specifically for state use, namely to support the surface estate. As a general test, Rubenfeld (1993, p. 1116) proposes that a regulation would not be classified as a using, and hence would not be compensable, "[i]f the state's interest in taking or regulating something would be equally well served by *destroying the thing altogether ...*" [emphasis in original].

Rose-Ackerman and Rossi (2000) propose a similar standard that calls for compensation when the government acts as a buyer that is in competition for resources with other market participants, but no compensation when the government acts as a policy maker (for example when it regulates land). The logic of this distinction is to preserve the investment incentives of landowners in the face of alternative possible uses of their land, whether those uses are public or private. The promise of compensation for takings ensures that landowners are (more or less) indifferent between a forced acquisition and a market exchange.[23]

---

[23] Rose-Ackerman and Rossi (2000, p. 1480) acknowledge the inadequacy of market value compensation with regard to idiosyncratic property values.

In contrast, no compensation would be due when the government acts in its policy-making capacity because the Takings Clause "is not designed to solve the deep problems that arise from a dysfunctional and predatory state" (Rose-Ackerman and Rossi, 2000, p. 1483). Rather, it should merely ensure that investors take into account the risk of government inefficiency by denying compensation for widely imposed policies. Landowners will therefore be dissuaded from compounding the inefficiency by overinvesting in their land, and will be encouraged to seek redress through the political process. Only when a particular policy precludes losers from a political remedy should courts step in to offer constitutional protection (Fischel, 1995a, pp. 114–115).

What is lacking in all of the preceding tests is a benchmark reflecting neutral conduct, which would serve as the basis for deciding when compensation would and would not be paid. Fischel (1985, pp. 158–160) offers such a benchmark in the form of his *normal behavior standard*, which is based on arguments first made by Ellickson (1973, 1977). According to this standard, no compensation is due for regulations that prevent landowners from engaging in "subnormal" behavior, but compensation is due for regulations that compel them to undertake "above-normal" behavior, where "normal" behavior is defined by community standards based on what landowners can reasonably expect to be able to do with their land. This "reasonableness standard" therefore replaces the arbitrary distinction between harms and benefits in the harm-benefit rule. For example, a landowner in a residential neighborhood could not reasonably expect to be allowed to open a gas station because of the external costs it would impose, and so a zoning law prohibiting him from doing so would not be a compensable taking. The law merely compels him to comply with normal behavior. By the same logic, a regulation forcing him to leave his land undeveloped so as to provide open space for other residents of the neighborhood to enjoy *would* be a compensable taking because it requires him to adopt above-normal behavior.

What makes this an economic standard (rather than another arbitrary distinction) is that it economizes on the transaction costs of achieving an efficient land use pattern. Specifically, by setting the "zero compensation point" at normal behavior, the costs of compliance will be minimized because most landowners will engage in normal behavior automatically (i.e., without the need for government action).

Wittman (1984) proposes a similar compensation rule that is based on the behavior of the government rather than landowners. Specifically, he argues that the transaction costs of paying compensation will be minimized if compensation is limited to cases in which the government acts inefficiently, based on the presumption that "we would expect the government to act efficiently more often than not" (Wittman, 1984, p. 74). An important drawback of both the Fischel and Wittman standards, however, is that they fail to account for the role of the compensation rule in *creating* the proper incentives for landowners and/or the government to act efficiently.

The final test for compensation that I will mention here is Michelman's standard, as previously discussed in both Chapters 3 and 4. Recall that this standard is based on a comparison of the settlement (or transaction) costs associated with paying compensation, and the demoralization costs of not paying compensation. Specifically, if the settlement costs are lower, compensation should be paid, whereas if demoralization costs are lower, compensation should not be paid. As suggested in the previous chapter, Michelman's standard anticipated the trade-off between arbitrary government behavior (as captured by demoralization costs) and landowner moral hazard (as captured by settlement costs) that forms the basis for the economic theory of eminent domain. The next section exploits this trade-off in developing an economic theory of regulatory takings.

5.3. An Economic Theory of Regulatory Takings: The Efficient Threshold Rule

The wide range of perspectives on how to answer the compensation question, as reflected by the preceding survey of the case law and academic scholarship, suggests a lack of consensus on the issue, if not outright confusion. For example, Rubenfeld (1993, p. 1080) refers to the case law in this area as "incoherent." This section therefore attempts to develop an economic theory aimed at synthesizing the conflicting views within a consistent framework. The basis for the analysis will be the trade-off, identified in Chapter 4, between the land use incentives of owners whose property is subject to a regulatory risk (moral hazard) and non-benevolent government regulators (fiscal illusion). In Chapter 4, we examined several compensation rules designed to resolve this trade-off in the context of physical takings. In view of the asserted mathematical equivalence between physical takings and regulations, all of these rules would also work equally well in the context of regulations. However, the goal here is more ambitious than simply proposing an efficient rule; rather, it is to develop an efficient rule that also explains actual legal practice. The particular challenge, as noted earlier, is to explain why courts adopt so-called corner solutions (Fischel, 1995a, pp. 1–2); that is, to explain why they routinely award full compensation for physical takings but rarely award any compensation for mere regulations.

The rule that I will propose as a response to this challenge involves a "threshold test" for compensation along the lines of the diminution of value test. The rule works as follows: If the government imposes a regulation inefficiently (that is, if it overregulates), it will be required to pay the landowner full compensation for the reduced value of the land (the diminution of value), but if the government imposes a regulation efficiently, it will not be required to pay any compensation.[24] Put somewhat more formally,

$$\text{Compensation} = \begin{cases} \text{Full, if the government acted inefficiently} \\ \text{Zero, if the government acted efficiently} \end{cases} \quad (5.1)$$

The compensation question thus turns on the efficiency of the government's regulatory decision.

Under this rule, a government that cares only about budgetary considerations (that is, one with fiscal illusion), or one that focuses only on the interests of the majority of landowners, will be restrained from overregulating by the threat of having to pay compensation. In this sense, compensation can usefully be interpreted at "penalizing" an overzealous government for regulating excessively. At the same time, the rule induces landowners to act efficiently because they will rationally anticipate that the government will only impose efficient regulations, in which case compensation will be zero. Thus, the moral hazard problem is also eliminated. In equilibrium, therefore, both parties will act efficiently, and no compensation will actually be paid. (As usual, the formal proof of this claim is provided in the Appendix to this chapter.) The remainder of this section illustrates this conclusion by means of an example, and subsequent sections draw implications for our understanding of actual regulatory takings law.

To illustrate the efficiency of the above rule, I will return to the example from Chapter 4 with a slight modification. The data for the landowner's investment options are reproduced in the first three columns of Table 5.1. As before, the landowner has a choice between two projects, which differ in their gross and net returns. In the absence of any regulatory threat, the landowner prefers Project 2 because it offers the higher net return (as shown by the third column of the table). Suppose, however, that development of the land creates the risk of an external cost that may justify a regulation

---

[24] The rule was first developed by Miceli and Segerson (1994). Also see Miceli and Segerson (1996) for a fuller treatment along with applications to a wide range of regulatory settings.

Table 5.1. *Data for the regulation example*

	Initial investment	Gross private return	Net private return	Net social return
Project 1	$25,000	$200,000	$175,000	$37,500
Project 2	$100,000	$300,000	$200,000	$12,500

prohibiting development. For example, engaging in coal mining may create the risk of surface cave-ins as in *Pennsylvania Coal*, or developing beach-front property may create the threat of beach erosion as in *Lucas*. The specific magnitude of the risk, however, cannot be known until after the landowner has made some irreversible investments. Thus, the landowner must commit to his land use decision before the regulator acts. While this sequence of events sounds restrictive, it is not since the threat of land use regulations can emerge at any point in time. Thus, landowners cannot simply wait until the regulatory threat is gone (for it never is).

To be concrete, suppose in the current example that when the landowner makes his project choice, he knows that the external cost associated with development will either be "high," imposing a social cost of $325,000, or "low," imposing a social cost of $75,000. The landowner also knows that both outcomes are equally likely; that is, each will occur with probability 0.5. Finally, assume that the only way to avoid the externality is to prohibit development altogether, which reduces the private value of the land to zero. (The conclusions would not change if the regulated land had some small residual value to the owner.)

Given the threatened externality, we begin by deriving the socially optimal outcome in reverse sequence of time. That is, we first derive the optimal regulatory decision of the government, conditional on which project was chosen, and then consider the optimal project choice by the landowner.

Generally speaking, it is efficient for the government to impose a regulation prohibiting development whenever the realized cost of the externality exceeds the private value of the land. In the current example, if Project 1 is chosen, which promises a gross return of $200,000, the government should prohibit development if the externality turns out to be high (considering that $325,000 > $200,000) but not if it turns out to be low (considering that $75,000 < $200,000). Likewise, if Project 2 is chosen, which yields a gross return of $300,000, the government should prohibit development if the externality is high (because $325,000 > $300,000) but not if it is low (because $75,000 < $300,000). Thus, regardless of the landowner's project choice, the probability of a regulation, given efficient government behavior, is 0.5.[25] (Note that in making the regulatory decision, the landowner's initial investment of $25,000 under Project 1, or $100,000 under Project 2, is irrelevant because at the time the regulatory decision must be made, these are sunk costs.)

Based on these conclusions, we can calculate the net social value of each project as follows:

Project 1: (0.5)($200,000–$75,000) – $25,000 = $37,500   (5.2)

Project 2: (0.5)($300,000–$75,000) – $100,000 = $12,500,   (5.3)

where in both cases, development is prohibited if the high external cost materializes. Project 1, which promises the higher expected return, is therefore the socially optimal land use. These values are shown in column four of Table 5.1. (Note that in the event of a regulation, the land has zero private value, but the external cost is avoided. Thus, the social return in that event is zero, which is its maximized value in that state.)

Consider next the actual choices by the government (assuming it has fiscal illusion) and the landowner under the proposed threshold rule for compensation. Recall that under the rule, compensation is full if the government overregulates but zero if it regulates efficiently. In the context of the example, compensation will therefore be zero if the government prohibits development when the high value of the externality is realized (because it is efficient to regulate in that case), but full if it prohibits development when the low value is realized (because it is not efficient to regulate in that case).[26]

A government with fiscal illusion is assumed to regulate if the benefit in terms of the prevented external cost exceeds the amount of compensation

---

[25] The assumption that the probability of a regulation is the same regardless of which project is chosen is made purely for simplicity.

[26] It is important to note that, in a more general model, the definition of efficient regulation must be based on when it is efficient to regulate under the *efficient* rather than the *actual* land use. For example, it may be the case under certain land uses that it would not be efficient to prohibit development for either value of the externality. This would be true in the current example if the high value of the externality were, say, $275,000 rather than $325,000, because then it would never be efficient to regulate under Project 2. In that case, efficiency of the regulatory decision for purposes of determining when compensation is due would be based on when it is efficient to regulate under Project 1, considering that this is the efficient land use. The reason for this aspect of the rule is that if the amount of compensation were conditioned on which project was *actually* chosen, the landowner would be able to affect the amount of compensation by his land use decision, thereby resurrecting the moral hazard problem. For example, by choosing Project 2, he could avoid the regulation altogether, but this would be an inefficient land use because the net social value of that choice would be $300,000 – (0.5)($75,000) – (0.5)($275,000)–$100,000 = $25,000 < $37,500. See the Appendix to this chapter for formal details.

that it must pay to the landowner. In the example, if the government prohibits development when the low value of the externality is realized, it will have to pay full compensation because the regulation is inefficiently imposed. But because in this case the amount of compensation exceeds the saved external cost under either project (i.e., both $200,000 and $300,000 are greater than the saved cost of $75,000), the government will be deterred from regulating. In contrast, if the high value of the externality is realized, compensation is zero because the regulation is efficient. Thus, in this case the government will impose the regulation under both projects. The proposed compensation rule therefore induces efficient regulatory behavior by the government.

Consider next the landowner's behavior. Given the preceding analysis of the government's behavior, the landowner rationally anticipates that the government will act efficiently – which means that it will regulate only when the high value of the externality is realized – and also that compensation will be zero in the event of a regulation. The landowner therefore calculates his expected private return under the two projects to be

$$\text{Project 1: } (0.5)(\$200,000) - \$25,000 = \$75,000 \qquad (5.4)$$
$$\text{Project 2: } (0.5)(\$300,000) - \$100,000 = \$50,000 \qquad (5.5)$$

He therefore chooses Project 1, which is the efficient choice. (Notice in particular that the difference in value between the two projects is necessarily the same, $25,000, whether we are comparing the social or private returns.) The threshold rule therefore succeeds in inducing efficient behavior by both the government and the landowner.

5.4. Implementation of the Threshold Rule

One might object that the threshold rule just described places a heavy informational burden on courts by requiring them to be able to determine the efficiency of the government's regulatory decision. (Some of the rules discussed in the previous chapter likewise required the court to be able to determine the efficiency of the land use decision.) Still, this burden does not seem out of line compared to rules that courts routinely implement in other areas of the law. The best example is the due care standard for determining negligence in tort law, which is based on the level of care that a reasonable person should have taken to avoid an accident. For example, in the famous case of *United States v. Carroll Towing Co.*,[27] Judge Learned Hand said that

---

[27]   159 F.2d 169, 2nd Cir. (1947)

an injurer should be found negligent if he or she failed to take a precaution whose cost was less than the expected harm that the action would have avoided.[28] This is referred to as the Hand test for negligence, and economic analysis has shown that it coincides with the efficient standard for determining negligence.[29] In effect, the Hand test requires the court to undertake a cost-benefit analysis of the injurer's care choice.

It should be apparent that the threshold test proposed here functions much like the Hand test in the sense that it asks the court to compare the cost of a government regulation in terms of the harm it imposes on the landowner (as measured by the loss in property value) to the social benefit in the form of avoided external harm. Specifically, the court would judge that the regulation is not efficient if the benefit is less than the cost (in which case the government is "negligent" and must pay compensation), but that it is efficient if the reverse is true (in which case the government is "not negligent" and owes no compensation). Based on this logic, it seems that implementation of the efficient threshold rule for regulatory takings should impose no greater computational burden on courts than the application of ordinary negligence rules. Indeed, the re-examination of the case law in the next section will make the argument that the various standards courts already use to answer the compensation question can be interpreted as threshold rules, like negligence, that require the court to undertake an analogous sort of balancing test.[30] In this sense, courts have already demonstrated their ability to implement the proposed rule.

5.5. Implications of the Efficient Threshold Rule for Regulatory Takings Law

In addition to providing a normative standard for efficient compensation, I will argue that the proposed threshold rule is appealing on positive grounds

[28] Judge Hand explicitly presented this standard in algebraic form. Specifically, he said that an injurer is negligent if he or she failed to take a precaution for which $B < PL$, where B is the cost (or burden) of the untaken precaution, P is the probability of the harm, and L is the resulting loss.

[29] See, for example, Landes and Posner (1987, chapter 4), who emphasize that the rule must be interpreted in marginal terms.

[30] Interestingly, Horwitz (1992, pp. 97–100) draws a correspondence between the rise of negligence in American law in the nineteenth century, which limited the liability of injurers, and judicial efforts to limit just compensation for government-sanctioned takings of property by private enterprises like mill builders and transportation companies. In contrast to the current analysis, however, which sees the efficiency of threshold rules as the common thread, Horwitz associated the correlation with legal efforts aimed at promoting economic development during the onset of the Industrial Revolution.

because it provides a unifying framework for understanding regulatory takings law. As the earlier survey of the law showed, courts have identified certain principles for answering the compensation question but have not been able (or willing) to articulate an objective standard for applying those principles. I will argue that the proposed rule offers such a standard.

Most obviously, the rule resembles the diminution of value test from *Pennsylvania Coal* in the sense that it establishes a threshold, based on efficiency, for determining when a regulation "goes too far," thus triggering compensation. In particular, the rule suggests that a regulation goes too far *when it is inefficiently imposed*. Note that this interpretation avoids the "parceling problem" associated with the diminution of value test because it does not rely on a ratio of the absolute loss in value to some arbitrary measure of the value of the landowner's parcel as a whole. Rather, it depends on a ratio of the landowner's loss to the social gain from the regulation. The proportional loss to the landowner, however that is measured, is therefore immaterial.

The threshold rule also provides a standard for applying the noxious use doctrine. Recall that one objection to that rule was that the meaning of "noxious" use was open to interpretation. The proposed rule, however, implies that a noxious use can be defined as *an activity that is efficiently regulated by the government*, and for which compensation is therefore not required. Note that according to this interpretation, the noxious use doctrine and the diminution of value test are therefore two ways of saying the same thing: The noxious use doctrine emphasizes cases where the government has acted efficiently in imposing a regulation and so compensation is not due (corresponding to the second line of [5.1]), whereas the diminution of value test emphasizes cases where the government has not acted efficiently and so compensation is due (corresponding to the first line of [5.1]).

Seen in this light, the Supreme Court's ruling in *Pennsylvania Coal* no longer necessarily appears to be the fundamental break in the law that it is conventionally portrayed as. Rather, it is simply another way of articulating the same standard as was used in *Mugler*. Likewise, the conflicting views in *Pennsylvania Coal* between Holmes, who argued for compensation based on the diminution of value suffered by the coal companies, and Brandeis, who argued against compensation based on the noxious use doctrine, can be interpreted as a *disagreement over facts rather than over law*.

To illustrate this point, let us suppose for sake of argument that both Holmes and Brandeis were approaching the case from the perspective of the rule in (5.1); that is, both were applying the same legal standard. However, they disagreed about whether or not the regulation in question was efficient.

In particular, let us suppose that Holmes believed that the benefit to society in terms of the protections afforded to surface owners was less than the value of the coal that had to be left in the ground, whereas Brandeis, in making the same calculation, believed that the reverse was true. As a result, the judges reached opposite conclusions regarding compensation, even though, according to this interpretation, they were applying the same rule. In other words, their disagreement was factual rather than legal.

Similar reasoning shows that the *Lucas* nuisance exception, which, recall, was really a refinement of the noxious use doctrine, fits easily into this framework. Recall that the nuisance exception allows the government to avoid paying compensation when it regulates activities that would be judged a nuisance under the state's common law. But how is a nuisance defined by the common law? The usual standard is reasonableness, which is defined by asking whether "a reasonable person would conclude that the amount of harm done outweighs the benefit."[31] In other words, it is based on a cost-benefit calculation. Thus, the threshold for compensation implied by the nuisance exception is identical to that under the proposed threshold rule.

Extending this logic shows that the threshold rule provides an alternative "neutral conduct" point for applying the harm-benefit rule. Specifically, by setting *neutral conduct* equal to *efficient conduct*, a regulation can be said to "confer a benefit" (and hence require compensation) when it imposes inefficient restrictions on landowners, whereas it can be said to "prevent a harm" (and hence not require compensation) when it imposes an efficient restriction. The threshold rule is also consistent with Fischel's normal behavior standard, which, recall, set normal behavior based on a landowner's reasonable expectations (i.e., based on community norms) about permissible land uses. And as has been emphasized, reasonableness standards in law (like the Hand test) are generally interpreted by economists as representing (or inducing) efficient behavior.

5.6. Epstein's View of Takings Law

The various forms of the noxious use doctrine, as just interpreted in light of the efficient threshold rule, can also be used to explicate Richard Epstein's view on takings law, which is based on the Lockean notion that the government should not stand in a preferred position compared to private citizens (Epstein, 1985, chapter 2). In this perspective, the government has no more rights in its interactions with private citizens than does any other private

---

[31] See, e.g., Keeton et al. (1984, p. 630). Also see Landes and Posner (1987, chapter 2) for an economic theory of nuisance law.

citizen, inasmuch as the government is merely an agent of those citizens when they act collectively (the viewpoint underlying the constitutional choice models discussed in Chapter 4). Thus, according to Epstein, when a government action wrongfully deprives a private citizen of valuable property, it should have to pay compensation, just as a private citizen would have to pay for imposing similar harm under nuisance (tort) law. In contrast, when a government action prevents a private citizen from imposing harm on other citizens – as, when it prevents that citizen from creating a nuisance (or noxious use) – it should not have to pay, based on the right that private citizens have to be free from nuisances caused by fellow citizens.[32] (I will return to this point in Section 5.9 later in this chapter.) In Epstein's view, therefore, the principal protection of landowner rights, and hence the key to understanding the function of the eminent domain clause, is the law of nuisance. Thus, to the extent that nuisance law provides an efficient standard of behavior for individual citizens, and by extension, for the government in its dealings with citizens, the proposed threshold rule is consistent with Epstein's view of takings.

The congruence is not perfect, however, as illustrated by the famous case of *Miller v. Schoene*.[33] The case concerned a law passed by the state of Virginia allowing government officials to cut down cedar trees within two miles of an apple orchard because the cedar trees were found to harbor a certain fungus that was known to destroy the fruit and foliage of apple trees. When the state ordered Miller to cut down his cedar trees and did not pay compensation (aside from the value of the cut wood, which he was allowed to keep), Miller sued, alleging a taking. The Supreme Court upheld the law (and hence denied compensation) based on the argument that apple growing was a valuable industry and thus deserved state protection (Fischel, 1995a, p. 152).

According to the efficient threshold rule, this ruling was correct, under the presumption that the regulation was efficiently proposed; that is, assuming that the value of the saved apple trees exceeded the value of the cedar trees to the owner. However, Epstein (1985, pp. 113–115) argues that, unless the Court could show that the cedar trees were a nuisance under the state's common law (a burden he clearly believed it could not have met), compensation should have been paid.

As argued earlier, nuisance law and efficiency generally converge to the same outcome, but not always. When they differ, the question is whether the standard for compensation should be based on efficiency or on the law of nuisance. Epstein argues for nuisance law, whereas the proposed threshold rule

[32] See Epstein (1985, p. 36) and Epstein (1995, p. 133).
[33] 276 U.S. 272 (1928).

argues for efficiency. Fundamentally, this reflects a difference in normative perspectives on the appropriate function of the takings clause, particularly its just compensation requirement. Epstein acknowledges that efficiency is an acceptable criterion for determining whether or not the government's action was *appropriate*, but he objects to its use for deciding whether or not compensation is due: "The question of relative values would go only to whether it would be prudent for the state to condemn the land and not to whether the state should pay for the land thus condemned" (Epstein, 1985, p. 115).

This logic reflects a valid perspective on the compensation question, which focuses on the role of compensation in achieving distributive justice (i.e., on making the landowner whole for the loss of his property rights, as required under nuisance law), as opposed to its incentive function. In some situations, these objectives are compatible with one another, but in others, like *Miller*, they may not be.[34] In Section 5.8, however, I will examine an alternative version of the threshold rule that is also efficient but is distributionally more in line with Epstein's view.

5.7. Did *Keystone* Overrule *Pennsylvania Coal*?

As a final point concerning the interpretation of the efficient threshold rule, consider the well-known case of *Keystone Bituminous Coal Assn. v. DeBenedictus*,[35] which the Supreme Court decided in 1987. The case is especially noteworthy because the facts are strikingly similar to those in *Pennsylvania Coal v. Mahon*. Specifically, the case was filed by an association of coal companies in response to a state law, the Subsidence Act, which required coal miners to leave sufficient coal in the ground to support the surface. Yet, in an apparent reversal of its earlier decision to award the coal company compensation for a similar law in *Pennsylvania Coal*, the Court held that no compensation was due! If there ever was a clear case where the Court abandoned established legal precedent, this case appears to be it.

Recognizing the apparent departure from its earlier ruling, Justice Stevens, writing for the majority, sought to distinguish the two cases. He noted in particular that the law at issue in *Pennsylvania Coal* protected only a few landowners, whereas

[h]ere, by contrast, the Commonwealth [of Pennsylvania] is acting to protect the public interest in health, the environment, and the fiscal integrity of the area ...

---

[34] The same issue arises in tort law, where the goal of compensating victims sometimes conflicts with its goal of deterring injurer and victim negligence. See the discussion of this point in relation to takings law in Miceli and Segerson (1996, pp. 54–55).

[35] 480 U.S. 470 (1987).

The Subsidence Act is a prime example that "circumstances may so change in time … as to clothe with such a [public] interest what in other times would be a matter of purely private concern."[36]

Although the number of owners occupying the surface may seem to be a frail basis on which to distinguish the two cases, the efficient threshold rule suggests that an inquiry into the relative benefits of the government's action in the two cases is in fact crucial for deciding the compensation question. If it is true that the value of the surface property was substantially larger in 1987 than it was in 1922 (as Stevens seems to be arguing), then the calculation of the efficiency of the regulation may well have shifted in the direction of making the regulation efficient. In other words, the change in property values on the surface increased the benefit of the regulation. Couple that with the fact that the loss to coal companies was probably substantially smaller in 1987 compared to 1922 as a result of the diminished value of coal to the economy, and it becomes entirely possible – indeed likely – that a regulation that was inefficient in 1922 had become efficient by 1987. According to Fischel (1995a, p. 48), "by the 1960s [when the Subsidence Act was passed], general growth in personal incomes had driven up the demand for housing and a pleasant environment. Technological changes over the same period had reduced concern over extraction of coal, because many substitutes for it had developed." Seen in this perspective, the opposing decisions in the two cases are perfectly compatible, reflecting a change in economic circumstances rather than a departure from established law. As in the Holmes-Brandeis disagreement, the difference here was again a factual rather than a legal one.

5.8. An Alternative Version of the Efficient Threshold Rule

Having illustrated the explanatory power of the efficient threshold rule with regard to the law of regulatory takings, it is worth pointing out that the specific form of rule is not unique in terms of its efficiency properties. In fact, an equally efficient version of the rule can be specified that conditions the payment of compensation on the efficiency of the landowner's investment decision rather than on the efficiency of the regulatory decision (as was the case with the rule in [5.1]). The specific form of this alternative version of the threshold rule is

$$\text{Compensation} = \begin{cases} \text{Full, if the landowner invested efficiently} \\ \text{Zero, if the landowner overinvested.} \end{cases} \quad (5.6)$$

---

[36] *Id.*, p. 488. The quoted passage is from *Block v. Hirsh*, 256 U.S. 135, 155 (1921).

Note that this rule differs from the one in (5.1) by the fact that here, compensation is full when the landowner acted *efficiently*, whereas compensation was full under the previous version when the government acted *inefficiently*. Thus, compensation acts here as a "reward" for efficient landowner behavior rather than as a "penalty" for inefficient government behavior. To distinguish between these two versions of the threshold rule, I will refer to the earlier version, under which compensation was conditioned on the regulator's behavior, as the *ex post* rule, and the current version, under which compensation is conditioned on the landowner's behavior, as the *ex ante* rule.[37]

To demonstrate the efficiency of the ex ante rule, let us return to the example in Table 5.1. Recall that there were two projects available to the landowner, Project 1, which promised a net private return of $175,000, and Project 2, which promised a net private return of $200,000, but both entailed the risk of an external cost. Although Project 2 offered the higher private return to the landowner, once the external cost was accounted for, Project 1 yielded the higher net social return and was therefore optimal.

Now consider the actual choices of the landowner and regulator under the ex ante threshold rule. As before, we consider their decisions in reverse order of time. Suppose first that the landowner acted efficiently and chose Project 1. Then, by (5.6), compensation will be full in the event of a regulation (that is, $C=\$200,000$), and as a result, the regulator, who compares the benefit of the regulation to the amount of compensation, will only enact the regulation if the high external cost ($325,000) is realized, which is the efficient decision. Suppose next that the landowner acted inefficiently and chose Project 2. In that case, compensation is zero, so the regulator will impose the regulation if either cost is realized; that is, it will overregulate.

Next consider the landowner's behavior, given that he correctly anticipates the behavior of the regulator as just described. First, if he chooses Project 1, he knows that the regulator will only impose the regulation if the high cost is realized (which occurs with probability 0.5), and that compensation in that case will be full. His expected return is therefore $175,000, or the full private return. In contrast, if the landowner chooses Project 2, he knows that the regulator will impose the regulation with certainty (that is, if either the high or the low cost is realized) and that compensation will be zero. His expected return in this case is –$100,000. Clearly, the landowner will prefer

---

[37] The two threshold rules and their efficiency properties were first examined in Miceli and Segerson (1994, 1996).

Project 1. As a result, the equilibrium involves efficient behavior by both the landowner and the regulator, as was the case under the efficient ex post rule. Thus, the two rules are identical in terms of their incentive effects.

Notice, however, that the rules have opposite distributional implications; whereas no compensation was paid in the efficient equilibrium under the ex post rule, full compensation is paid in equilibrium under the ex ante rule. An analogy to this result exists in the area of tort law, where economists have shown that several different versions of the negligence rule can induce efficient care by both injurers and victims in bilateral care accident settings.[38] (Recall our comparison of the ex post rule to negligence law in Section 5.4 earlier in this chapter.) The intuition for this finding is that negligence rules combine two methods for inducing parties to take the proper level of care. One is to set a standard of behavior (the "due standard") that allows one party to *avoid liability* by meeting the standard, and the other is to impose the actual damages on the other party, which induces that party to fully internalize the harm. And considering that, from a mathematical (and Coasian) perspective, the identities of the parties to an accident (injurer or victim) are irrelevant with regard to the impact of these incentives, the two devices are perfectly reversible; that is, the due standard can be set for either party, with the full damages being imposed on the other party. As a result, different distributional outcomes are possible without distorting incentives.[39]

This same reversibility carries over to the proposed compensation rules. Thus, given our earlier interpretation of landowners as takings "victims" and the government as the "injurer," the ex post rule, under which compensation is not paid in equilibrium, corresponds to a pure negligence rule, which sets a due standard for injurers. In contrast, the ex ante rule corresponds to a rule of strict liability with a defense of contributory negligence, which sets a due standard for victims (Miceli and Segerson, 1996, p. 55).

Given the equivalence between the two rules in terms of incentives, it is worth asking, on both a positive and normative grounds, what basis one might use to choose between them. One obvious reason for favoring the

---

[38] See, for example, Landes and Posner (1987) and Shavell (1987).

[39] One might therefore be tempted to attribute this "irrelevance" of the assignment of liability to the Coase Theorem, which, recall, asserts that efficiency can be achieved in externality settings under different assignments of liability provided that the parties can bargain (Coase, 1960). However, this would not be true here because there is no bargaining needed to demonstrate the efficiency of the ex ante and ex post rules, or of the various negligence rules. Rather, the irrelevance arises from the existence of the two methods for inducing care, which, as noted, are completely reversible as between injurers and victims, or (in the takings context) between landowners and the government.

ex ante rule is fairness or distributional justice, given that compensation is paid in equilibrium, and one purpose of just compensation is surely to make landowners whole. However, as the earlier discussion revealed, the actual case law appears more consistent with the ex post rule given the general denial of compensation for most regulations.

Alternatively, one might choose between the rules by appealing to the administrative costs of paying compensation (a component of Michelman's settlement costs). These consist of the legal costs incurred by both the plaintiff and the government in litigating a takings claim, as well as the deadweight costs of the taxes necessary to finance compensation (Fischel, 1995a, p. 96). Such costs represent the economic counterpart of friction in physics, and therefore choosing the legal rules so as to minimize such costs, all else equal, is consistent with efficiency. In this regard, the ex post version of the threshold rule may be preferred on the grounds that denial of compensation in equilibrium will tend to discourage inverse condemnation suits by landowners because they would expect to lose on average.[40] As a result, once administrative costs are taken into account, a case can be made that the ex post rule is the more efficient of the two.

Finally, the choice between the two rules could depend on which places a heavier informational burden on courts. In this case, the question is whether it would be easier for courts to determine when a regulation was efficiently imposed (as under the ex post rule), or when a landowner invested efficiently (as under the ex ante rule). Both are difficult calculations that require a large amount of information (a point I discussed in Section 4.9 of the previous chapter), but which courts are often asked to undertake. In practice, the easier rule to implement will likely vary on a case-by-case basis, thus offering no obvious basis for choosing between them.

5.9. In-Kind Compensation: Neighborhood Externalities Revisited

Government regulations are pervasive, and in many cases they impose substantial burdens on property owners in terms of lost value. Yet, as has been noted, courts have rarely found them to be takings requiring compensation. It does not follow, however, that property owners as a whole are necessarily made worse off by the imposition of such regulations, or even that they are uncompensated. The reason for this paradoxical assertion is

---

[40] Condemnation occurs when the government initiates a taking in order to physically acquire a piece of land. In most regulatory takings cases, however, it is the landowner who initiates the claim for compensation by filing an "inverse condemnation" suit.

that the constitutional requirement of just compensation does not specify that compensation must always be *monetary*; it can also be *in-kind* (Epstein, 1985, chapter 14).

To see what this means, note that in cases where regulations are widely imposed, as in the case, for example, of zoning restrictions, all property owners are equally burdened by the regulations, but they are also equally benefited by them. And if the regulations are efficiently imposed, the collective benefits should in principle outweigh the costs, thereby providing a form of implicit, in-kind compensation to all affected landowners. This argument implies that a compensable taking has not occurred when a regulation secures an "average reciprocity of advantage" across all property owners, based on the idea first advanced by Justice Holmes in *Pennsylvania Coal*[41] and later reiterated by Justice Rehnquist in *Penn Central*. It also reflects Michelman's fairness standard, which, recall, says that "[a] decision not to compensate is not unfair as long as the disappointed claimant ought to be able to appreciate how such decisions might fit into a consistent practice which holds forth a lesser long run risk to people like him than would any consistent practice which is naturally suggested by the opposite decision."[42]

The economics of this perspective is based on the problem of "neighborhood externalities," which we discussed in Chapter 2 in connection with urban renewal policies (see Section 2.9). Recall that neighborhood externalities represent the spillover effects (costs or benefits) that neighboring property owners impose on one another as a result of their land use decisions. For example, the manner in which owners use or maintain their property obviously affects their own values but also the values of neighboring property owners. And because owners generally ignore these spillover effects, they may engage in socially inefficient practices. For example, they may skimp on maintenance, or paint their houses unusual colors. More substantially, a landowner may try to open a gas station in the middle of a residential neighborhood so as to maximize his or her own property value, even though it is an inefficient land use from a social perspective owing to the resulting noise and congestion.

Often, the problem of neighborhood externalities can be solved privately by means of agreements, explicit or implicit, among residents. For example, condominium residents often enter into complex contracts specifying

---

[41] 260 U.S. 393, 415 (1922).

[42] Michelman (1967, p. 1223). Also see Fischel (1985, p.152), who discusses this standard in light of the non-compensability of zoning laws.

certain obligations and restrictions on the use and upkeep of their properties (Cannaday, 1994). Similarly, land deeds sometimes contain restrictive covenants that constrain the owner's lifestyle or land use (Hughes and Turnbull, 1996). More commonly, though, neighborhood externalities in suburban settings are controlled through implicit or informal agreements among neighbors to maintain their properties in a reasonable condition and to refrain from overly disruptive behavior.

In some cases, however, transaction costs limit the ability of these sorts of private responses to the problem of neighborhood externalities. This is especially true for large-scale externalities, such as those created by gas stations or other business operations, or in very dense neighborhoods where residents are strangers, and the sort of multilateral agreements that would be necessary to internalize the resulting externalities would be impractical. As we argued in Chapter 2, the likely result in such settings is inefficient land use, and in the extreme case, severe neighborhood decline. Thus, it is in the interests of property owners to allow the government, acting on their collective behalf, to impose regulations that allow (or rather "force") them to achieve an efficient land use pattern.

Based on this logic, regulations aimed at achieving this outcome would not be compensable takings because landowners as a group actually benefit from them. Thus, for example, a zoning regulation that prevents a landowner from opening a gas station in a residential neighborhood would *not* give rise to a taking claim because, even though the aggrieved owner might be able to claim a loss in value due to the restriction, this loss would only exist relative to a background in which all other landowners are prevented from engaging in such use. In other words, the claimant's "loss" is calculated based on his unilateral departure from the efficient land use pattern. Thus, he would have no claim for compensation. Indeed, if the regulation is efficiently structured, it actually *raises* the claimant's property value relative to the situation where no regulation is in place, and all landowners are free to pursue their private interests unimpeded. It is in this sense that all landowners are said to receive in-kind compensation for the restrictions imposed by broad (and efficient) government actions.[43]

We began this chapter by suggesting that, from an economic perspective, regulatory takings lie on a continuum with physical takings, and therefore should in principle be treated the same. The preceding argument, however, provides a possible economic basis for the dissimilar treatment of the two

---

[43] The logic is similar to that underlying the benefit-offset principle discussed Section 3.4 of Chapter 3.

types of cases (Fischel's corner solutions). Specifically, the nearly universal payment of compensation for physical takings, which typically involves the acquisition of only a few parcels, reflects the concentration of costs on those owners whose land is taken, and for which they receive little or no in-kind compensation. Thus, monetary compensation is necessary to satisfy the just compensation requirement. In contrast, the denial of compensation for most regulations reflects their broad impact across property owners, with its promise of in-kind compensation through increased property value, as measured relative to a world in which no regulations are imposed on individual land use decisions.[44]

5.10. The Essential Nexus and Proportionality Requirements: *Nollan* and *Dolan*

A different sort of argument for in-kind compensation was evaluated by the Supreme Court in the case of *Nollan v. California Coastal Commission*.[45] The case concerned the buyer of a beachfront cottage, Patrick Nollan, who wanted to build a larger house on the lot. The California Coastal Commission granted permission for the expansion, but only on the condition that Nollan would agree to allow public access to the adjoining beach. The basis for the Commission's argument was that the larger house would obstruct the view of the beach, and so direct access to the beach was necessary to mitigate the obstruction. Although beach access would clearly represent a physical invasion of the owner's property, and hence would constitute a taking under ordinary circumstances, the Commission's logic was that the requisite compensation was implicit in the Commission's granting of the development right. In other words, the government's granting of the development right was in-kind compensated for the invasion. Thus, it maintained, no further compensation was due.

The Supreme Court disagreed with this logic based on the argument that there had to be an "essential nexus" between any conditions attached by the government to the development permit and the impact of the proposed

---

[44] Levinson (2002), however, might argue that the distinction proposed here is arbitrary in regard to the "transactional frame" that is used to calculate harms and benefits. For example, in *Poletown Neighborhood Council v. City of Detroit* (304 N.W.2d 455, Mich. 1981), one could use this logic to deny compensation to individual landowners based on the average-reciprocity-of-advantage argument by "offsetting the economic benefits stemming from the plant against the dispossession and dislocation of residents" (Levinson, 2002, p. 1342). Such a ruling, however, would substantially burden the displaced residents relative to other citizens.

[45] 483 U.S. 825 (1987)

development. In this case, it found that no such nexus existed in the sense that the proposed expansion of the house would not in fact have blocked the view of the beach, as the Commission had contended. Thus, the implicit transaction was not legally acceptable.

The important thing to notice here is that the Court's ruling did not seem to invalidate the logic of the government's argument; rather it suggested that the proposed transaction was not acceptable based on the *facts* of the case.[46] That is, the implicit compensation that Nollan was being asked to accept in return for giving up exclusive rights to his beach – namely, the right to re-develop his property – was not in fact something that would have been harmful to the community. As a result, the proposed "transaction" involved a sacrifice by Nollan that was not matched by a corresponding sacrifice by the community.

According to Fischel's normal behavior standard, Nollan's proposed use was consistent with normal (efficient) behavior, and so asking him to give up something of value in return for permission to do it was properly invalidated by the Court. Based on the argument in the previous section, landowners can be compelled to conform to the efficient land use pattern without compensation, but they cannot be required to exceed it. In terms of the ex post version of the efficient threshold rule, we would argue that the regulation imposed on the landowner (public use of his beach) was inefficient, and so explicit compensation was required.

The Supreme Court further refined its position on this issue seven years later in the case of *Dolan v. Tigard*,[47] which involved a requirement by the City of Tigard that the owner of a hardware store had to deed a portion of her property to the city for use as a bike path and open space as a condition for its allowing her to expand the store and pave a larger parking lot. The city's argument in making this request was that the open space and bike path would mitigate the costs to the community arising from the expanded business operation. The Court in this case found that, in contrast to *Nollan*, there did exist a nexus between the city's demand and the proposed expansion. That is, the bike path and open space would in fact mitigate the damage from the proposed expansion. However, it also found that the costs imposed on the landowner by the demand were disproportionate in comparison to the social benefits. In order to avoid the need for explicit compensation, the Court said, the government had to demonstrate a "rough proportionality" between the social harm from the

---

[46] The argument in this section is largely based on Fischel (1995a, pp. 342–355). Also see Miceli and Segerson (1996, pp. 55–59) for a somewhat different perspective.

[47] 512 U.S. 374 (1994)

proposed development and the value of the property that was being taken in exchange. In other words, the in-kind benefit received by the landowner had to provide sufficient compensation for her losses in order to meet the requirement of just compensation.

Note that the difference between the rulings in *Nollan* and *Dolan* is merely one of degree. Whereas *Nollan* found *no* relation between the government's demand and the landowner's proposed development, *Dolan* found an *inadequate* relation (Fischel, 1995a, p. 349). In any case, both rulings fit comfortably into the economic framework described in this chapter in the sense that they involve an explicit balancing of the costs and benefits of a regulation in answering the compensation question.

Been (1991) nevertheless criticized the Court's awarding of compensation in *Nollan* (and presumably would have likewise criticized it in *Dolan*) based on the argument that the claimant was protected against what he deemed to be an unreasonable government demand by his option to exit the jurisdiction. As discussed in Chapter 3 (Section 3.5), this logic makes sense provided that the claimant could have avoided the inefficiency by moving. However Fischel (1995a, p. 345) notes that in *Nollan*, the regulation in question was tied to the particular location – namely the beachfront – rather than to an activity that the claimant could easily have resumed in a different location. Thus, exit did not provide an adequate escape for Nollan. The exit argument against compensation applies better to the facts of *Dolan*, which involved a business that the claimant presumably could have relocated without substantially diminishing its value.[48] Still, as argued in Chapter 3, the exit option is also limited to the extent that landowners, on selling, will suffer a loss in property value equal to the capitalized cost of the regulation to prospective buyers.

5.11. Some Applications of the Theory

This final section discusses in more detail the application of the economic theory developed in this chapter to various areas where regulatory takings issues have most commonly arisen. The discussion is meant to be illustrative rather than exhaustive. The specific areas I will discuss are mining regulation, zoning, historic landmark designation, wetland preservation, and protection of endangered species.[49]

---

[48] Of course, businesses often have location-specific goodwill that would be lost in the event of exit.

[49] This section is based on Miceli and Segerson (1996), chapters 9–10; and Meltz et al. (1999), parts IV and V.

Mining. The process of mining, while clearly necessary for economic development, often results in environmental damages and other risks, both to persons and property. Because the most of the resulting costs are external, however, mine owners and operators will generally ignore them in making their economic decisions, thus providing an economic justification for government regulation of mining. The taking issue arises when mine owners seek compensation for the resulting loss in profits. The issue is complicated by the common practice in mining of separating ownership of the surface estate from subsurface mining rights. Although this practice creates the possibility of mutual advantage to the mine and surface owners by allowing both users to exploit the property simultaneously, potential conflicts arise when the mining operation compromises the integrity of the surface, thus creating the risk of subsidence, or cave-ins.[50]

As we have seen, this was precisely the issue in the famous case of *Pennsylvania Coal v. Mahon* (1922).[51] Recall that this case involved a challenge by mine owners of the Kohler Act, which had been enacted by the State of Pennsylvania to prevent extraction of coal to the point where it would risk subsidence of the surface. The fact that the mining company's ownership was limited to the mineral interest, however, essentially guaranteed that the Court would find that the regulation had substantially reduced the value of that interest. The severance of rights therefore worked to the advantage of the mining company in terms of its claim that the regulation resulted in a complete loss in the value of its rights.

Apparently, however, the Court found a way around this provision when it ruled that a similar anti-subsidence statute was not a taking in the case of *Keystone Coal Assn v. DeBenedictus* (1987). In endeavoring to distinguish the two cases, the Court argued that the statute in *Keystone* protected a broader public interest as compared to the earlier statute, which had been aimed at protecting only a few private parties. Although the distinction between public and private interests is not strictly valid from an economic point of view, the implication that the value of the surface rights had substantially increased during the intervening decades is a relevant consideration and relates to the externality argument for government regulations.

---

[50] Surface cave-ins are not the only risk associated with mining, however. For example, in *Goldblatt v. Town of Hempstead* (369 U.S. 590, 1962), the Court upheld an ordinance preventing the mining of sand and gravel below the water table because of the danger created by the resulting lake.

[51] See the fascinating discussion of this case and its aftermath in Fischel (1995a, chapter 1).

In particular, as I previously argued, the two cases can be reconciled in terms of the efficient ex post threshold rule, where compensation is only due when the government overregulates, or when the harm prevented by the regulation is less than the loss to the landowner. As I suggested, it is perfectly plausible to argue that between 1922 and 1987, the value of the surface estate had risen while the value of the mineral estate had declined to such an extent that what was an inefficient regulation in the earlier case had become efficient. The opposite rulings in *Pennsylvania Coal* and *Keystone* are therefore consistent with this logic and together suggest that the Court based its decisions, not on a calculation of the percentage decrease in the value of the mineral estate alone (which presumably was equally large in the two cases regardless of the nominal value of the coal), but on a comparison of the decrease in value relative to the social benefit gained by the regulation, which apparently was vastly different in the two cases.

Another takings question that arises in mining concerns the extent to which mining rights on federal (publicly owned) lands are legally protected by the eminent domain clause. Under the Mining Act of 1872,[52] prospectors were allowed to enter federal lands, explore for minerals, and establish vested rights in a "discovery," where the legal test for discovery was that a prudent person could expect to earn a reasonable return in conducting the mining operation. With discovery comes the further legal right to exclude others and to apply for a patent. Even before a patent is issued, however, courts have ruled that the mining claim itself enjoys the legal status of property, and is therefore subject to the usual limitations on government takings. However, courts have also put mine owners on notice that new government restrictions are always possible in areas like mining where unforeseen dangers and environmental risks can arise unexpectedly (Meltz et al., 1999, p. 417). Thus, as with any potentially harmful activity, mine owners are subject, in an ongoing way, to reasonable (efficient) limitations on their property rights in the interest of public safety (echoing the noxious use doctrine).

Zoning. Zoning is perhaps the most pervasive form of government regulation of land in the United States.[53] From an economic perspective, zoning is generally justified as a means of minimizing the externalities associated with incompatible land uses. To some extent, a smoothly functioning land market should be able to achieve an efficient land use pattern without

---

[52] 30 U.S.C. §§21–54.

[53] Fischel (1985) provides a comprehensive economic treatment of zoning, including its relation to the takings issue.

the need for government intervention because land users will voluntarily seek out, and pay higher prices for, locations that are most suited to their intended use or are sufficiently distant from offending uses. Thus, for example, residential users will generally outbid industrial users in a predominantly residential area (and vice versa), thereby resulting in a voluntary segregation of land uses that minimizes spillover costs.[54]

Still, transaction costs will likely prevent a fully efficient configuration of land uses from being achieved purely by market forces (Henderson, 1985, pp. 92–96). (Our discussion of neighborhood externalities and urban sprawl in Chapter 2 suggested some reasons why.) When this is true, zoning can improve efficiency by requiring the separation of differing uses based on the theory "that similar land uses have no (or only small) external effects on each other whereas dissimilar land uses may have large effects" (White, 1975, p. 32). Such a regulatory policy is referred to as "externality zoning."

A different sort of zoning is also commonly used by local governments, primarily within residential areas, to restrict population density, for example by setting minimum lot sizes and excluding high-density (usually rental) housing. Whereas this practice can also be justified as minimizing neighborhood externalities, it has the further budgetary effect of ensuring that all residents within a jurisdiction consume property of sufficient value that they will pay their fair share of property taxes to finance local public goods. For this reason, zoning restrictions whose primary effect is to guarantee that all residents consume a minimum property value (for example, minimum lot size zoning) are sometimes referred to as "fiscal zoning" (Fischel, 1985, p. 60–61; Miceli, 1991b).

Regardless of their purpose, zoning regulations raise the taking issue because, by limiting the things a landowner can do with his or her property, they potentially lower its value. Although landowners have repeatedly challenged the legitimacy of zoning on this basis, courts have historically upheld the practice as a valid exercise of the government's right under the police power to protect the public's welfare. The first case to reach such a conclusion was *Village of Euclid v. Ambler Realty*,[55] which involved a challenge by Ambler Realty Company of a city ordinance that zoned a portion of property owned by the plaintiff for residential use only. Ambler had intended to sell the property for industrial use, which would have fetched a substantially higher price, so it sought to have the ordinance overturned.

[54] See, for example, Posner (2003, p. 66) and Siegan (1970, 1972).
[55] 272 U.S. 365 (1926).

The Supreme Court nevertheless upheld the regulation as falling within the city's police power. In so doing, it relied on the common law of nuisance to provide a "fairly helpful clew [sic]" regarding the limits of that power.[56] Notice that this appeal to the common law anticipated the nuisance exception from *Lucas v. South Carolina Coastal Council* (1922), which held that a regulation preventing a common-law nuisance is not a compensable taking. To the extent that nuisance law is efficient, the resulting standard is also consistent with the non-compensability of zoning under the ex post version of the efficient threshold rule.

The legitimacy of a zoning ordinance that required some amount of land to be set aside for open space (a third form of zoning) was challenged in the case of *Agins v. City Tiburon*.[57] Again, the U.S. Supreme Court upheld the action as a proper exercise of the government's police power on the grounds that the regulation "substantially advance[d] legitimate government goals" of "assuring careful and orderly development of residential property with provision for open-space areas."[58] In this case, however, the non-payment of compensation cannot be justified on the grounds that it was preventing a nuisance (residential development). Rather, it essentially asked the landowner to provide a public good.

This distinction harkens back to the harm-benefit rule, which, recall, said that compensation is not required when a regulation prevents the landowner from imposing a harm (nuisance), but compensation is required when the regulation compels the landowner to confer a benefit. We have argued, however, that economic theory does not support this viewpoint because it relies on an arbitrary distinction – that is, harms can always be defined as foregone benefits and benefits as foregone harms. The relevant distinction is instead between efficient and inefficient government actions, with compensation being due only in the latter case (according to the ex post rule). Based on this standard, zoning ordinances that compel landowners to set aside a certain amount of land for open space can be construed as legitimate exercises of the police power (and hence, as being non-compensable) if the social benefit of leaving the land vacant exceeds the value of developing it. Note that the departure in *Agins* from a strict reliance on nuisance law for determining the compensation question (echoing the case of *Miller v. Schoene*, but contrary to Epstein's view) is again evidence that the court seems inclined toward a standard based on economic

[56] *Village of Euclid v. Ambler Realty*, 272 U.S. 365, 387 (1926). Also see Meltz et al. (1999, p. 214).

[57] 447 U.S. 255 (1980).

[58] *Id.*, pp. 261–262.

efficiency rather than nuisance law when the conditions defining a nuisance and efficiency diverge.

Historic landmark designation. All fifty states and many municipalities have enacted laws that allow the designation of privately owned buildings as historic landmarks. Generally, these laws impose restrictions on what owners can and cannot do with the designated structure, rather than taking public ownership of it. For example, owners are typically required to maintain the structure in good repair and to obtain approval from an oversight commission before undertaking any exterior alterations. Because these restrictions often reduce the private value of the building, however, landmark designation has sometimes been challenged as a taking by owners of designated buildings.

The most famous such case was *Penn Central Transportation Co. v. New York City* (1978), which, recall, involved a claim by the owners of Grand Central Terminal that the city's designation of the structure as a historic landmark, and the consequent denial of an application to build a multi-storied office building above it, was a taking of the owner's development rights. The Supreme Court denied the claim on the grounds that the regulation did not interfere with the primary use of the building, thus allowing the owners to continue to earn a reasonable return on it. Further, the Court argued that the owner was allowed to transfer the development rights to another parcel, or even to propose a different plan for an addition to the terminal that would "harmonize" with the existing structure, thus further weakening its claim.

From an economic perspective, the desirability of designating a building a historic landmark involves a comparison of the value of the building in its preserved state to its value in its best alternative use. The reason that the owner of the building may not make the socially optimal decision in this regard is that the component of the building's value attributable to its historic nature will be largely external; that is, it will consist mostly of the value that non-owners attach to it. (In essence, the historic nature of the building is a public good.) Further, there generally is no practical way that the owner can capture all of this value because much of it resides in the mere knowledge among the public that the building has been preserved. Thus, by requiring the building to be left in its historic state, the government is essentially requiring the owner to provide a public good at his or her own expense (Gold, 1976).

In this sense, landmark designation is like the open-space zoning ordinance in *Agins*. Thus, from an economic perspective, the compensation question again turns on a consideration of the efficiency of the designation decision; specifically, was the social value of the building enhanced by the requirement that it had to be left in its historic condition? If so, the Court's decision not to award compensation was consistent with efficiency under the efficient ex post rule.

A related issue concerns the distinction between the designation of a single building as a historic landmark and the designation of a group of buildings as a "historic district." Although the two situations appear to be the based on the same economic considerations, there is an important economic difference between them. As Gold (1976, p. 355) notes, the economic rationale for a historic district is that an "individual historic structure gains in value by being surrounded by *other* historic structures so that all structures gain in value from mutual restriction" (emphasis in original). Thus, individual properties may actually gain in value from being included in the historic district. In this sense, historic district designation (in contrast to individual designation) may fall into the category of regulations that, as a result of the interdependencies across properties, confer in-kind compensation by making everyone better off.[59] As a result, claims for compensation based on inclusion in a historic district are even weaker than claims based on individual historic designation.

The little empirical evidence that exists on historic designation seems to bear out the distinction between individual designation and designation of a historic district. For example, Ford (1989) found that historic district designation raised the value of individual properties in Baltimore, and Asabere and Huffman (1994) likewise found that historic district designation in Philadelphia resulted in a 26 percent price premium. In contrast, studies of the impact of historic designation on the value of individual buildings reveal mixed results. Whereas Norwell, Sandy, and Tu (2008) found that designation of individual buildings resulted in a 16 percent increase in the designated building's value in San Diego, Asabere, Huffman, and Mehdian (1994) found that it caused a 24 percent loss in the designated building's value in Philadelphia.[60]

Wetlands preservation. Wetlands represent a natural resource that has only recently been recognized as providing important social benefits. These benefits include providing a habitat for wildlife, flood control, water quality maintenance, and both recreational and commercial use. The recent recognition of these values has led to the enactment of government

---

[59] This situation is therefore an example of a beneficial neighborhood externality.

[60] But see Meltz et al. (1999, p. 319), who notes that the *Penn Central* court was not persuaded by the argument that individual designation is more detrimental to property values than is inclusion in an historic district.

regulations at both the state and federal levels aimed at preserving wet-lands. However, because wetlands predominantly exist on privately owned land, and because their primary value to the owner is usually for future development, these regulations have naturally generated a large volume of takings claims.[61]

Efficiency dictates that conversion of wetlands to development should occur to the point where the marginal value of land in development equals its marginal value if left in an undeveloped state. Thus, although it is prob-ably efficient to convert some wetlands to alternative uses, especially in early stages of economic development, private landowners almost certainly would go beyond that efficient point if unrestrained because they would not internalize the full social value of the resource. Regulation is therefore nec-essary to achieve the efficient balance. Still, the question remains whether landowners are entitled to compensation for their resulting loss.

Generally, courts have held that the denial of permit to develop a wetland does not constitute a compensable taking of the owner's property. One argu-ment in support of this position has been to claim that the proposed use of the land would represent a nuisance. However, in *Florida Rock Industries v. United States*, the U.S. Claims Court held that "the assertion that a proposed activity would be a nuisance merely because Congress chose to restrict, regulate, or prohibit it for the public benefit indicates circular reasoning that would yield the destruction of the fifth amendment."[62] As a result, the Court found that a taking had occurred. This argument is consistent with the *Lucas* nuisance exception in its reliance on the common law for defin-ing a nuisance, but it fails to recognize the possible efficiency benefits that a departure from nuisance law would allow, as suggested by our discussion of the open-space zoning ordinance in the *Agins* case.

Nuisance law is not the only applicable legal doctrine in wetlands cases; the "public trust doctrine" is also relevant. The public trust is an ancient doctrine that grants ownership of navigable waterways, shorelines, and the open sea to the public. According to this doctrine, landowners do not have a right to impair resources, like water, that fall within its purview (Lueck and Miceli, 2007, p. 237). In *Just v. Marinette County*, for example, the court held that "[a]n owner of land has no absolute and unlimited right to change the essential character of his land so as to use it for a purpose for which it was unsuited in its natural state and which injures the rights of others."[63]

---

[61] According to Meltz et al. (1999, p. 366, note 5), there were about 400 cases involving wetlands regulations between 1960 and 1990, of which about half raised the takings issue.

[62] 21 Cl.Ct. 161, 168 (1990).

[63] 201 N.W.2d 761, 768 (Wisc. 1972).

Based on this logic, the court found that a regulation preventing the land-owner from filling a wetland was not a taking, even though the proposed use would not have constituted a nuisance.

Epstein (1985, pp. 121–123) has criticized the ruling in *Just* on the grounds that the regulation was not aimed at preventing a nuisance under ordinary common-law standards, but was instead designed to preserve a wildlife habitat. In this sense, he argues that the ruling compelled the owner to confer a social benefit rather than to prevent a harm. As we have repeat-edly argued, however, under the ex post version of the threshold rule, the relevant consideration for determining whether or not compensation is due (at least in terms of efficiency) is to ask if the benefits from the regulation, in whatever form they take, outweigh the costs to the landowner. Although Epstein's argument that compensation should be paid appears consistent with the logic of the *Lucas* nuisance exception, the fact that a proposed land use is not a nuisance under the common law does not necessarily make it an efficient use. The proper economic standard is whether the regulation produces a larger social gain than loss, a calculation that does not turn on the distinction between a harm and a benefit, and that can only be made on a case-by-case basis. And although we argued earlier that nuisance law will often provide a useful approximation, this will not always be the case. Indeed, the fact that wetlands were once themselves thought to be nuisances worthy of removal, but are now highly valued as an important natural resource by many, illustrates the point (Meltz et al., 1999, p. 365).

Endangered species protection. Like resource preservation, the protection of endangered species, especially those endangered by human activity, has become an important objective of government policy. The most important legislative action in this regard was the passage of the Endangered Species Act (ESA) in 1973.[64] Under this act, the Fish and Wildlife Service (FWS) was authorized to "list" a species as endangered or threatened, and to des-ignate the "critical habitat" of that species for special protection or manage-ment. The Act further stipulated that the criterion for listing a species was to be based on "the best scientific and commercial data, without reference to economic costs or private property impacts." In contrast, habitat designa-tion was to be based on both scientific data and "economic impact and any other relevant impact," thus theoretically allowing consideration of land-owners' interests (Meltz et al., 1999, p. 392).

As with wetlands, the preservation of endangered species warrants gov-ernment intervention because of the externalities involved (Harrington,

---

[64] 16 U.S.C. §§ 1531–1544.

1981). However, the takings issue also arises because of the loss suffered
by landowners as a result of the various restrictions on their allowed activities. For example, owners are prohibited from "taking" individuals of a
listed species unless it is done in a good-faith attempt to protect a person,
where a "take" is defined to include harassing, harming, pursuing, or hunt-
ing a listed animal. More ominously for landowners, the FWS has defined
"harm" to include significant habitat modification or degradation (Meltz
et al., 1999, p. 393), and in 1995, the Supreme Court upheld that interpretation as reasonable.[65]

On the other hand, land use restrictions under the ESA have generally
produced relatively modest impacts on landowners' value, which, based on
the prevailing legal standard requiring a landowner to show a virtual total
loss in value, does not bode well for the success of taking claims.[66] Of course
there are exceptions to this, such as when the owner of a stand of timber
is prevented from harvesting it. The risk here, as described in Chapter 4, is
that the threat of an uncompensated regulation can result in perverse (and
costly) landowner incentives, such as a decision to clear-cut the stand early
to avoid its being declared a habitat, or to conceal the fact that an endangered species might reside in a certain locale.

In terms of applying the efficient threshold rule to this situation, the compensation question again depends on a balancing of the benefits and costs
of the relevant restrictions. The particular challenge in this regard, as in the
case of wetlands (or in the regulation of any untraded resource), is to establish the proper measure of the economic value of the protected resource.
This is a difficult question that is open to much debate. In the context of
endangered species, the usual method is contingent valuation, which is a sur-
vey-based approach designed to elicit the dollar amount that people attach
to a resource. Although subject to various criticisms, such an approach is
normally the only practical way of valuing non-market goods.[67]

---

[65] *Sweet Home Chapter of Communities for a Great Oregon v. Babbitt*, 515 U.S. 687 (1995).
[66] Meltz et al. (1999, p. 396) note that as of 1999, not a single court decision finding a taking
under the ESA had been reported.
[67] See Freeman (1993) for a general discussion of the problem of valuing a natural resource.
For a discussion of this problem specifically in the context of endangered species, see
Boyle and Bishop (1987).

SIX

Conclusion

What Does Economic Theory Teach Us about Eminent Domain?

The issue of eminent domain is at the heart of debates about the limits of government control over private property. At one extreme are private property rights advocates who believe that the role of the government should be limited to protecting property rights and enforcing contracts for the exchange of property. On the other are those who would grant the government expansive powers to regulate or take property in the public interest, which they broadly define to include the provision of essential public goods, protection of the environment, and the fostering of economic development. The case law and scholarly literature seeking to reconcile these competing views within the context of constitutionally imposed guidelines are voluminous. The purpose of this book has been to survey and synthesize the contributions economic theory has made to this important area of law. This chapter summarizes the conclusions of that effort in the form of lessons economics can teach us about the scope and practice of eminent domain.

Lesson 1: The proper economic justification for eminent domain is to overcome the holdout problem. When viewed from an economic perspective, eminent domain is a forced sale of property from the current owner to another owner, either the government or another private party, in an effort to achieve some public objective. The question is, why does the sale have to be forced? According to economic theory, the purpose of exchange, whether voluntary or involuntary, is to transfer resources to higher-valued uses; in other words, to realize some gains from trade. Under ideal conditions, that goal is best achieved through ordinary market exchange, with the government's role being limited to the protection of property rights and the enforcement of contracts. Any departure from this paradigm is therefore justifiable only if there is some reason to believe that the market will fail to operate efficiently.

151

One possibility, suggested by the plain meaning of the public use requirement of the Fifth Amendment, is that forced exchange under eminent
domain is necessary to overcome a market failure associated with the provision of public goods. If, for example, privately owned land becomes more
valuable in public use, for example as a highway, park, or wildlife preserve,
then it may be necessary for the government to step in and forcibly purchase the land from the owner to ensure that these goods are provided in
the efficient quantity. Although intuitively appealing, this interpretation
is not supported by economic theory. To be sure, public good provision
does result in market failure due to the free-rider problem, but this is the
consequence of a demand-side problem that results in inadequate financing of public goods, given that consumers can enjoy the benefits of those
goods without having to contribute to their cost. The usual remedy for this
free-rider problem is therefore for the government to coerce payment from
consumers by means of its powers of taxation, thereby effecting a forced
purchase of the public good. The manner in which the land and other
necessary inputs are acquired, however, is a separate problem.

The proper economic justification for forcing the *sale* of land is instead
to overcome a supply-side failure, the holdout problem, which is a form of
monopoly power that can impede the efficient assembly of land. The source
of this problem is a scale economy, or complementarity, associated with
assembly, which gives individual sellers the ability to bargain for prices
in excess of what they would ordinarily have been willing to accept in a
voluntary, or market, transaction. Eminent domain allows the would-be
buyer to overcome this problem, and thus to achieve the gains from assembly, by depriving sellers of the right to refuse the purchases.

The problem with this explanation for eminent domain, however, and
the source of much of the resulting debate over the meaning of the public
use requirement, is that it does not provide a logical basis for limiting use of
the takings power to public projects. This is true because private and public
land assemblers alike can be plagued by holdouts. Recognizing this, courts
have historically tended to rule in a manner consistent with economic theory by generally allowing the extension of eminent domain power to private
entrepreneurs facing significant holdout problems, such as railroad builders
and urban re-developers. However, in an effort to satisfy the literal meaning
of the public use requirement, courts have typically rationalized their rulings in terms of the spillover benefits that would inure to the public from
these projects (the "public purpose") rather than pointing to the need to
overcome holdouts. The resulting confusion over ends versus means – what
I called the paradox of public use – has only served to muddy the debate.

In identifying the holdout problem as the proper economic rationale for eminent domain, however, economic theory does not necessarily sanction its use for any and all private projects facing holdouts. Indeed, there are at least two legitimate arguments for circumscribing the extension of eminent domain power to private developers. The first is that developers often have the ability to use alternative strategies (like secret buying agents) to overcome holdouts, whereas the government, because of its need to act in the open, does not. Second, private parties who stand to benefit from the use of eminent domain will have an incentive to engage in rent seeking or other inefficient (and possibly illegal) actions in an effort to acquire the power. In contrast, such risks are smaller for truly public projects because the gains are, by definition, widely dispersed. Taken together, these factors argue for a balanced approach to public use under which courts would treat the holdout problem as a necessary, but not a sufficient, condition for extending the power of eminent domain to private parties.

Lesson 2: The use of fair market value as the measure of just compensation undercompensates most landowners compared to what they would have received in a consensual transaction. According to economic theory, the benchmark for an efficient transfer is consensual exchange, but the requirement of consent can be a double-edged sword when it comes to efficiency. On the one hand, consent ensures that both parties must expect to receive a benefit from any transaction that is completed, but on the other, it potentially prevents some otherwise efficient transactions from taking place at all if bargaining is costly. Thus, consensual exchange may result in some foregone gains. The substitution of a forced sale for a consensual exchange will likely have the opposite effect; that is, it will enhance efficiency by overcoming impediments to bargaining (like the holdout problem), but it may also result in too many transfers if the price of the exchange is set too low. Thus, in any forced exchange, setting the proper price is a crucial requirement for ensuring efficiency; this is the economic function of the just compensation requirement of the eminent domain clause.

The problem, however, is that a third party (the court) has to set the price, and the legally accepted definition of just compensation, fair market value, is systematically biased downward compared to what a landowner would voluntarily accept. The reason for this is that market value reflects what someone else is willing to pay for a particular piece of property (as measured, for example, by recent sales of comparable properties), not what the current owner would ask in a consensual exchange. Thus, by forcing a sale at this price, eminent domain deprives a seller of that portion of his or her true valuation in excess of the property's market value (the subjective value component), as well the opportunity to bargain for a share of the surplus from the transaction.

In terms of efficiency, the resulting undercompensation has several consequences. First, it can lead to the excessive transfer of land to public use because buyers do not face the true opportunity cost of the land they acquire. Second, it imposes an uninsurable loss on risk-averse landowners, given that market insurance against takings is not generally available. And third, it creates an incentive for local governments to force sales that may be inefficient but would nevertheless increase their tax bases by allowing them to capture a share of the current owner's subjective value, which under market value assessment is effectively exempted from taxation.

The chief difficulty in ensuring that "just" compensation equals "full" compensation in an economic sense is that subjective value is unobservable and hence can be misrepresented by owners (one consequence of which is the holdout problem). Economists have devised various mechanisms that could theoretically induce truthful revelation, but none is really a practical solution. And, even if subjective value could be observed, there are some good economic arguments against paying it. One arises in the context of private development projects for which eminent domain is allowed (for example, urban redevelopment). Because these projects often involve external benefits that are not fully captured by the developer, there is an economic justification for subsidizing them. Paying less than full compensation is one way to do that, but because the optimal subsidy will not generally coincide with the unpaid subjective value, it is probably not the best way.

Another argument against paying full compensation is that the land market implicitly compensates owners at the time of purchase in the form of a price discount reflecting the risk of undercompensation from a future taking (or regulation). The logic of this capitalization argument is sound, but it only works once the threat of a taking is "in the air." Thus, owners at the time the threat first becomes public suffer an uncompensated loss. A third economic argument against paying full compensation is that it can lead to a moral hazard problem for owners of land that may be taken. This is the subject of the next lesson.

Lesson 3: Full compensation for takings creates a moral hazard problem that causes landowners to overinvest in land that is subject to a taking risk. Perhaps the most important contribution economists have made to the literature on eminent domain has been to point out the impact of compensation on land use incentives, and in particular to show that full compensation causes landowners to overinvestment in land that may be suitable for a taking (or regulation) at some point in the future. This conclusion, attributable to the moral hazard problem, is a standard result from the economics of insurance. Specifically, when a party is fully insured against the loss from an uncertain event, he or she has a reduced incentive to avoid that event or to mitigate any losses that might arise from it. And since full compensation is like insurance against a taking, landowners behave as if the risk of a taking – and the resulting loss of any improvements to their land – were zero. As a result, they overinvest.

One implication of this result is that a rule of paying zero compensation is efficient regarding landowner incentives because it eliminates the moral hazard problem. However, this prescription is both controversial and inconsistent with the constitutional requirement of just compensation. Thus, several counterarguments have been proposed. The most common one, noted earlier, is that positive compensation is necessary to prevent, or mitigate, the risk of excessive takings by the government. Although this suggests that the incentives of landowners and the government are in opposition, subsequent research has shown that there exist several compensation rules that can simultaneously induce efficient behavior by both parties. Such rules are based on a model of the government that views it as responding more or less as a private entrepreneur would in response to the cost of acquiring resources, rather than acting reflexively to maximize social welfare.

A somewhat different approach to the problem of choosing an optimal compensation rule views the government acting, not as a separate economic entity with its own objectives, but as an agent of citizens acting collectively to provide public goods, subject to the constraints imposed by a constitution which the citizens themselves had previously designed from behind a veil of ignorance regarding which particular parcels will be taken. In this original position, citizens know that they are both potential takings victims and taxpayers who will have to finance the cost of any compensation that the constitution authorizes. According to this argument, rational individuals will therefore design the compensation rule to balance the risk of excessive takings by the government if compensation is set too low, against the incentive of landowners to overinvest in land that may be suitable for a taking if compensation is set too high.

The particular rule that emerges from this constitutional choice approach is sensitive to the assumptions that one makes regarding the objectives of the government (i.e., whether it is majoritarian or benevolent), and the manner in which taxes are assessed (i.e., whether they are proportional or lump sum). One noteworthy result is that if compensation and taxes are both calculated as proportions of market value (as they generally are in practice), and if taxes are used solely to finance compensation, then the amount of compensation will be irrelevant with regard to land use incentives and public good provision, both of which will be efficient. The reason for this surprising conclusion is that the tax and compensation distortions are exactly offsetting through the government's balanced budget condition.

Lesson 4: The efficient threshold compensation rule provides a unifying framework for understanding regulatory takings within the larger context of eminent domain law. An important debate in takings law concerns the question of whether government regulations that reduce the value of a piece of property without actually seizing title to it should ever result in compensation for the owner. In other words, do regulations ever cross the threshold separating police power actions that do not require compensation from physical takings that do? The extensive case law and scholarship in this area have offered mixed conclusions. One perspective has focused on the intent of the regulation, arguing that as long as it is aimed at protecting the health, safety, or welfare of the public, no compensation is required, regardless of how onerous the regulation is on landowners. The idea behind this view is that the law does not recognize a property right in those activities – whether they are called noxious uses or nuisances – that impose costs on others.

An opposing perspective looks instead at the impact of the regulation on the landowner and says that, regardless of the intent of the regulation, if it causes a sufficiently large reduction in the owner's property value, compensation is due. This perspective is epitomized by the diminution-of-value test. The current state of regulatory takings law appears to involve a balancing of these factors on a case-by-case basis, along with various other considerations, with no clear standard for how to weigh them.

The contribution of economic theory to this debate has been to provide a framework for applying this balancing test in a coherent and objective way. The approach is based on the fundamental trade-off, previously noted, between landowner moral hazard on the one hand and excessive government regulation (fiscal illusion) on the other, that has become a recurrent theme in the recent economics literature on takings. The particular insight that this approach has brought to the regulatory takings question is that efficiency of both the land use and regulatory decision can be achieved by a threshold rule that conditions the payment of compensation on whether or not the regulatory decision was efficiently made. According to this rule, compensation would be required if the regulation were inefficiently imposed, but not otherwise. Although the efficiency of this rule is not unique, this particular version (referred to as the ex post rule) has considerable appeal on both normative and positive grounds.

First, as a prescription of how courts should decide regulatory takings cases, the efficient ex post rule provides an objective test for determining when compensation should be awarded based on a straightforward cost-benefit calculation. It also minimizes the administrative costs associated with compensation because payment is not required for efficient regulations. And even though one may quibble about the ease with which courts can undertake the necessary balancing test, the approach is in principle no more demanding than what is required under ordinary negligence law. Second, as a positive matter, the proposed rule goes a long way toward explaining actual legal doctrine within a coherent framework, as discussed at length in Chapter 5. Most notably, the fact that no compensation is required in an efficient equilibrium is consistent with the refusal of courts to award compensation in most regulatory takings cases.

The preceding lessons were by no means intended to suggest that economic theory offers a complete account of how eminent domain law is or should be applied. To the extent that the law as a social institution serves purposes besides efficiency, like fairness or justice, economics will never be able to achieve that objective, no matter what area of law is being considered. (Of course, the same can be said of any theory that attempts to explain the whole of law from a single perspective.) Nor will economic theory adequately capture the political dimensions of the takings debate, which have come to dominate much of the popular discussion of the issue in recent times. Rather, the value of economics resides in its ability to provide a coherent and objective framework for understanding broad elements of legal doctrine, predicting its consequences, and proposing useful improvements. The reader may judge whether the arguments set forth in this book have met those criteria with respect to eminent domain law.

Appendix

This appendix provides technical details underlying the results presented in the various chapters, as well as notes on the relevant literature.

Chapter 1
Introduction: A Framework for Analysis

This section provides a brief review of the key efficiency concepts that economists typically employ in evaluating alternative allocations of resources. The first and most fundamental concept is Pareto efficiency (also referred to as Pareto optimality).

Pareto Efficiency

Consider the decision of how to divide a fixed quantity of goods or services between two individuals.[1] The Pareto-efficient divisions, or "allocations," are the best among all possible allocations in the sense that they meet the following two criteria. First, an allocation A is said to be *Pareto superior* to any other allocation B if both (all) individuals are at least as well off under A as compared to B, and at least one individual is strictly better off under A. Second, an allocation A is said to be *Pareto efficient* if there exists no other allocations that are Pareto superior to it. Pareto superiority thus provides a means of ranking any two allocations, whereas Pareto efficiency identifies the best among all feasible allocations.

An appealing feature of Pareto efficiency, as the previous definitions suggest, is that it is based on unanimous approval of any proposed

---

[1] The discussion here focuses on *exchange efficiency*, meaning the distribution of a fixed quantity of goods. *Production efficiency* concerns the manner in which the available resources (inputs) are most efficiently allocated to the production of various goods (outputs).

159

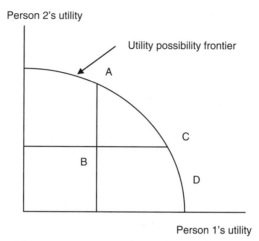

Figure A1.1. The utility possibility frontier and the definition of Pareto efficiency.

reallocation, given some initial entitlement point. In other words, any changes that are consistent with the Pareto criteria must be consensual in the sense that all individuals must approve of them (or at least not object to them). It is easy to show, however, that this unanimity requirement is also an important drawback of Pareto.

To see why, consider Figure A1.1, which illustrates the determination of the set of Pareto-efficient allocations in a two-person, pure exchange economy. The horizontal axis measures the satisfaction (or utility) of Person 1, and the vertical axis measures the satisfaction of Person 2. Starting from the origin, movements upward and to the right therefore yield higher levels of satisfaction for both individuals. The feasible points are limited, however, by the available resources, as indicated by the negatively sloped convex curve, called the utility possibility frontier. Only those points on or inside this frontier are attainable.

Now consider an arbitrary starting point inside the frontier, labeled B in the graph. Starting from this point, we can use the Pareto criterion to show that the "triangular" area ABC represents the set of allocations that are Pareto-superior to B. Notice, for example, that if we fix the utility of Person 1 and move vertically along the line segment BA, Person 2 becomes better off while leaving Person 1 no worse off. Likewise, if we fix the utility of Person 2 and move horizontally along segment BC, Person 1 becomes better off while Person 2 is no worse off. Movement to points inside the triangle obviously makes both people better off. It follows that point B cannot be Pareto efficient. The same logic applies to all points strictly inside area

ABC. Thus, the set of Pareto-efficient points, given the initial point B, are all of the points on the utility possibility frontier along the segment AC, considering that there is no further reallocation that can make both people better off. The only possible movements are along the frontier, which necessarily make one person better off and one person worse off. Such changes, however, cannot be evaluated using the Pareto criterion, so we say that these points are *non-comparable*.

The non-comparability of points on the utility frontier – the set of Pareto-efficient points – is an important shortcoming of the Pareto criterion, but the non-comparability problem is worse than that. Consider, for example, a comparison between point D, which is on the frontier and hence is Pareto efficient, and point B, which we have already seen is not Pareto efficient. Notice that they are also non-comparable by the Pareto criterion because movement from B to D makes Person 2 worse off. Thus, we arrive at the paradoxical conclusion that point D, an efficient point, and point B, an inefficient point, cannot be ranked by Pareto. The reason for this problem is that the definition of Pareto efficiency depends on the initial allocation, which establishes the minimally acceptable level of utility for all individuals in relation to any proposed reallocation away from that initial point.

The non-comparability problem is especially significant when it comes to evaluating actual legal or economic policy questions because most (if not all) interesting proposals involve changes that would help one group of individuals at the expense of others. For this reason, Pareto efficiency is not very useful in evaluating policy changes that involve both winners and losers.

Kaldor-Hicks efficiency

To address this problem, economists have developed a modified version of Pareto efficiency, referred to as Kaldor-Hicks efficiency or potential Pareto efficiency. To understand the logic of this criterion, consider the proposed movement from B to D in Figure A1.1. If that movement required Person 1 (the gainer) to compensate Person 2 (the loser) and still left Person 1 with a net gain, then it would represent a Pareto-superior change. For example, suppose the movement from B to D yielded Person 1 a gain of $500 but cost Person 2 $400. Person 1 would thus still enjoy a surplus of $100 after fully compensating Person 2.

In many cases, of course, the actual payment of compensation is either impractical or impossible. Recognizing this, we say that point D is more efficient than point B in a Kaldor-Hicks sense because the movement produces a positive net gain. That is, the gainers could *potentially* compensate the losers and still be better off. Notice, therefore, that the Kaldor-Hicks criterion essentially involves a cost-benefit analysis – changes in policy or law are viewed as efficient if they produce larger aggregate gains than losses. By extension, the "best" (most efficient) policy or law according to Kaldor-Hicks is one that maximizes net wealth in the sense that it exhausts all value-enhancing changes.

A Word on Efficiency, Fairness, and Takings

The economic theory of eminent domain as surveyed in this book will employ the Kaldor-Hicks notion of efficiency. It is worth noting, however, that the requirement of "just compensation" in the Fifth Amendment Takings Clause can be interpreted as ensuring that losers are actually compensated – in other words, that any takings satisfy the more stringent criteria of Pareto. If this is true, then the taking effectively becomes consensual because, in theory, the landowner should not object to it. In reality, of course, compensation is not always full (see Chapter 3), and in the case of some regulations, is not paid at all (see Chapter 5). In consequence, the analysis in this book will separate questions of efficiency, which will be judged based on the Kaldor-Hicks criterion, and compensation, which will be treated more as a distributional, or fairness question (though with possible efficiency consequences).

   Notes on the literature. The material in this section is adapted from Miceli (2009a, chapter 1). For a more detailed discussion of economic efficiency, also in a law and economics context, see the Appendix to chapter 1 in Mercuro and Medema (1997).

Chapter 2
Public Use

This section presents a formal model of the holdout problem in the context of land assembly, where the cost of holdouts is modeled as a delay in completion of the project. It also shows how the threat of eminent domain can prevent holdouts.

The Holdout Problem

Consider a development project (public or private) that requires the assembly of two contiguous parcels of land. Let

   V = gross value of the project if completed;
   v = value of each parcel to its current owner (and also the value of a single parcel to the developer);

where

$$V > 2v. \tag{A2.1}$$

Thus, the project is socially valuable in the sense that the aggregate value of the parcels, once assembled, is larger than the sum of their individual values.

Suppose that bargaining between the developer and the owners for purchase of the parcels can take place in two periods: "now" (period one) and "later" (period two). The project can proceed if both parcels are acquired by the end of period two; otherwise, it must be scrapped. However, completion of the project now rather than later is more valuable. To capture this, assume there is a cost of delay of δ dollars for each parcel acquired later, though assembly is still valuable. That is,

$$V - 2\delta > 2v. \tag{A2.2}$$

After period two, however, the project is worthless.

The equilibrium is derived in reverse sequence of time. Thus, suppose that both sellers refused to sell in the first period (i.e., both were holdouts). Because period two is the last period during which the project can be completed, it is in the joint interests of the parties to reach an agreement. Assume, therefore, that both owners sell. Also assume, for simplicity, that the sellers acquire all of the surplus from the sale and divide it equally. Thus, each receives a price of $V/2-\delta$, which, by (A2.2), is greater than their individual reservation prices, v.

Now consider the case where one seller – call her Seller 1 – sold in period one for a price equal to P_1, while the other seller, Seller 2, held out. Again, it is in the interest of Seller 2 to sell in period two so that the project can go forward. To determine the maximum amount the developer is willing to pay for the second parcel, denoted P_2, note that his return if he completes the sale is $V-\delta-P_1-P_2$ (since acquisition of only parcel two was delayed), whereas if he fails to acquire the second parcel, his return is simply $v-P_1$ (since the project is scrapped). Equating these returns and solving for P_2 yields

$$P_2 = V - \delta - v. \tag{A2.3}$$

Substituting this expression into the developer's overall return from the project and setting the result equal to zero yields the expression for P_1:

$$P_1 = v. \tag{A2.4}$$

Comparison of (A2.3) and (A2.4) immediately reveals that $P_2 > P_1$ by (A2.2). Thus, it is better to be the lone holdout rather than to be the lone seller in period one.

Table A2.1. *Payoff matrix for the sellers' entry game*

		Seller 2	
		Now	Later
Seller 1	Now	$V/2, V/2$	$v, V-\delta-v$
	Later	$V-\delta-v, v$	$V/2-\delta, V/2-\delta$

Finally, suppose that both sellers agree to sell in period one. Because there is no cost of delay in this case, each seller obtains a price of $V/2$. It follows that it is better for both sellers to sell in period one rather than for both to sell in period two because this avoids the cost of delay. However, it is also the case that $P_2 > V/2$ by (A2.2), and $P_2 > V/2-\delta$ by (A2.1). Thus, it is better to be the lone holdout than to sell jointly in either period one or two.

We are now in a position to derive the equilibrium strategies of the two sellers. Assume that in deciding when to bargain with the developer, the sellers do not cooperate with each other but instead pursue their individual self-interests, taking the behavior of the other seller as given. That is, they play a non-cooperative "entry" game. The available strategies to each player are "now" and "later," where "now" means sell in period one and "later" means hold out in period one and sell in period two. Table A2.1 contains the payoffs to each player from the various combinations of strategies. (This payoff matrix is a general version of Table 2.2 in the text.) Given these relationships, it is easy to verify that this game has the structure of a prisoner's dilemma. Thus, the dominant strategy for both sellers is to sell later, even though both would be better off if they sold now.

It is important to note that this holdout problem is a result of strategic behavior by the two sellers during the entry game rather than a breakdown in bargaining in any given period. (Indeed, we have assumed that whenever a seller chooses to enter, she successfully completes a bargain with the developer.) Thus, for example, if there were a single seller, there would be no advantage of waiting to sell. This illustrates the point that a true holdout problem can only occur in the case of land assembly.

Bargaining in the Shadow of Eminent Domain

Now suppose that the buyer first tries to bargain with the sellers in period one, but also has the power to use eminent domain in period two to take any parcels that he could not acquire in a consensual trade. Let the amount of compensation sellers receive under eminent domain be given by m, where $m \leq v$, reflecting the fact that market value compensation is generally less than the owner's true valuation. It may also reflect the transaction costs associated with a non-consensual sale.

As above, we begin in period two and assume that neither parcel sold in period one. In that case, the buyer will take both parcels by eminent domain if

$$V - 2\delta > 2m \qquad (A2.5)$$

which holds by (A2.2) given $m \leq v$. Likewise, if one parcel sold in period one at price P_1, the buyer will take the second parcel in period two by eminent domain if

$$V - \delta - P_1 - m > v - P_1,$$

or if

$$V - \delta > m + v, \qquad (A2.6)$$

which again holds by (A2.2). Thus, the buyer's threat to use eminent domain in period two to take one or both parcels is credible.

Now move back to period one. If both sellers bargain, we assume, as previously mentioned, that they each obtain a price of $V/2$. Alternatively, if one sells at P_1 while the other holds out, the buyer will take the second parcel in period two for m, as just described. The buyer's overall return in that case is $V - \delta - P_1 - m$. Equating this to zero and solving for P_1 yields

$$P_1 = V - \delta - m. \qquad (A2.7)$$

Comparing this price to the expressions in (A2.3) and (A2.4) shows that, in contrast to the above model, the bargaining advantage now resides with the first-period seller rather than with the first period holdout, given that any seller who holds out loses all bargaining power.

The resulting payoff matrix for the sellers' entry game is given by Table A2.2. It should be easy to verify that the unique Nash equilibrium of this game is for both sellers to enter and bargain in period one. Thus, the holdout problem is eliminated, and eminent domain is never actually used.

As a final point, note that although eminent domain overcomes holdouts, it may allow inefficient projects to go forward. To see this, recall that the condition for the project to be efficient in the current model is (A2.2), whereas the condition for the threat of eminent domain to be credible is (A2.5). As noted, the assumption that $m \leq v$ implies that (A2.2) is sufficient, but not necessary, for (A2.5) to hold. In other words, eminent domain will allow all efficient projects to go forward, but it may

Table A2.2. *Payoff matrix for the sellers' entry game when the buyer has eminent domain power in period two*

		Seller 2	
		Now	Later
Seller 1	Now	$V/2, V/2$	$V–\delta–m, m$
	Later	$m, V–\delta–m$	m, m

allow some inefficient ones to proceed as well if $m < v$. This risk of excessive acquisitions under market-value compensation is addressed in more detail in Chapter 3.

Notes on the literature. The model in this section is a simplified version of one developed in Miceli and Segerson (2007). The current model is simpler in the sense that it does not allow the buyer to capture any of the surplus from period one bargaining. The basic conclusions, however, are unaffected by this simplification. Also see Menezes and Pitchford (2004), Dixit and Olson (2000), and Strange (1995) for related models. Shavell (2010) develops a model in which eminent domain may be justified even if sellers do not behave strategically to exploit their monopoly power. The value of eminent domain in his model is to overcome the developer's inability to observe the reservation prices of sellers, which may prevent assembly of all necessary parcels by consensual means. Malaith and Postlewaite (1990) study the more general problem of several individuals trying to reach an agreement to share the cost of providing a public good when individual valuations are private knowledge. Finally, Heller (1998, 1999, 2008) notes that the holdout problem is a special case of the more general anti-commons problem. For a formal model of the anti-commons problem, see Buchanan and Yoon (2000).

Chapter 3

Just Compensation

Tax-motivated Takings and the Proposed Reassessment Scheme
Consider a proposed development project that requires the assembly of n identical parcels. Let

V = aggregate value of the project;
R = reservation price of each parcel (i.e., the true value to each owner);
A = assessed value of each parcel, where $A < R$;

t = property tax rate;

G = level of government spending.[2]

Let X be the amount that the developer offers for each of the parcels. Thus, if the project goes forward, the aggregate assessed value of the parcels will be nX, whereas its current assessed value is nA. The government will therefore receive increased revenue, and hence, will want the project to go forward, if $X > A$ (holding the tax rate fixed). In contrast, the condition for the project to be efficient is $V > nR$. Generally, these two conditions will not coincide. To see this, note that the maximum amount the developer will offer for each parcel is given by

$$X = V/n - tX, \qquad (A3.1)$$

which represents his zero-profit condition.

As for the individual sellers, if we ignore the holdout problem, the minimum amount each will accept to sell is $R - tA$, which is the owner's true value of his parcel net of its tax liability. Thus, the owners will sell if $X \geq R{-}tA$, or, substituting from (A3.1), if

$$V \geq nR + nt(X{-}A). \qquad (A3.2)$$

According to this condition, if $X > A$, some projects that are efficient – that is, for which $V > nR$ – will not go forward. In other words, there will be too few transactions from a social perspective. This reflects the implicit subsidy that landowners enjoy as a result of the exemption of their subjective value from taxation. On the other hand, the government has an incentive to force any transactions for which $X > A$ in order to increase its tax revenue. This could result in some projects going forward even if $V < nR$.

To eliminate these possible inefficiencies, suppose that any owner who turns down a legitimate offer, X, will have his or her property reassessed at that amount. Now, the minimum amount the owner will accept is $R - tX$. Thus, given the developer's offer of X, a transaction will occur if $X \geq R{-}tX$. Substituting once again from (A3.1), this condition becomes $V \geq nR$, which is the efficient condition.

The preceding analysis relied on the assumption that all parcels were identical. Suppose, more realistically, that owners differ in their reservation

[2] I assume here that both the tax rate and level of government spending would be unaffected by the redevelopment project. This will be true for t if n is small relative to the overall number of parcels in the jurisdiction, and it will be true for G if the redevelopment does not put significant demands on the public budget in the form of infrastructure, demand for police protection, and so on.

prices, denoted R_j for owner j, though (for simplicity) assume that they all have the same assessment, A. In this case, the condition for an efficient sale is

$$V \geq \Sigma_j R_j$$

or

$$V/n \geq (\Sigma_j R_j)/n. \tag{A3.3}$$

That is, the per-parcel value of the project must exceed the average reservation price of the owners. The developer's maximum offer for each parcel continues to be given by (A3.1). As for owner j, she will accept the offer if $X \geq R_j - tX$ under the proposed reassessment scheme. After substituting for X from (A3.1), this condition becomes

$$V/n \geq R_j. \tag{A3.4}$$

Thus, even if (A3.3) holds, meaning that the project is efficient, owners with above-average reservation prices may turn down the developer's offer. In contrast to the case of identical parcels, therefore, the proposed scheme may result in too few projects going forward. In this case, eminent domain may still be necessary to allow efficient projects to proceed. Nevertheless, the scheme retains the virtue of eliminating the government's incentive to use eminent domain to promote inefficient projects purely for tax purposes.

   Notes on the literature. The analysis of tax motivated takings is based on Miceli, Segerson, and Sirmans (2008).

Compensation and Insurance
If landowners are risk averse, then compensation for takings can serve as a form of social insurance against takings risk. To show this formally, suppose landowners have utility over wealth given by $U(w)$, where $U' > 0$ and $U'' < 0$. In the presence of a takings risk, the wealth of landowners in the "no-takings" and "takings" states, respectively, are given by

$$w_N = y - T + V, \tag{A3.5}$$
$$w_T = y - T + C, \tag{A3.6}$$

where
   $y =$ income;
   $V =$ land value;
   $T =$ taxes assessed to pay compensation in the event of a taking;[3]
   $C =$ compensation in the event of a taking.

---

[3]   I assume that taxes are assessed in both the taking and no-taking states.

Suppose that p is the probability of a taking. Then the landowner's expected utility is

$$EU = pU(y-T+C) + (1-p)U(y-T+V). \qquad (A3.7)$$

Because the public budget must be balanced,

$$T = pC. \qquad (A3.8)$$

The optimal compensation rule is found by maximizing (A3.7) subject to (A3.8). Substituting (A3.8) into (A3.7) and differentiating with respect to C yields the first-order condition

$$U'(w_T) = U'(w_N), \qquad (A3.9)$$

from which it follows that $w_T = w_N$. Using (A3.5) and (A3.6), we obtain $C = V$, or compensation should be full.

Notes on the literature: Blume and Rubinfeld (1984, 1987) and Kaplow (1986, 1992) examine the insurance argument for compensation.

Capitalization and Compensation
To demonstrate the capitalization argument formally, let

V = market value of a piece of property if unregulated;
V_R = market value of the property if regulated, where $0 \le V_R < V$;
p = probability that a regulation will be imposed;
C = compensation paid to the owner in the event of a regulation.

Suppose that the current owner wishes to sell the property after the regulatory threat has become public knowledge. Assuming that both buyers and sellers are risk neutral, the maximum amount a rational buyer would be willing to pay for the property would be

$$(1-p)V + p(V_R+C), \qquad (A3.10)$$

which reflects both the risk of the regulation and the expected compensation.

In the case of zero compensation, the buyer would only pay $(1-p)V + pV_R < V$. Thus, if the regulation were subsequently imposed, he would not have a good argument for compensation because the sale price was appropriately discounted. The seller, on the other hand, *would* have a good argument because at the time the possibility of the regulation was announced, he suffered a capital loss equal to the difference between the discounted sale price and V, the value of the land in the absence of a regulatory threat. His loss in this case would be $V - [(1-p)V + pV_R] = p(V - V_R)$.

One way to eliminate the original owner's loss would therefore be to pay full compensation, or $C = V - V_R$, to the buyer at the time the regulation is actually enacted. Substituting this amount into (A3.10) yields V, which means that the seller suffers no loss at the time of sale. Alternatively, suppose the original owner/seller is given the right to assert a takings claim at the time of sale. In that case, the buyer would pay a price equal to $(1-p)V + pV_R$ because he would have no takings claim later (i.e., $C = 0$), but the seller would receive compensation equal to $p(V - V_R)$ at the time of sale, yielding him an overall return of $(1-p)V + pV_R + p(V - V_R) = V$. Again, his loss is eliminated.

Notes on the literature. Michelman (1967) first made the argument that capitalization eliminates the need to compensate buyers of land because the discounted price provides implicit compensation. Epstein (1985, pp. 151–158) and Fischel and Shapiro (1988, pp. 287–289) pointed out the error in his reasoning. Stein (2000) discussed the two remedies aimed at compensating the original owner. Miceli and Segerson (1996, chapter 6) analyzed capitalization and takings more formally.

Chapter 4
Land Use Incentives

This section develops a simple version of the BRS model and then examines the various extensions to it. The basic model uses the following notation:

$V(x)$ = market value of a piece of land after x dollars of improvements have been made, where $V' > 0$, and $V'' < 0$;

p = probability that the land will be taken for public use;

B = fixed value of the land in public use if taken;

$C(x)$ = compensation paid to the owner in the event of a taking.

The timing of events is as follows: First the landowner decides how much to invest in improving his land, and then the taking decision occurs. The owner's initial investment is irreversible, so if the land is taken, its value in private use, $V(x)$, as well as the cost of the investment, x, are lost.

In the simple model where the taking occurs randomly, the only economic decision is the owner's choice of x. The socially optimal investment maximizes the expected social value of the land:

$$pB + (1-p)V(x) - x. \tag{A4.1}$$

The resulting first order condition is

$$(1-p)V'(x) = 1, \tag{A4.2}$$

which defines the optimal investment, x^*. Note that the amount of investment is decreasing in p. Thus, as the probability of a taking increases, the landowner should invest less so as to reduce the loss in the event of a taking.

The No-compensation Result
Now consider the actual choice of x by the landowner. His goal is to maximize his expected private return from the land, which is given by

$$pC(x) + (1-p)V(x) - x. \tag{A4.3}$$

Note that this expression differs from (A4.1) by the first term. The first order condition defining the owner's optimal investment is

$$pC'(x) + (1-p)V'(x) = 1. \tag{A4.4}$$

Comparing (A4.4) and (A4.2) shows that $C'=0$ is a sufficient condition for efficiency; that is, lump sum compensation induces efficient investment. A special case of lump sum compensation is $C \equiv 0$, or zero compensation. Intuitively, zero compensation prevents the owner from overinvesting in his land because he thereby internalizes the loss that would result if the land is taken. This is the "no-compensation result" of BRS.

Arguments in Favor of Compensation
Several counterarguments have been advanced in favor of compensation. These arguments can be categorized based on the assumption that is made about the government's behavior.

(*i*) *Endogenous probability of a taking: benevolent (Pigovian) government.* Consider first the case where the government makes the taking decision to maximize social welfare. To capture this formally, let the value of the land in public use, B, now be a random variable whose value is only learned after the landowner invests x. A benevolent government will only take the land if it turns out to be worth more in public than in private use, given x. Thus, once B, is realized, a taking will occur if and only if $B \geq V(x)$. Let $F(B)$ be the distribution function of B, where $F'(B) \equiv f(B)$ is the density. The landowner is assumed to know $F(B)$, so that at the time he makes his investment decision, he knows that the probability of a taking is equal to $1 - F(V(x))$ for any x.

The socially optimal choice of x now maximizes

$$F(V(x))V(x) + [1 - F(V(x))]E[B \mid B \geq V(x)] - x$$

$$= F(V(x))V(x) + \int_{V(x)}^{\infty} BdF(B) - x \tag{A4.5}$$

The resulting first order condition is

$$F(V(x))V'(x) = 1, \qquad (A4.6)$$

which has the same interpretation as (A4.2), with $F(V(x))$ replacing $1-p$ as the probability that the land will not be taken. The expected private value of the land in this case is given by

$$F(V(x))V(x) + [1-F(V(x))]C(x) - x. \qquad (A4.7)$$

The resulting first order condition for x is

$$F(V(x))V'(x) + [1-F(V(x))]C'(x)$$
$$+ F'(V(x))V'(x)[V(x)-C(x)] = 1. \qquad (A4.8)$$

Comparison of (A4.8) and (A4.6) shows that lump-sum compensation ($C'=0$) is no longer sufficient for efficiency. Instead, compensation must be equal to the full value of the land at its efficient level of investment, or $C=V(x^*)$. Intuitively, full compensation is necessary to prevent the landowner from either overinvesting or underinvesting to alter the probability of a taking. Specifically, if $C(x) < V(x)$, the final term on the left-hand side of (A4.8) is positive. Thus, the landowner will have an incentive to overinvest in order to reduce the probability of a taking because he expects to be undercompensated. Conversely, if $C(x) > V(x)$, he will have an incentive to underinvest to increase the probability of a taking because he expects to be overcompensated. Only a rule of full compensation, or $C(x) = V(x)$, will eliminate this incentive. Combining this result with the lump-sum requirement yields the efficient rule, $C = V(x^*)$.[4]

The preceding compensation rule is not the only one that induces efficient investment in this case. Suppose instead that $C=B$; that is, the government must pay the landowner the full value of the public project in the event of a taking (the gain-based compensation rule). In this case, the landowner internalizes the social value of the land, as given in (A4.5), and therefore makes the efficient investment choice. Alternatively, suppose that compensation is zero in the event of a taking, but the owner has the option to keep the land by paying the government its social value, B. A rational owner will exercise this "buy-back" option if and only if $B < V(x)$.

---

[4] If Cooter's (1985) option approach were used, the option price, P, would replace $C(x)$ in (A4.7). The first order condition in (A4.8) would thus become $F(V(x))V'(x)+F'(V(x))$ $V'(x)[V(x)-P]=1$. (Note that the C' term drops out here because the price is viewed as fixed with respect to the investment choice, x.) It follows that $P=V(x^*)$ for efficiency.

Thus, only efficient takings will go forward. (Note, therefore, that the government's decision about when to initiate a taking is immaterial, as long as it truthfully reveals B to the landowner. I assume that a benevolent government does this.) Under this rule, the landowner's expected return is equal to

$$F(V(x))E[V(x)-B \mid V(x) > B] + [1-F(V(x))] \cdot 0 - x$$

$$= \int_0^{V(x)} [V(x)-B]dF(B)-x \qquad (A4.9)$$

Maximizing (A4.9) with respect to x yields the first order condition in (A4.6). Thus, the landowner makes the efficient investment choice.

(*ii*) *Endogenous probability of a taking: non-benevolent government.* Suppose now that the government makes its taking decision by comparing the value of the public project to the amount of compensation that it must pay in the event of a taking rather than to the opportunity cost of the land. Such a government is said to have "fiscal illusion" in that it only considers the budgetary impacts of its actions. In this case, the government will initiate a taking if and only if $B \geq C(x)$, which implies that the probability of a taking is $1-F(C(x))$, given x.

An obvious way to induce the government to make the correct taking decision in this case is to set $C = V(x)$ (full compensation), but this rule will revive the moral hazard problem. One solution is to set $C = V(x^*)$, which solves both the fiscal illusion problem (because compensation is full), and the moral hazard problem (because compensation is a lump sum). Alternatively, let $C = B$, which, as we saw earlier, solves the moral hazard problem. As for the government's taking decision, because the gain-based rule requires it to pay the full value of any project, it will be indifferent between undertaking the project and not undertaking it. The landowner, however, will only want the taking to occur if $B \geq V(x)$, which is the efficient condition (given x). Thus, if the government follows the wishes of the landowner, the rule will be (weakly) efficient regarding the taking decision.

Finally, consider the buy-back rule. Again, the landowner will control the taking decision in this case, and will do so efficiently because he or she will buy back the land if and only if $B < V(x)$. And because we showed earlier that this rule also solves the moral hazard problem, it will achieve efficiency of both the land use and takings decisions.

The Constitutional Choice Model
Let:

> n = total number of identical parcels subject to a taking risk;
> s = number of parcels actually taken for public use, $s \leq n$;
> $B(s)$ = social value of the taken land, $B' > 0$, $B'' < 0$.
> T = per-person tax liability to finance compensation.

All other variables are defined as previously presented. The public good, B, is assumed to be pure in the sense that it is enjoyed by all landowners, including those whose land is taken. The tax is also assessed on all landowners. (Neither of these assumptions is essential.)

In this model, landowners, acting collectively from behind a veil of ignorance, choose the number of parcels to take. However, which particular parcels will be taken is only revealed after landowners have made their investment decisions. Thus, in the initial state, each landowner assesses an equal probability, p, that his or her parcel will be taken, where $p = s/n$. The probability that a parcel will not be taken is therefore $1 - p = (n-s)/n$.

Given this model, the wealth of landowners in the "no-taking" and "taking" states, respectively, are given by

$$w_N = V(x) - T + B(s) - x \tag{A4.10}$$
$$w_T = C(x) - T + B(s) - x. \tag{A4.11}$$

The expected wealth of each landowner is therefore

$$E(w) = (1-p)V(x) + pC(x) - T + B(s) - x. \tag{A4.12}$$

The public budget must be balanced, so $nT = sC$, or, using the definition of p,

$$T = pC. \tag{A4.13}$$

(This assumes that the tax is assessed solely to finance compensation for takings.)

As in the BRS model, landowners choose x to maximize their expected wealth, taking the compensation rule as a given. In the current model, they also take as a given the amount of land to be taken, s (or, equivalently, the probability of a taking). The new element here is the tax payment, T. If landowners also treat T as fixed (as if it were a lump-sum tax), then the first order condition emerging from (A4.12) would be identical to that in (A4.4), and the BRS result would obtain. (That is, $C' = 0$ is a sufficient condition for efficient investment.) But suppose, more realistically, that taxes are assessed proportionately on property values. That is, let $T = tV(x)$, where t is the property tax rate. Also, suppose that compensation is defined as a proportion of land value, or $C(x) = \alpha V(x)$ for some parameter α. Substituting these expressions for T and $C(x)$ into (A4.12), and taking the derivative with respect to x yields the first order condition

$$(1-p)V'(x) + p\alpha V'(x) - tV'(x) = 1,$$

or

$$(1-p)V'(x) + (p\alpha - t)V'(x) = 1. \tag{A4.14}$$

Now observe that, according to the balanced-budget condition in (A4.13), $tV(x) = p\alpha V(x)$, or $t = \alpha p$. Thus, the second term on the left-hand side of (A4.14) vanishes, yielding (A4.2). The landowner therefore makes the efficient investment choice for any value of α. In other words, *the compensation rule is irrelevant with respect to the land use decision.* The reason for this result is that the compensation and tax distortions exactly offset through the balanced-budget condition.

Finally, consider the decision about how much land to take. As noted, landowners, acting from behind a veil of ignorance, choose s, the amount of land to devote to public use, to maximize their expected wealth in (A4.12), subject to the balanced budget condition in (A4.13). Note that in making this choice, they recognize the fact that $p(s) = s/n$. The resulting first order condition for s, after canceling terms, is

$$nB'(s) = V(x), \tag{A4.15}$$

which is the Samuelson condition for a pure public good. That is, land should be devoted to public use until the marginal benefit of the last unit taken equals its opportunity cost in private use. Thus, landowners authorize the efficient amount of takings for any given x. As was true of the land use decision, this result is independent of the form of the compensation rule and for the same reason.

Notes on the literature. The moral hazard problem associated with compensation was first examined in the seminal paper by Blume, Rubinfeld, and Shapiro (1984). They used a general equilibrium model to derive their famous no-compensation result, which is actually a special case of their more general conclusion that compensation must be a lump sum. They also considered various extensions, including the case of a government with fiscal illusion. Papers that have followed up on BRS include Miceli (1991a), Miceli and Segerson (1994), Hermalin (1995), Giammarino and Nosal (2005), Tideman and Plassmann (2005), and Niemann and Shapiro (2008). The constitutional choice approach to the takings question was developed by Fischel and Shapiro (1989). Subsequent papers in this vein include Nosal (2001) and Miceli (2008).

The Timing of Development

To investigate the impact of compensation on the timing of development, consider the following two-period model of the land use decision. Let

V_N = present value of the land if developed now;

V_L = present value of the land if developed later;

p = probability that there will be a social benefit from preventing development in the future, given no development now;

B = the resulting social benefit from prohibiting development in the future (either in the form of an explicit benefit or a foregone harm);

V_0 = residual value of the land to the landowner if development is prohibited, where $0 \leq V_0 < V_L$;

C = compensation paid to landowners who are prohibited from developing in the future.

Assume that development in the present period cannot be prevented, and that once it goes forward, the social benefit from prohibiting development can never be realized. Also assume that if the land is not developed in period one and B is not realized in period two, then the optimal course of action is to develop the land (i.e., there is no chance that B will be realized in some future period).

The key question in this setting is whether or not it is optimal for the landowner to develop the land now or to wait. If he develops now, the social (and also private) value of the land is fixed at V_N, whereas if he waits, the expected social value is $p(B+V_0)+(1-p)V_L$. Thus, waiting preserves the option to use the land for the public project. It is therefore socially optimal to wait if and only if

$$p(B+V_0) + (1-p)V_L > V_N. \qquad (A4.16)$$

From the landowner's perspective, if he develops now, his return is V_N, whereas if he waits, it is $p(C+V_0)+(1-p)V_L$, which differs from the social value by the inclusion of C rather than B in the first term. He will therefore choose to wait if and only if

$$p(C+V_0) + (1-p)V_L > V_N. \qquad (A4.17)$$

Comparing (A4.16) and (A4.17) reveals that the only compensation rule that guarantees that the landowner will make the correct decision is $C=B$. Any lesser amount of compensation, including zero compensation, runs the risk of causing premature development. (The minimal amount of compensation needed to forestall early development would be found by writing [A4.17] as an equality and solving for *C*.)

Alternatively, the government could tax "early" development. That is, if the landowner develops now, he must pay a tax *T*. In this case, the landowner will wait if and only if

$$pV_0 + (1-p)V_L > V_N - T. \tag{A4.18}$$

Again, comparing (A4.18) with (A4.16) shows that setting $T = pB$ – that is, setting the tax equal to the expected value of future development – induces the correct decision by the landowner.

Notes on the literature. The timing issue was first examined by Miceli and Segerson (1996, chapter 8). Also see Innes (1997), Riddiough (1997), Turnbull (2002), and Lueck and Michael (2003).

The Model of Precaution as Applied to Torts, Contracts, and Takings

The model of precaution as originally developed in the context of tort, or accident law, is described as follows. Let

$x =$ victim's dollar investment in precaution;
$y =$ injurer's dollar investment in precaution;
$L(x,y) =$ expected dollar loss suffered by the victim in the event of an accident, where $L_x < 0$, and $L_{xx} > 0$, $L_y < 0$, $L_{yy} > 0$.[5]

The social problem is to choose *x* and *y* to minimize social costs as given by

$$x + y + L(x,y). \tag{A4.19}$$

The first order conditions simultaneously defining the optimal levels of precaution, x^* and y^*, are therefore

$$1 + L_x = 0, \tag{A4.20}$$
$$1 + L_y = 0. \tag{A4.21}$$

Now consider the actual levels of precaution under strict liability (full compensation for victims) and no liability (no compensation for victims). Under strict liability, the injurer will expect to face the victim's full loss, *L*, and hence will choose efficient precaution (conditional on the victim's choice of care), whereas the victim will bear none of the damages and will choose zero precaution. Conversely, under no liability, the injurer will take

---

[5] The expected loss is sometimes decomposed into the probability of an accident, $p(x,y)$ and the damages in the event of an accident, $D(x,y)$. Thus, $L(x,y) \equiv p(x,y)D(x,y)$.

zero precaution and the victim will take efficient precaution (conditional on the injurer's choice of care).[6] Thus, neither rule induces efficient care by both parties.

It turns out, however, that efficient care by both parties can be achieved by a negligence rule that sets a due standard of care for the injurer at his efficient level of care, y^*. To see why, note first that the injurer can avoid liability altogether by meeting the due standard, so that is his optimal strategy.[7] As a result, the victim expects to bear her own damages and so she chooses x to minimize $x + L(x,y^*)$, which yields x^*. Thus, the Nash equilibrium involves efficient care by both parties. Given the symmetry of the model, the same result can be achieved by a rule that sets a due standard for the victim at x^* (a contributory negligence standard), which could then be paired with the above "simple" negligence rule or with strict liability.

Consider next the application of this model to contract law. First redefine the variables as follows:

x = investment in reliance by the promisee;
y = probability of a breach by the promisor;
$V(x)$ = value of performance to the promisee, $V' > 0$, $V'' < 0$;
$B(y)$ = value of breach to the promisor, where B is first rising and then falling in y, and $B'' < 0$.

The social problem in this case is to choose x and y to maximize the joint value of the contract (including the possibility of a breach):

$$B(y) + (1-y)V(x) - x. \tag{A4.22}$$

The resulting first order conditions defining x^* and y^*, respectively, are

$$(1-y)V'(x) - 1 = 0. \tag{A4.23}$$
$$B'(y) - V(x) = 0. \tag{A4.24}$$

Now consider the impact of alternative remedies for breach. Under an expectation damages remedy, the promisee receives full compensation for

---

[6] Under both rules, the party taking care will adjust his or her care level up or down compared to the first best level (as defined by [A4.20] and [A4.21]) in response to the anticipated underinvestment in care by the other party. In the most likely scenario where injurer and victim care are substitutes (that is, $L_{xy} > 0$), the party taking care will raise his or her care level to compensate for the lower expected care level of the other party. For example, under strict liability, the injurer will choose y to solve $1 + L_y(0,y) = 0$, where, given $L_{xy} > 0$, the resulting level of y will exceed y^* because $x = 0 < x^*$. Conversely, under no liability, the victim will choose x to solve $1 + L_x(x,0) = 0$, where $x > x^*$ because $y = 0 < y^*$.

[7] Specifically, the injurer's best response to the victim's choice of x^* is y^* because $y^* < y^* + L(x^*,y^*) \leq \min_{y>y^*} y + L(x^*,y)$.

her loss in the event of breach (as under strict liability). That is, the amount of damages is set at $V(x)$. In this case, the promisor will choose the efficient probability of breach (conditional on the victim's reliance choice), but the promisee will choose reliance as if the probability of breach were zero. Specifically, she will choose x to maximize $V(x) - x$, which, in comparison to (A4.23), results in an excessive level of reliance. In contrast, when damages for breach are zero (no liability), the promisor will choose y to maximize $B(y)$, which leads to excessive breach, whereas the promisee will choose the efficient reliance, conditional on the promisor's choice of y. Thus, as in the tort case, neither damage measure induces efficient behavior by both parties.

Again, however, the efficient outcome can be achieved by a "limited" expectation damage remedy that fixes the amount of damages at the promisor's efficient level of reliance, or $V(x^*)$. Under this rule, the promisor will choose y to maximize $B(y)+(1-y)V(x^*)$, which yields y^*, whereas the promisee will choose x to maximize $yV(^*x)+(1-y)V(x)-x$, which yields x^*. Note that the promisee does not overrely in this case because she will not be compensated for any losses in excess of $V(x^*)$.

Finally, consider the application of this model to takings law. The formal structure of the model is identical to that for contract breach (that is, the expected social value of the land is given by [A4.22]), with the variables redefined as follows:

x = investment by the landowner;
y = fraction of privately owned land taken by the government for public use (or equivalently, the probability of a taking);
$V(x)$ = value of land in private use;
$B(y)$ = value of land in public use.

The conclusions of the contract model carry over directly. Specifically, under full compensation, the government will take the efficient amount of land (conditional on the landowner's investment), but the landowner will overinvest. In contrast, under zero compensation, the government will take too much land, and the landowner will invest efficiently, conditional on the probability of a taking. This reflects the trade-off between moral hazard and fiscal illusion as examined in the previously presented takings models.

As shown earlier, however, efficient behavior by both parties can be achieved by a variety of compensation rules. As one example, note that the lump-sum rule, $C = V(x^*)$, is mathematically equivalent to the limited expectations damage remedy for breach of contract as just examined.

Notes on the literature. The model of precaution as applied to torts was first developed by Brown (1973). Cooter (1985) generalized the model to reveal the commonalities among torts, contracts, and takings. For fuller treatments of the tort models, see Shavell (1987) and Landes and Posner (1987). For models of breach of contract, see Shavell (1980, 1984).

Balancing risk and Incentives

Consider the insurance model from Chapter 3, extended to allow the landowner to invest in his or her land. Recall from the earlier model that landowners are risk averse and have utility over wealth given by $U(w)$, where $U' > 0$ and $U'' < 0$. We now extend that model such that $V(x)$ is the value of the land after an investment of x dollars has been made, where $V' > 0$ and $V'' < 0$. Also, let compensation take the form $C = C(x)$. Wealth in the "no takings" and "takings" states is therefore given by

$$w_N(x) = y - T + V(x) - x, \qquad (A4.25)$$
$$w_T(x) = y - T + C(x) - x, \qquad (A4.26)$$

where y is income and T is the tax paid to finance compensation. Also let p be the probability of a taking (which I assume here is fixed), which implies that $T = pC(x)$ for a balanced budget. Expected utility in this case is

$$EU = pU(y-T+C(x)-x) + (1-p)U(y-T+V(x)-x). \qquad (A4.27)$$

The landowner's optimal choice of x maximizes (A4.27), taking $C(x)$ and T as given. The first order condition is

$$pU'(w_T)(C'(x)-1) + (1-p)U'(w_N)(V'(x)-1) = 0, \qquad (A4.28)$$

which defines $\hat{x}$

Suppose first the compensation is full, or $C(x) = V(x)$. Then, since $w_N = w_T$, insurance is full, but because $C'(x) = V'(x)$, (A4.28) reduces to $V'(x) = 1$. Thus, the landowner invests as if there were no taking risk. This reflects the moral hazard problem associated with full insurance. At the other extreme, let $C = 0$. In this case, there is no insurance, so $w_T < w_N$. Thus, (A4.28) becomes

$$-pU'(w_T) + (1-p)U'(w_N)(V'(x)-1) = 0,$$

which implies that $V'(x) > 1$, so the landowner invests less than under full insurance.

Consider next the lump-sum compensation rule $C = V(x^*)$, where x^* is the level of investment that maximizes the expected value of the land (i.e., the solution to [A4.2] presented earlier). If we assume that x^* is the land-owner's actual choice of x, then $w_N = w_T$, and the landowner is fully insured. Given this result and the fact that $C' = 0$, (A4.28) reduces to

$$(1-p)V'(x) = 1, \tag{A4.29}$$

which verifies that the landowner in fact chooses x^* under this rule. This shows that lump-sum compensation equal to $C = V(x^*)$ achieves the first best outcome wherein the landowner is fully insured against takings risk, and the expected value of the land is maximized (i.e., there is no moral haz-ard problem).

Because a rule that conditions compensation on the efficient (as opposed to the actual) level of landowner investment is impractical, we finally con-sider a compensation rule of the form $C = \alpha V(x)$, where α is a non-negative parameter. That is, compensation is proportional to the value of the land. Given this rule, condition (A4.28) becomes

$$pU'(w_T)(\alpha V'(x)-1) + (1-p)U'(w_N)(V'(x)-1) = 0, \tag{A4.30}$$

which defines $\hat{x}(\alpha)$. (Note that $\alpha = 1$ and 0 produce the special cases of full and zero compensation examined above.) Based on the logic of the consti-tutional choice arguments discussed earlier, we suppose that landowners would choose α to maximize their expected utility in (A4.27), subject to the balanced-budget condition, $T = pC$, and their anticipated investment behavior, as reflected by $\hat{x}(\alpha)$. Taking the derivative of the expected utility expression in (A4.27) with respect to α and substituting from (A4.30), we obtain the first order condition

$$\frac{\partial EU}{\partial \alpha} = -p\alpha V'(x)[(1-p)U'(w_N) + pU'(w_T)]\left(\frac{\partial \hat{x}}{\partial \alpha}\right)$$
$$+(1-p)pV(x)[U'(w_T)-U'(w_N)] \tag{A4.31}$$

To prove that the optimal α, denoted α^*, is positive, set $\alpha = 0$ in (A4.31). The result is

$$\frac{\partial EU}{\partial \alpha} = (1-p)pV(x)[U'(w_T)-U'(w_N)] > 0 \tag{A4.32}$$

where the sign follows from the facts that $U'' < 0$ and $w_N > w_T$ when $\alpha = 0$. Thus, $\alpha^* > 0$. Now set $\alpha = 1$ in (A4.31). Since $w_T = w_N = w$ in this case (because insurance is full), the second term of (A4.31) vanishes, while the first term becomes

$$\frac{\partial EU}{\partial \alpha} = -pV'(x)U'(w)\left(\frac{\partial \hat{x}}{\partial \alpha}\right)$$

(A4.33)

It can be shown that $\partial \hat{x}(\alpha)/\partial \alpha > 0$ when $\alpha = 1$, implying that (A4.33) is negative. This proves that $\alpha^* < 1$. Combining this with the above result establishes that $0 < \alpha^* < 1$.

Notes on the literature. Blume and Rubinfeld (1984, 1987) advanced the insurance argument for compensation. Kaplow (1986) argued that because private companies would almost certainly be able to provide takings insurance more efficiently than the government, the government should never pay compensation for takings. Miceli and Segerson (2007a, Appendix) derived the partial compensation result based on the trade-off between risk and incentives. For formal analyses of the trade-off between risk sharing and incentives in different contexts, see Stiglitz (1974), Holmstrom (1979), Shavell (1979), and Kaplow (1992).

Chapter 5

Regulatory Takings

Efficiency of the ex Post Version of the Threshold Compensation Rule
The threshold compensation rule in (5.1) in the text (the ex post version of the threshold rule) can be written in mathematical terms as follows:

$$C = \begin{cases} V(x), & \text{if } E < V(x^*) \\ 0, & \text{if } E \geq V(x^*) \end{cases}$$

(A5.1)

where

$V(x)$ = value of the land given investment level x, $V' > 0$, $V'' < 0$;
   x = dollar investment by the landowner;
   x^* = efficient level of investment (to be derived below);
   E = external cost from development, which is a random variable;
$F(E)$ = distribution function of E, where $F' \equiv f(E) > 0$ is the density function.

The derivation of the efficient regulatory and land use decisions is similar to that in the model of physical takings from Chapter 4. The difference is that here, the external cost, E, is incurred if the development goes forward and avoided if development is prohibited. The two formulations are economically identical, however, given the equivalence between a benefit and a foregone harm.

Specifically, for any choice of x by the landowner, it is efficient for the government to enact a regulation prohibiting development if $E \geq V(x)$, but it is not efficient to impose the regulation if $E < V(x)$. Given this behavior by the government, the socially optimal choice of x maximizes

$$\int_0^{V(x)} (V(x)-E)dF(E)-x, \qquad (A.5.2)$$

where the integral expression is the expected value of the land in the event that the regulation is not imposed. (When the regulation is imposed, the value of the land is zero; that is, the private value of the land is lost, but the externality is avoided.) The first order condition implied by (A5.2) is

$$F(V(x))V'(x)=1, \qquad (A5.3)$$

which is identical to that in the takings model in the Appendix to Chapter 4, and it has the same interpretation. (See equation [A4.6].)

To prove the efficiency of the compensation rule in (A5.1), we need to derive the equilibrium of the sequential choice problem between the landowner and the government, where the landowner moves first and chooses x, and then the government, which is subject to fiscal illusion, moves second and makes its regulatory decision. Using backward induction, we first consider the behavior of the government, given the prior choice of x by the landowner.

Once the government realizes the value of E, it will enact the regulation if and only if $E \geq C$ (given fiscal illusion). Suppose first that $E \geq V(x^*)$, or that the regulation is efficient. Then, by (A5.1), $C=0$, in which case the government will enact the regulation with certainty for any x. The landowner's return in this case is $-x$. Alternatively, suppose that $E < V(x^*)$, or that the regulation is not efficient. Now $C = V(x)$, or compensation is full. In this case, the government may or may not enact the regulation, depending on the landowner's actual choice of x. If $x \geq x^*$, $C = V(x) \geq V(x^*) > E$, and the government will not enact the regulation. However, if $x < x^*$, the government will enact the regulation, even though compensation is full, if the following condition holds: $C = V(x) < E < V(x^*)$. Either way, however, the landowner's return is $V(x)-x$.

Now consider the landowner's choice of x. His expected return, given the preceding description of the government's behavior, is

$$F(V(x^*))V(x) - x, \qquad (A5.4)$$

which yields the first order condition

$$F(V(x^*))V'(x) = 1. \qquad (A5.5)$$

Because this condition has x^* as its solution, we conclude that the landowner makes the efficient land use decision. As a result, the government also makes the efficient regulatory decision since $C = V(x^*)$ when $E < V(x^*)$. Together, these results show that the compensation rule in (A5.1) induces efficient behavior by both parties in equilibrium.

Efficiency of the ex Ante Version of the Threshold Compensation Rule
Define the ex ante version of the threshold compensation rule (the counterpart to (5.6) in the text) as follows:

$$C = \begin{cases} V(x), & \text{if } x \leq x^* \\ 0, & \text{if } x > x^*. \end{cases} \qquad (A5.6)$$

Proceeding as above, we begin by considering the government's behavior. Suppose first that the government observed that the landowner invested an amount $x \leq x^*$. Then, by (A5.6), compensation for any regulation will be full; that is, $C = V(x)$. When the government realizes E, it will therefore enact the regulation if and only if $E \geq V(x)$, which is the efficient criterion, conditional on the landowner's choice of x. In this case, the ex ante probability of a regulation from the landowner's perspective is $1 - F(V(x))$, but because compensation is full, the landowner's gross return is $V(x)$ whether or not the regulation is imposed. Next suppose that the government observed that the landowner invested an amount $x > x^*$. Then, by (A5.6), $C = 0$, and the government enacts a regulation whenever $E \geq 0$. In effect, it will regulate with certainty, and the landowner's gross return is zero.

Now consider the landowner's behavior. Given (A5.6) and the expected behavior of the government as just described, the landowner's problem is to choose x to

$$\max \begin{cases} V(x) - x, & \text{if } x \leq x^*, \\ -x, & \text{if } x > x^*, \end{cases} \qquad (A5.7)$$

where the first line corresponds to the case of full compensation and the second corresponds to no compensation. Because the expression $V(x)-x$ is increasing at $x=x^*$, the first line is maximized at x^*. And because $V(x^*)-x^* > -x$ for all $x>x^*$, the solution to this problem is x^*, which again proves that both parties act efficiently in equilibrium. Finally, note that in contrast to the ex post version of the threshold rule, compensation is full in equilibrium under the rule in (A5.6).

Notes on the literature. The two forms of the threshold rule (the ex post and ex ante versions) were first proposed by Miceli and Segerson (1994) and elaborated on in Miceli and Segerson (1996, 2007a).

List of Cases

Agins v. Tiburon, 157 Cal. Rptr. 373 (1979), *affirmed* 447 U.S. 255 (1980).
Armstrong v. United States, 364 U.S. 40 (1960).
Berman v. Parker, 348 U.S. 26 (1954).
Block v. Hirsh, 256 U.S. 135 (1921).
Boomer v. Atlantic Cement Co., 309 N.Y.S.2d 312 (1970).
Callender v. Marsh, 18 Mass. (1 Pick.) 418 (1823).
City of Oakland v. Oakland Raiders, 183 Cal. Rptr. 391 (Ct. App. 1969).
County of Wayne v. Hathcock, 684 N.W.2d 765, 471 Mich. 445 (2004).
Dayton Mining Co. v. Seawell, 11 Nev. 394 (1876).
Dolan v. City of Tigard, 512 U.S. 687 (1994).
Florida Rock Industries v. United States, 18 F.3d 1560 (Fed. Cir. 1994), *cert. denied* 115 S. Ct. 898 (1995).
Goldblatt v. Town of Hempstead, 369 U.S. 590 (1962).
Hawaii Housing Authority v. Midkiff, 467 U.S. 229 (1984).
Head v. Amoskeag Mfg. Co., 113 U.S. 9 (1885).
H.F.H. Ltd. v. Superior Court, 125 Cal. Rptr. 365 (1975).
Just v. Marinette County, 56 Wis.2d 7, 201 N.W.2d 761 (1972).
Kelo v. New London, 545 U.S. 469 (2005).
Keystone Bituminous Coal Assn. v. DeBenedictus, 480 U.S. 470 (1987).
Loretto v. Teleprompter Manhattan CATV, 423 N.E.2d 320 (N.Y. 1981), *reversed* 458 U.S. 419 (1982).
Lucas v. South Carolina Coastal Council, 505 U.S. 1003 (1992).
Miller v. Schoene, 276 U.S. 272 (1928).
Mugler v. Kansas, 123 U.S. 623 (1887).
Nollan v. California Coastal Council, 483 U.S. 825 (1987).
Palazzolo v. Rhode Island, 533 U.S. 606 (2001).
Peevyhouse v. Garland Coal & Mining Co., 382 P.2d 109, *cert. denied*, 375 U.S. 906 (1962).
Penn Central Transportation Co. v. City of New York, 366 N.E.2d 1271 (N.Y. 1977), *affirmed*, 438 U.S. 104 (1978).
Pennsylvania Coal v. Mahon, 260 U.S. 393 (1922).
Poletown Neighborhood Council v. City of Detroit, 304 N.W.2d 455 (Mich. 1981).
Porter v. United States, 473 F.2d 1329 (5th Cir. 1973).
Pumpelly v. Green Bay Co., 80 U.S. (13 Wall.) 166 (1871).

References

Adelstein, R. (1974) "Just Compensation and the Assassin's Bequest: A Utilitarian Approach," *University of Pennsylvania Law Review* 122: 1012–1032.

Asabere, P. and F. Huffman (1994) "Historic District Designation and Residential Market Value," *Appraisal Journal* 62: 396–401.

Asabere, P., F. Huffman, and S. Mehdian (1994) "The Adverse Impacts of Local Historic Designation: The Case of Small Apartment Buildings in Philadelphia," *Journal of Real Estate Finance and Economics* 8: 225–234.

Atkinson, A. and J. Stiglitz (1980), *Lectures on Public Economics*. New York: McGraw-Hill.

Ayres, I. and J. M. Balkin (1997) "Legal Entitlements and Auctions: Property Rules, Liability Rules, and Beyond," *Yale Law Journal* 106: 703–750.

Baxter, W. and L. Altree (1972) "Legal Aspects of Airport Noise," *Journal of Law and Economics* 15: 1–113.

Been, V. (1991) "'Exit' as a Constraint on Land Use Exactions: Rethinking the Unconstitutional Conditions Doctrine," *Columbia Law Review* 91: 473–545.

Bell, A. (2009) "Private Takings," *Univ. of Chicago Law Review* 76: 517–585.

Benedict, J. (2009) *Little Pink House: A True Story of Defiance and Courage*. New York: Grand Central Publishing.

Berliner, D. (2003) *Public Power, Private Gain: A Five Year State-by-State Report Examining the Abuse of Eminent Domain*, Washington, DC: Castle Coalition. (http://www.CastleCoalition.org)

Blume, L. and D. Rubinfeld (1987) "Compensation for Takings: An Economic Analysis," *Research in Law and Economics* 10: 53–104.

  (1984) "Compensation for Takings: An Economic Analysis," *California Law Review* 72: 569–628.

Blume, L., D. Rubinfeld, and P. Shapiro (1984) "The Taking of Land: When Should Compensation Be Paid?" *Quarterly Journal of Economics* 99: 71–92.

Boyle, K. and R. Bishop (1987) "Valuing Wildlife in Benefit-Cost Analysis: A Case Study Involving Endangered Species," *Water Resources Research* 23: 943–950.

Brennan, G. and J. Buchanan (1980) *The Power to Tax: Analytical Foundations of a Fiscal Constitution*. Cambridge: Cambridge Univ. Press.

Bromley, D. (1993) "Regulatory Takings: Coherent Concept or Logical Contradiction?" *Vermont Law Review* 17: 647–682.

Brown, J. (1973) "Toward an Economic Theory of Liability," *Journal of Legal Studies* 2: 323–349.

Brueckner, J. (2000) "Urban Sprawl: Diagnosis and Remedies," *International Regional Science Review* 23: 160–171.

(1993) "Inter-Store Externalities and Space Allocation in Shopping Centers," *Journal of Real Estate Finance and Economics* 7: 5–16.

Buchanan, J. and Y. Yoon (2000) "Symmetric Tragedies: Commons and Anticommons," *Journal of Law and Economics* 43: 1–13.

Cadigan, J., P. Schmitt, R. Shupp, and Kurtis Swope (2010) "An Experimental Study of the Holdout Problem in a Multilateral Bargaining Game," *Southern Economic Journal*, 76: 444–457.

Calabresi, G. and A. D. Melamed (1972) "Property Rules, Liability Rules, and Inalienability: One View of the Cathedral," *Harvard Law Review* 85: 1089–1128.

Cannaday, R. (1994) "Condominium Covenants: Cats, Yes; Dogs, No." *Journal of Urban Economics* 35: 71–82.

Castle Coalition (2008) *50 State Report Card: Tracking Eminent Domain Reform Legislation since Kelo* (http://www.castlecoalition.org).

Chang, Y. (2010a) "An Empirical Study of Compensation Paid in Eminent Domain Settlements: New York City, 1990–2002," *Journal of Legal Studies* 39: 201–244.

(2010b) "An Empirical Study of Court-Adjudicated Takings Compensation in New York City: 1990–2002," manuscript.

Coase, R. (1960) "The Problem of Social Costs," *Journal of Law and Economics* 3: 1–44.

(1937) "The Nature of the Firm," *Economica* 4: 386–405.

Cohen, L. (1991) "Holdouts and Free Riders," *Journal of Legal Studies* 20: 351–362.

Coleman, J. (1988) *Markets, Morals, and the Law*. Cambridge: Cambridge University Press.

Colwell, P. (1990) "Privatization of Assessment, Zoning, and Eminent Domain," *ORER Letter* 4: 1–7.

Colwell, P. and H. Munneke (1999) "Land Prices and Assembly in the CBD," *Journal of Real Estate Finance and Economics* 18: 163–180.

Cooter, R. (2000) *The Strategic Constitution*. Princeton, NJ: Princeton University Press.

(1985) "Unity in Tort, Contract, and Property: The Model of Precaution," *California Law Review* 73: 1–51.

Davis, O. and A. Whinston (1961) "The Economics of Urban Renewal," *Journal of Contemporary Problems* 26: 105–117.

Demsetz, H. (1972) "When Does the Rule of Liability Matter?" *Journal of Legal Studies* 1: 13–28.

Diop, M., S. Lanza, T. Miceli, and C.F. Sirmans (2010) "Public Use or Abuse? The Use of Eminent Domain for Economic Development in the Era of *Kelo*," Working paper, Department of Economics, University of Connecticut.

Dixit, A. and M. Olson (2000) "Does Voluntary Participation Undermine the Coase Theorem?" *Journal of Public Economics* 76: 309–335.

Ellickson, R. (1993) "Property in Land," *Yale Law Journal* 102: 1315–1400.

(1991) *Order without Law: How Neighbors Settle Disputes*. Cambridge, MA: Harvard University Press.

(1979) "Public Property Rights: Vicarious Intergovernmental Rights and Liabilities as a Technique for Correcting Intergovernmental Spillovers," in: D. Rubinfeld (ed.), *Essays on the Law and Economics of Local Government*. Washington, DC: The Urban Institute.

(1977) "Suburban Growth Controls: An Economic and Legal Analysis," *Yale Law Journal* 86: 385–511.

(1973) "Alternatives to Zoning: Covenants, Nuisance Rules, and Fines as Land Use Controls," *University of Chicago Law Review* 40: 681–782.

Epstein, R. (1995) *Simple Rules for a Complex World*. Cambridge, MA: Harvard University Press.

(1985) *Takings: Private Property and the Power of Eminent Domain*, Cambridge, MA: Harvard University Press.

Feldman, A. (1980) *Welfare Economics and Social Choice Theory*. Boston: Kluwer-Nijhoff Publishing.

Fennell, L. (2004) "Taking Eminent Domain Apart," *Michigan State Law Review* 2004: 957–1004.

Fischel, W. (2004) "The Political Economy of Public Use in *Poletown*: How Federal Grants Encourage Excessive Use of Eminent Domain," *Michigan State Law Review* 2004: 929–955.

(1996) "The Political Economy of Just Compensation: Lessons from the Military Draft for the Takings Issue," *Harvard Journal of Law and Public Policy* 20: 23–63.

(1995a) *Regulatory Takings: Law, Economics, and Politics*. Cambridge, MA: Harvard University Press.

(1995b) "The Offer/Ask Disparity and Just Compensation for Takings: A Constitutional Choice Approach," *International Review of Law and Economics* 9: 115–128.

(1985) *The Economics of Zoning Laws: A Property Rights Approach to American Land Use Controls*. Baltimore: Johns Hopkins University Press.

Fischel, W. and P. Shapiro (1989) "A Constitutional Choice Model of Compensation for Takings," *International Review of Law and Economics* 9: 115–128.

(1988) "Takings, Insurance, and Michelman: Comments on Economic Interpretations of 'Just Compensation' Law," *Journal of Legal Studies* 17: 269–293.

Fleck, R. and F. A. Hanssen (2010) "Repeated Adjustment of Delegated Powers and the History of Eminent Domain," *International Review of Law and Economics* 30: 99–112.

Ford, D. (1989) "The Effect of Historic District Designation on Single-Family Home Prices," *Journal of the American Real Estate and Urban Economics Association* 17: 353–362.

Freeman, A. M. (1993) *The Measurement of Environmental and Resource Values: Theory and Methods*. Washington, DC: Resources for the Future.

Friedman, L. (1986) "A Search for Seizure: *Pennsylvania Coal v. Mahon* in Context," *Law and History Review* 4: 1–22.

(1985) *A History of American Law*, 2nd edition. New York: Touchstone Books.

Friedmann, D. (1989) "The Efficient Breach Fallacy," *Journal of Legal Studies* 18: 1–24.

Galster, G., R. Hanson, M. Ratcliffe, H. Wolman, S. Coleman, and J. Freihage (2001) "Wrestling Urban Sprawl to the Ground: Defining and Measuring an Elusive Concept," *Housing Policy Debate* 12: 681–717.

Gennaioli, N. and A. Shleifer (2007) "The Evolution of the Common Law," *Journal of Political Economy* 115: 43–68.

Ghosh, S. (1997) "Takings, the Exit Option and Just Compensation," *International Review of Law and Economics* 17: 157–176.

Giammarino, R. and E. Nosal (2005) "Loggers versus Campers: Compensation for the Taking of Property Rights," *Journal of Law, Economics, and Organization* 21: 136–152.

Gold, A. (1976) "The Welfare Economics of Historic Preservation," *Connecticut Law Review* 8: 348–369.

Goldberg, V. (1985) "Relational Exchange, Contract Law, and the *Boomer* Problem," *Journal of Institutional and Theoretical Economics* 141: 570–575.

Gould, S. (1985) *The Flamingo's Smile*. New York: W.W. Norton & Co.

Hamilton, B. (1975) "Zoning and Property Taxes in a System of Local Governments," *Urban Studies* 12: 205–211.

Harding, J., T. Miceli, and C. F. Sirmans (2000) "Do Owners Take Better Care of Their Housing Than Renters?" *Real Estate Economics* 28: 663–681.

Harrington, W. (1981) "The Endangered Species Act and the Search for Balance," *Natural Resources Journal* 21: 71–92.

Heller, M. (2008) *The Gridlock Economy: How Too Much Ownership Wrecks Markets, Stops Innovation, and Costs Lives*. New York: Basic Books.

(1999) "The Boundaries of Private Property," *Yale Law Journal* 108: 1163–1223.

(1998) "The Tragedy of the Anticommons: Property in the Transition from Marx to Markets," *Harvard Law Review* 111: 621–688.

Heller, M. and R. Hills (2008) "Land Assembly Districts," *Harvard Law Review* 121: 1465–1527.

Henderson, J. V. (1985) *Economic Theory and the Cities*, 2nd edition. Orlando, FL: Academic Press.

Henderson, J. V. and Y. Ioannides (1983) "A Model of Housing Tenure Choice," *American Economic Review* 73: 98–113.

Hermalin, B. (1995) "An Economic Analysis of Takings," *Journal of Law, Economics, and Organization* 11: 64–86.

Holmes, O. (1897) "The Path of the Law," *Harvard Law Review* 10: 457–478.

Holmstrom, B. (1979) "Moral Hazard and Observability," *Bell Journal of Economics* 10: 74–91.

Horwitz, M. (1992) *The Transformation of American Law, 1780–1860*. New York: Oxford University Press

Hovenkamp, H. (1991) "Legal Policy and the Endowment Effect," *Journal of Legal Studies* 20: 225–247.

Hughes, W. and G. Turnbull (1996) "Restrictive Land Covenant," *Journal of Real Estate Finance and Economics* 12: 9–21.

Innes, R. (1997) "Takings, Compensation and Equal Treatment for Owners of Developed and Undeveloped Property," *Journal of Law and Economics* 40: 403–432.

Johnson, M. (1977) "Planning without Prices: A Discussion of Land Use Regulation without Compensation," in: B. Siegan (ed.): *Planning without Prices*. Lexington, MA: Lexington Books.

Jolls, C., C. Sunstein, and R. Thaler (2000) "A Behavioral Approach to Law and Economics," pp. 13–58, in C. Sunstein (ed.): *Behavioral Law and Economics*. Cambridge: Cambridge University Press.

Kaplow, L. (1992) "Government Relief for Risk Associated with Government Action," *Scandinavian Journal of Economics* 94: 525–541.

(1986) "An Economic Analysis of Legal Transitions," *Harvard Law Review* 99: 509–617.

Kaplow, L. and S. Shavell (1996) "Property Rules versus Liability Rules," *Harvard Law Review* 103: 713–790.

Keeton, W. P ., D. Dobbs, R. Keeton, and D. Owen (1984), *Prosser and Keeton on Torts*, 5th edition. St. Paul, MN: West Publishing Co.

Kelly, D. (2006) "The 'Public Use' Requirement in Eminent Domain Law: A Rationale Based on Secret Purchases and Private Influence," *Cornell Law Review* 92: 1–65.

Klevorick, A. (1985) "On the Economic Theory of Crime," in J. Pennock and J. Chapman (eds.): *NOMOS XXVII: Criminal Justice*. New York: New York University Press.

Knetsch, J. and T. Borcherding (1979) "Expropriation of Private Property and the Basis for Compensation," *University of Toronto Law Journal* 29: 237–252.

Krier, J. and C. Serkin (2004) "Public Ruses," *Michigan State Law Review* 2004: 859–875.

LaCroix, S . and L. Rose (1995) "Public Use, Just Compensation, and Land Reform in Hawaii," *Research in Law and Economics* 17: 7–82.

Landes, W. and R. Posner (1987) *The Economic Structure of Tort Law*. Cambridge, MA: Harvard University Press.

Levinson, D. (2002) "Framing Transactions in Constitutional Law," *Yale Law Journal* 111: 1311–1390.

(2000) "Making Government Pay: Markets, Politics, and the Allocation of Constitutional Costs," *University of Chicago Law Review* 67: 345–420.

Lopez, E., R. Jewell, and N. Campbell (2009) "Pass a Law, Any Law, Fast! State Legislative Responses to the *Kelo* Backlash," *Review of Law and Economics* 5: 101–135.

Lueck, D. and T. Miceli (2007) "Property Law," in: A. M. Polinsky and S. Shavell (eds.): *Handbook of Law and Economics*, Amsterdam: Elsevier.

Lueck, D. and J. Michael (2003) "Preemptive Habitat Destruction under the Endangered Species Act," *Journal of Law and Economics* 46: 27–61.

Malaith, G. and A. Postlewaite (1990) "Asymmetric Information Bargaining Problems with Many Agents," *Review of Economic Studies* 57: 351–367.

Mandelker, D. (1987) "Investment-Backed Expectations: Is There a Taking?" *Journal of Urban and Contemporary Problems* 31: 3–43.

McFarlane, A. (1999) "Taxes, Fees, and Urban Development," *Journal of Urban Economics* 46: 416–436.

Meltz, R., D. Merriam, and R. Frank (1999) *The Takings Issue: Constitutional Limits on Land Use Control and Environmental Regulation*. Washington, DC: Island Press.

Menezes, F. and R. Pitchford (2004) "A Model of Seller Holdout," *Economic Theory* 24: 231–253.

Mercuro, N., and S. Medema (1997) *Economics and the Law: From Posner to Post-Modernism*. Princeton, NJ: Princeton University Press.

Merrill, T. (1986) "The Economics of Public Use," *Cornell Law Review* 72: 61–116.

Miceli, T. (2010) "Holdouts, Free Riders, and Public Use: A Tale of Two Externalities," *Public Choice*, forthcoming.

(2009a) *The Economic Approach to Law*, 2nd edition, Stanford, CA: Stanford University Press.

(2009b) "Legal Change: Selective Litigation, Judicial Bias, and Precedent," *Journal of Legal Studies* 38: 157–168.

(2008) "Public Goods, Taxes, and Takings," *International Review of Law and Economics* 28:287–293.

(1991a) "Compensation for the Taking of Land under Eminent Domain," *Journal of Institutional and Theoretical Economics* 147: 354–363.

(1991b) "Free Riders and Distortionary Zoning by Local Communities," *Journal of Urban Economics* 30: 112–122.

Miceli, T. and L. Minkler (1995) "Willingness to Accept versus Willingness to Pay Measures of Value: Implications for Rent Control, Eminent Domain and Zoning," *Public Finance Quarterly* 23: 255–270.

Miceli, T. and K. Segerson (2007a) *The Economics of Eminent Domain: Private Property, Public Use, and Just Compensation*, Volume 3 in Foundations and Trends in Microeconomics, W. Kip Viscusi (ed). Boston: Now Publishers.

(2007b) "A Bargaining Model of Holdouts and Takings," *American Law and Economics Review* 9: 160–174.

(1996) *Regulatory Takings: An Economic Analysis with Applications*. Greenwich, CT: JAI Press.

(1994) "Regulatory Takings: When Should Compensation Be Paid?" *Journal of Legal Studies* 23: 749–776.

Miceli, T., K. Segerson, and C.F. Sirmans (2008) "Tax Motivated Takings," *National Tax Journal* 61: 579–591.

Miceli, T. and C. F. Sirmans (2007) "The Holdout Problem, Urban Sprawl, and Eminent Domain," *Journal of Housing Economics* 16: 309–319.

(2000) "Partition of Real Estate; or, Breaking Up is (Not) Hard to Do," *Journal of Legal Studies* 29: 783–796.

Miceli, T. and C. F. Sirmans (1995) "Contracting with Spatial Externalities and Agency Problems: The Case of Retail Leases," *Regional Science and Urban Economics* 25: 355–372.

Michelman, F. (1967) "Property, Utility, and Fairness: Comments on the Ethical Foundations of 'Just Compensation' Law," *Harvard Law Review* 80: 1165–1258.

Morriss, A. (2009) "Symbol or Substance? An Empirical Assessment of State Responses to *Kelo*," *Supreme Court Economic Review* 17: 237–278.

Munch, P. (1976) "An Economic Analysis of Eminent Domain," *Journal of Political Economy* 84: 473–497.

Narwold, A., J. Sandy, and C. Tu (2008) "Historic Designation and Residential Property Values," *International Real Estate Review* 11: 83–95.

Nechyba, T. and R. Walsh (2004) "Urban Sprawl," *Journal of Economic Perspectives* 18: 177–200.

Niemann, P. and P. Shapiro (2008) "Efficiency and Fairness: Compensation for Takings," *International Review of Law and Economics* 28: 157–165.

Nosal, E. (2001) "The Taking of Land: Market Value Compensation Should be Paid," *Journal of Public Economics* 82: 431–443.

O'Flaherty, B. (1994) "Land Assembly and Urban Renewal," *Regional Science and Urban Economics* 24: 287–300.

O'Sullivan, A. (2009) *Urban Economics*, 7th edition. Boston: McGraw-Hill.

Parisi, F. (2002) "Entropy in Property," *American Journal of Comparative Law* 50: 595–632.

Plassmann, F. and T. N. Tideman (2008) "Accurate Valuation in the Absence of Markets," *Public Finance Review* 36: 334–358.

Polinsky, A. M. (1980) "On the Choice between Property Rules and Liability Rules," *Economic Inquiry* 18: 233–246.

Posner, R. (2003), *Economic Analysis of Law*, 6th edition. New York: Aspen Law & Business.

Poundstone, W. (1992) *Prisoner's Dilemma*. New York: Doubleday.

Priest, G. (1977) "The Common Law Process and the Selection of Efficient Rules," *Journal of Legal Studies* 6: 65–82.

Rawls, J. (1971) *A Theory of Justice*. Cambridge, MA: Belknap Press.

Riddiough, T. (1997) "The Economic Consequences of Regulatory Taking Risk on Land Value and Development," *Journal of Urban Economics* 41: 56–77.

Rose, C. (1983) "Planning and Dealing: Piecemeal Land Controls as a Problem of Local Legitimacy," *California Law Review* 71: 837–912.

Rose-Ackerman, S. (1992) "Regulatory Takings: Policy Analysis and Democratic Principles," in N. Mercuro (ed.): *Taking Property and Just Compensation: Law and Economic Perspectives of the Takings Issue*. Boston: Kluwer Academic Publishers.

Rose-Ackerman, S. and J. Rossi (2000) "Disentangling Deregulatory Takings," *Virginia Law Review* 86: 1435–1495.

Rosen, S. (1974) "Hedonic Prices and Implicit Markets: Product Differentiation in Pure Competition," *Journal of Political Economy* 82: 34–55.

Rubenfeld, J. (1993) "Usings," *Yale Law Journal* 102: 1077–1163.

Rubin, P. (1977) "Why Is the Common Law Efficient?" *Journal of Legal Studies* 6: 51–63.

Sanchez, N. and J. Nugent (2000) "Fence Laws vs. Herd Laws: A Nineteenth Century Kansas Paradox," *Land Economics* 76: 518–533.

Sax, J. (1971) "Takings, Private Property, and Public Rights," *Yale Law Journal* 81: 149–186.

(1964) "Takings and the Police Power," *Yale Law Journal* 74: 36–76.

Schall, L. (1976) "Urban Renewal Policy and Economic Efficiency," *American Economic Review* 66: 612–628.

Scheiber, H. (1973) "Property Law, Expropriation, and Resource Allocation by Government: The United States, 1789–1910," *Journal of Economic History* 33: 232–251.

Shapiro, P. and J. Pincus (2007) "Efficiency and Equity in the Assemblage of Land for Public Use: The L2H2 Auction," Working Paper, Department of Economics, Univ. of California, Santa Barbara.

Shavell, S. (2010) "Eminent Domain versus Government Purchase of Land Given Imperfect Information about Owners' Valuations," *Journal of Law and Economics* 53: 1–27.

(2004) *Foundations of Economic Analysis of Law*. Cambridge, MA: Harvard University Press.

(1987) *Economic Analysis of Accident Law*. Cambridge, MA: Harvard University Press.

(1984) "The Design of Contracts and Remedies for Breach," *Quarterly Journal of Economics* 99: 121–148.

(1980) "Damage Measures for Breach of Contract," *Bell Journal of Economics* 11: 466–490.

(1979) "On Moral Hazard and Insurance," *Quarterly Journal of Economics* 93: 541–562.

Siegan, B. (1972) *Land Use without Zoning.* Lexington, MA: Lexington Books.

(1970) "Non-Zoning in Houston," *Journal of Law and Economics* 13: 71–147.

Somin, I. (2004) "Overcoming *Poletown: County of Wayne v. Hathcock*, Economic Development Takings, and the Future of Public Use," *Michigan State Law Review* 2004: 1005–1039.

Stein, G. (2000) "Who Gets the Takings Claim? Changes in Land Use Law, Pre-Enactment Owners, and Post-Enactment Buyers," *Ohio State Law Journal* 61: 89–165.

Stiglitz, J. (1974) "Incentives and Risk Sharing in Sharecropping," *Review of Economic Studies* 79: 578–595.

Strange, W. (1995) "Information, Holdouts, and Land Assembly," *Journal of Urban Economics* 38: 317–332.

Tideman, T. and F. Plassmann (2005) "Fair and Efficient Compensation for Taking Property under Uncertainty," *Journal of Public Economic Theory* 7: 471–495.

Tiebout, C. (1956) "A Pure Theory of Local Public Expenditure," *Journal of Political Economy* 64: 416–424.

Treanor, W. (1985) "The Origins and Original Significance of the Just Compensation Clause of the Fifth Amendment," *Yale Law Journal* 94: 694–716.

Turnbull, G. (2005) "The Investment Incentive Effects of Land Use Regulations," *Journal of Real Estate Finance and Economics* 17: 233–244.

(2002) "Land Development under the Threat of Taking," *Southern Economic Journal* 69: 468–501.

Turnbull, G. and R. Salvino (2009) "Do Broader Eminent Domain Powers Increase Government Size?" *Review of Law and Economics* 5: 785–806.

Ulen, T. (1992) "The Public Use of Private Property: A Dual Constraint Theory of Efficient Government Takings," pp. 163–198 in N. Mercuro (ed.): *Taking Property and Just Compensation: Law and Economic Perspectives of the Takings Issue.* Boston: Kluwer Academic Publishers.

(1984) "The Efficiency of Specific Performance: Toward a Unified Theory of Contract Remedies," *Michigan Law Review* 83: 341–403.

Vickrey, W. (1961) "Counterspeculation, Auctions, and Competitive Sealed Tenders," *Journal of Finance* 16: 8–37.

White, M. (1975) "Fiscal Zoning in Fragmented Metropolitan Areas," in E. Mills and W. Oates (eds.): *Fiscal Zoning and Land Use Controls.* Lexington, MA: Lexington Books.

Wittman, D. (1984) "Liability for Harm or Restitution for Benefit?" *Journal of Legal Studies* 13: 57–80.

Wyman, K. (2007) "The Measure of Just Compensation," *University of California Davis Law Review* 41: 239–287.

Index

Accident costs, 105–106
  Hand rule, 106
Ad coelum rule, 115
Adverse selection
  insurance, 76
Agins v. Tiburon, 118, 145, 146, 148
Anti-commons problem, 28, 166
  partition statutes, 39
Armstrong v. United States, 79
Auctions, 63, 65
Average reciprocity of advantage, 118

Behavioral economics, 57
  fairness, 79
Benefit offset principle, *see* Just compensation
Berman v. Parker, 22, 40
Bilateral monopoly, 34–35, 36, 37, 60
  as rationale for eminent domain, 35
Block v. Hirsh, 133
Blume, Lawrence, 19, 76
Boomer v. Atlantic Cement Co., 35–37
Brandeis, Louis, 113, 117, 129–130, 133
Bromley, Daniel, 120
Brown, John, 105–106

Calabresi, Guido, 9
Callender v. Marsh, 49, 80
Capitalization, 18, 72, 80, 154, 169–170
  investment backed expectations, 118
City of Oakland v. Oakland Raiders, 23, 51
Coase, Ronald, 5, 28
Coase Theorem, 5–14
  causation, 7, 13
  distribution of wealth, 7
  general transaction structure, 11–14
  impact of transaction costs, 8–9
  threshold rules, 135

Coming to the nuisance, 13
Common law, 3, 119
Compensation, *see* Just compensation
Condominiums, 137
Constitution, U.S., xi, 3, 22, 56, 88
Constitutional choice model, 96–101,
  174–175, 181
Contract law, 35, 37, 92, 107, 178–179
Cooter, Robert, 92, 105–107
County of Wayne v. Hathcock, 22, 51

Dayton Mining Co. v. Seawell, 38
Demand revealing mechanisms, 17
  for discovering owners' true valuations,
  62–66
  public good provision, 27, 63
Demoralization costs, 18, 19, 77–78,
  110–111, 123
Diminution of value test, 116–117, 119, 156
  parceling problem, 117, 120, 129
  threshold rule, 124, 129
Dolan v. City of Tigard, 140–141
Dominant strategy, 26, 41

Economic efficiency, 2, 4
  Kaldor-Hicks as criterion for, 111,
  161–162
  Pareto optimality as criterion for, 111,
  159–161
Ellickson, Robert, 1, 57, 122
Eminent domain, 2, 3, 4
  as forced sale, 30, 164–166
  as liability rule, 13–14
  as spur for economic growth, 49–50,
  52–53
  urban renewal, 40–42
  urban sprawl, 44–46